SOUR M.A.S.H. AT SEA - SECOND WAVE

By

Walter "Bud" Stuhldreher

For Herman Thompson

Merry Christmas!

Bud Stuhldreher

December 25, 2004

This book is a work of non-fiction. Names and places have been changed to protect the privacy of all individuals. The events and situations are true.

© 2004 by Walter "Bud" Stuhldreher. All rights reserved.

No part of this book may be reproduced, stored in a retrieval system, or transmitted by any means, electronic, mechanical, photocopying, recording, or otherwise, without written permission from the author.

First published by AuthorHouse 04/19/04

ISBN: 1-4140-5432-7 (e-book)
ISBN: 1-4184-4436-7 (Paperback)
ISBN: 1-4184-4435-9 (Dust Jacket)

Library of Congress Control Number: 2003099678

This book is printed on acid free paper.

Printed in the United States of America
Bloomington, IN

Also by Walter "Bud" Stuhldreher

****

SOUR M.A.S.H. AT SEA — And Other Stories

ACKNOWLEDGMENTS

Many think writing is a lonely job. Balderdash! It's a team effort from A to Z. First you must understand I'm not a writer. I'm a storyteller. I tell the story, typing in my two-finger style, letting the words flow as they will. Spelling, typing mistakes, and, most important, correct grammar aren't my bag. Wife Bettie takes over at this point and fixes these shortcomings plus puts the stories in a more logical sequence. Then back and forth between us the embryo story goes, each working to improve the finished product. Key aides are *Webster's Dictionary* and *Prentice-Hall Handbook for Writers*, plus a thesaurus, and intelligent, non-acrimonious disagreements between us. Bettie is very careful to leave the story as close to the original effort as possible, in order to preserve my unique perspective on the details, yet insistent that the final edition be correct as far as language and proper grammar requires. One story in this book, one of the shorter ones, took *seventeen* iterations before we both signed off. And then the tough work starts.

If there's a tougher writing job than proofreading I don't know what it is. It's simply brutal. The stories have to be laid out in the sequence desired for the book. Inconsistencies, not apparent in single stories have to be corrected. Redundant material becomes apparent and must be fixed. Each paragraph must be reviewed for proper spelling and grammar. Sometimes the same word will be reused too often and must be changed to avoid putting the reader to sleep. Bettie and I were assisted in this tough assignment by daughter Lisa Durham, the same as the last book. However a new proofreader, Dick Schreitmueller, of Kensington, MD., generously offered to help, and he too proofread every word. Dick, a Notre Dame classmate of mine, proved invaluable in offering a different perspective on the stories. A big time THANKS is due Dick for his efforts. Dick suggested an estimated 1,000 plus changes, truly an outstanding effort. Retired Florida State University Professor Gene Tanzy offered to help do this. He also suggested over 1,000 changes, and his perspective was extremely helpful. Thanks, Gene.

Next, the pictures to be used have to be identified and inserted in the book. Then, finally, off goes the manuscript to the publisher and the fun begins. It's amazing how different the first set of galleys look from the manuscript. Again, every word must be examined to ensure accuracy. Corrections made, perhaps a change in font size, etc., and the corrected pages are returned. My Personal Author's Representative is involved every step of the way. The second set of galleys, plus the two suggested book covers, one for the hardback, another for the paperback, arrive and back we go into the sweat box. Fun, it ain't! But absolutely necessary. Even so, we are resigned to the inescapable fact that some errors will remain in the finished product. Our objective is to reduce them to as close to zero as possible.

Special thanks are due Gene Tanzy of Tallahassee. In spite of battling a virulent form of cancer, in addition to proofreading, Gene wrote a book review for our local newspaper, the *Tallahassee Democrat* and another for Amazon.com. For an author, hardly anything is more important than a favorable book review. *Molte grazie*, Gene.

Thanks to Laura Phillips, Branch Office Administrator of the Tallahassee office of Edward D. Jones & Co. who dug through their research files for the stock split and price history of Golden Valley Microwave Foods.

As mentioned in the book, Dick Ruehlin and Frank Shemanski, both of California, supplied many of the details used in the chapter regarding the *USS Haven's* epic voyage around the world. Both were members of the ship's crew and furnished the operating details. Special help was furnished by Mary Shafer Cermak of Tallahassee, a former nurse on the *Haven*. Through personal interviews, she provided details from the medical side of the voyage. Also, many details, and pictures, were obtained from her cruise book of the voyage which she kindly lent me. Fading with age, tattered and worn, it was invaluable. Without their help this story would not have been told, since I wasn't on the ship during the trip. But ever since hearing about it several years ago, I was determined to tell it. Thanks Mary, Frank and Dick!

And thanks to Durward "Dusty" Rhodes of Tallahassee, FL who supplied the fascinating details of the sinking of the *USS Benevolence* off San Francisco within sight of the Golden Gate Bridge. Dusty interviewed a survivor of that sinking.

Hospital ship historian Ray Seiple supplied much of the history of hospital ships, including the picture of the U.S. Hospital ship *Red Rover*.

My former shipmate on the *Haven*, Paul Fisher, supplied the pictures for the *Spam* story.

Bob Riley of Newcastle, California supplied the details of the *Kleinsmith's* 1956 Med cruise. Great story, Bob, and we thank you for it.

A special thanks to the readers of my first book who encouraged me to write another.

It was wonderful to hear, for the first time in fifty years, from several of my former shipmates on the *Haven* and the *Kleinsmith*. Friendships were forged that the years could not break. It was also wonderful to be able to make new friends from former crew members of both the *Haven* and the *Kleinsmith*. I heard from many, both when ordering the book and after they had read it. For many, the book seemed to act as a catharsis, reminding them of their military experiences, memories they hadn't thought about for a long time. I'm sorry that, with one exception, I couldn't locate missing shipmates they wanted to find.

Wife Bettie named this book. She was involved all the way with the writing of each story and deserves much credit for it being completed. Many thanks and my love.

CONTENTS

ACKNOWLEDGMENTS v

AUTHOR'S NOTE xiii

STORIES FROM THE USS HAVEN (AH-12) 1
   VD DAY 3
   WHO ATE MY SHRIMP? 11
   THE PURPLE ORANGE CAPER 17
   WHERE'S THE CAPTAIN'S GIG? 23
   SPAM 27
   AROUND THE WORLD IN SIXTY DAYS 41

STORIES FROM THE USS KLEINSMITH (APD-134) 75
   HONEY, WHERE'S MY CAR? 77
   A MONKEY NAMED LAZARUS 85
   RANK HATH ITS PRIVY 95
   COLONEL BO PEEP HAS LOST HIS JEEP 103
   HOW BACHELORS LIVE 113
   THE VIRGIN MARY 127
   THE UNHAPPY ADMIRAL 135

STORIES FROM THE STATES 141
   SERGEANT STUHLDREHER OF THE PINKERTONS 143
   THE STING 159
   EARTHQUAKE! 171
   TRANSFER THE BASTARDS 183
   THE COAST GUARD, A DOG AND A DRUNK 195
   UNCLE TIM'S WAKE 211
   THE CATHOLIC CADILLAC 217
   THE PATRIOTIC SWIMMING POOL 229
   MY FIRST COLLEGE FOOTBALL GAME 233

THE BADGER GAME	239
IT'S STRADIVARIUS TIME!	261
MOOSE MISCHIEF	273
THE PSA PGA	283
THE SECRET SOCIETY	303
POPCORN ANYONE?	311
LETTERS FROM IRAQ	315
A SCREENPLAY TREATMENT	355
THE MAZATLAN INCIDENT	359
SCRAPBOOK	375

This book is dedicated, with love, to

Our Children

Lisa   Andy   Linda   Beth

and Our Grandchildren

Jessie   Sarah   Jason   James

AUTHOR'S NOTE

These are true stories with real people.
Real names were used, except in one story, due to libel laws.

STORIES FROM THE USS HAVEN
(AH-12)

VD DAY

It was a cold winter day in Inchon, Korea, aboard the hospital ship *USS Haven*. A raw, wet cold that cut through our winter clothes. If you ever ask a Korean veteran what he remembers most about Korea, chances are it will be, "The cold of winter and the stink of summer." Even on clear winter days the ever-present winds were nasty.

Not only was it another day of disagreeable weather, it promised to be hectic, as usual. The helicopters bringing wounded aboard were arriving at a fast pace. As the ship's Helicopter Landing Officer, I was busy running back to the aft helicopter pad to help them land. A Helicopter Landing Officer was required by Navy regulations, but I'm not sure what help I afforded the pilots. Even though our ship was not originally designed for landing helicopters, our landing pad was large and not encumbered by dangerous wires. I would stand there, shivering, and guide them in with two paddles swiped from the ping-pong supply box. No one missed the paddles; we didn't have a ping-pong table, but we had the supplies ready just in case we ever got one. (I had gotten the idea of the paddles from the nightly movies.) The pilots were not allowed to loiter on the pad. Another helicopter might be coming, so each one took off as soon as it was unloaded.

Another reason I faced a busy day was that I had a rehearsal with the ship's band, and would also be teaching two correspondence classes. I know that's an oxymoron, but that's the way some Navy correspondence classes were handled in those days. The Navy wanted people knowledgeable in the subject matter to assist the swabbies taking the courses. I didn't mind. I actually enjoyed such duty, but it was one more task on top of my normal duties.

And since this was VD Day, I had more extra work in front of me. If you're a certain age I'm sure you remember VE Day and VJ Day. WW II abbreviations, VE stood for Victory in Europe, and VJ was for Victory in Japan. But VD Day? Let me explain. Every month or so the Army required the medical personnel on the *Haven* to inspect the local prostitutes for venereal disease. The Army would bus them in from all over. We would run boats to and from the pier, and our shipboard doctors, nurses and corpsmen would do the inspections. The prostitutes would readily agree to participate. If found clean, they would then be entitled to cards attesting to this fact. These cards were highly desirable, since the more knowledgeable troops would insist on seeing them prior to conducting their business. (I saw this procedure in only one other country, pre-Castro Cuba. There the local doctors would do the inspection, issuing yellow cards to the women.)

I well remember the attitude of the doctors on VD days. Angry. Angry that they were separated from their families for many months, thousands of miles from home, and for what: to inspect whores. Angry that their hard-earned skills were being ill-used to do this. Angry that their expensive training had caused debts up to their ears, and that they were not making the large sums they had anticipated when they had incurred the debts. Angry? You bet! We didn't have any general practitioners on board. The 56 doctors were board-certified surgeons, plus a psychiatrist and a pathologist. Our four dentists weren't involved in VD day.

My first roommate on the *Haven*, Dr. Ben Gregory, an orthopedic surgeon, had explained their feelings on this to me. Ben had served in WW II, then had gone to medical school, then did his required residency. Shortly after he went into private practice he was called up for the "police action." At a time when he was at the peak of his earning power, here he was, earning a small military pay many miles from home. And this story was the same for many of our doctors.

My extra assignment on VD days was ensuring the sugar bowls on the tables in the crew's mess hall were removed. That's right — making sure the sugar bowls, which were always left out between meals for the coffee drinkers, were removed. Why? Because, in addition to the free medical inspections, the prostitutes were treated to a nice meal. As they took over the mess hall with their long, colorful scarves flowing around them, they made a colorful change to the usual scene of blue-covered swabbies. They would grab the sugar bowls and quickly empty them. Not using spoons, they would simply upend them into their mouths. So we learned the hard way to remove the bowls on VD days. At the time we were disgusted by the whores' despicable behavior in doing this. I now believe they had a deficiency in their diet, and their bodies were starved for sugar.

So in addition to my normal disbursing duties, I was busy that day landing helicopters, teaching, practicing in the band, managing my 120-man division, and removing sugar bowls. What I sure didn't need was Paul Fisher, a fellow officer, asking me, "Hey, Bud, you running a special at your office?"

What was he talking about?

"Well, Bud, there's a long line of guys standing outside your office door. I was just wondering what was going on since the door's closed."

Well, I started wondering too. A long line of sailors standing outside a closed door? What is going on back there? Without answering Paul, I hurried back to my office. Sure enough the door was closed, and a bunch of swabbies were standing outside. Strangely, they melted away as I came down the corridor. I became more curious.

My office had a "Dutch" door, that is, an upper and lower door. Each half door could be locked independently, and the lower door had a shelf built in. This allowed us to conduct business with the lower door closed, talking and handling documents through the open upper door. We didn't need any extra people in the office, small as it was, and I didn't need unauthorized personnel around my money. OK, strictly speaking, it was the Navy's money, but since I was *personally* responsible for it, and had to make up any shortfall out of my pocket, I took a very possessive attitude toward it. So, wondering what was up, I unlocked the upper door and peered in.

The usually well-lit office was dark, with only one dim reading lamp on. In a bunk at the rear of the office, usually chained up against the bulkhead during the business day, was a Korean woman and a swabbie. She was naked; he had his trousers and shorts down around his ankles. I was staggered; speechless. My office a whorehouse? And apparently doing a landslide business, judging by the line outside. How had this happened?

Just then, my chief disbursing clerk, Barbee, clutched my shirt. "Mr. Stuhldreher," he whispered, "we have to talk."

Indeed we did, as soon as the whore and swabbie left my office.

"OK, Barbee, you better level with me. I'm as ticked off as I can ever remember. What in hell are you running here?" As if I hadn't guessed. He was using VD day to his advantage. But in my office? That news getting out would put me in a pot of very hot soup. Our Captain was really naive about certain things, sex being one of them. Unusual for a Navy ship, we had two elevators on board which were used to transport the wounded to the operating rooms at the bottom of the ship. The two operating rooms were located on the lowest deck to minimize the rocking motion. The elevators were rarely used by the regular crew, but one day the Captain had ridden in one. He naively asked what a mattress was doing in it. He didn't know the elevators could be stopped between decks, thus providing a rare place of seclusion for making out. And if he would have been shocked with a truthful answer about the mattress, which he didn't get, imagine what he would have felt upon learning I had my own private sex operation in business on his ship! This deal would top all the other scrapes I had gotten into on the *Haven*.

Barbee, a 1st Class Petty Officer, Disbursing Clerk, operated on the shady side at times. He was from a rural area in West

Virginia, and, according to him, a really hard-scrabble place up in the hills. Although possessing more mental smarts than many college graduates I knew, Barbee hadn't finished high school. In fact, he went only one year until his uncles needed him in the family business which was making and selling "White Lightning," their name for moonshine. He was caught running a load by the State Troopers. The car had no back seat, was weighted down at the rear, and had a hell of an engine. Normally Barbee could outrun the police, but this time he blew a tire. Since he was so young, sixteen, the judge offered him a choice: military service or jail. So the Navy got him on what we called a "kiddie" enlistment: out in four years, or his twenty-first birthday, whichever came first. But Barbee enjoyed Navy life, and had re-enlisted three times by the time we started working together.

My first inkling that Barbee wasn't opposed to skirting the law came when he approached me with a deal. It seemed there was an imbalance in what the Japanese yen was worth in Japan compared to Hong Kong. This was a long time ago, and communications in money matters between countries was very slow. Today such an imbalance would be corrected in a hurry. Somehow, I never knew how, Barbee had learned there was a 20 percent difference in the exchange rates between Japan and Hong Kong. His proposition was simple. I would give him money (scrip) from the ship's safe, and he would convert it into yen in Japan. When we got to Hong Kong he would sell it for American dollars, which I would then put back into the safe. The next time we hit Korea he would have no difficulty in selling it for scrip. As he put it, this would be a "victimless" crime. The Navy would have the same amount of scrip it started with, and no funds would have been stolen from anyone. *He knew other ships in the Far East were doing it and making great gobs of dough!* He thought we would be nuts to pass up a golden opportunity like this. He proposed we invest $100,000, half of the scrip in the safe. I would pocket the $20,000 profit; his cut would come from selling the American dollars for scrip in Korea to black marketeers.

Well, maybe it was a "victimless" crime, but crime it was, and I wanted no part of it. I was in enough hot water most of the time as it was. I didn't need another way to tick off the Navy. Regretfully, I turned Barbee's proposition down, much to his disgust and dismay.

Therefore, while I knew Barbee cut things close to his vest, this whorehouse operation was pretty brazen. My office a whorehouse? The CO would initiate punishment without even letting me get a word in. But it was easy to figure out Barbee's scheme. He had simply seen a way to make some extra money, taking advantage of two coincidences. One, when space permitted, the Navy required a bunk be placed in Disbursing Officer's office, where the safe containing large amounts of money was located, $200,000 in 1954 dollars in my case. The senior petty officer in the disbursing office always claimed the bunk for himself. Such privacy was hard to come by for enlisted men. Two, our ship having VD days completed the unholy alliance. A private place and willing whores? On a Navy ship? Too good to pass up as Barbee explained. "Hey," he asked, "who's the loser? The girls are happy, the sailors are, too, and I make a little money."

I glared at him. As I started to speak Barbee said, "Mr. Stuhldreher, let's talk this over." He went on to explain that silence might be the best course of action, both for him, naturally, and, surprisingly, for me.

"You better do some tall talking," I told him, "your ass is hanging out over the rail on this one." And he did.

Walter "Bud" Stuhldreher

He convinced me that spilling this dirty laundry over the ship was certain to rebound unfavorably on me. Yes, it was true I didn't know about it, but with my track record, who would believe it? Especially after the 48-hour party in a whorehouse in Yokosuka for the crew which everyone knew I had produced. Since I was the officer in charge of both Barbee and the disbursing office space, wasn't I equally guilty? And so on. Mad as I was, I realized Barbee had me between a rock and a hard place. No news was going to be good news.

I did kick him out of his bunk in the Disbursing Office, replacing him with the next highest ranking clerk. And I prayed every night that none of my fellow officers would get wind of this exploit. I shuttered to think of the inventive nicknames which would have been applied to me. Luckily, I never heard anything further on it.

Paul Fisher, the one who had told me about the line outside my office, asked me about it soon after. "No big deal, Paul, nothing to explain." My, what a whopper!

WHO ATE MY SHRIMP?

The Fight

The officers in the wardroom aboard the hospital ship the *USS Haven* had just enjoyed a special lunch: fried shrimp. The serving trays had been removed, but the wonderful smell of fried shrimp lingered in the air. Only a few officers were still present in the wardroom when our chief pathologist, LCDR L. Walter Fix, came in late. He was mighty displeased when he was told there was no more shrimp. Would a cheese sandwich do?

"No, it damn well would not," Dr. Fix exclaimed. He shoved back his chair and stormed into the galley, apparently to check up on the mess steward's statement. He quickly canvassed the galley and found Robby, one of the stewards, eating some shrimp. (The stewards often ate food leftover from our mess rather than go to the enlisted men's mess.) Dr. Fix flew into a rage, yelling, "Damnit! I was told there wasn't any! How dare you eat my shrimp!" Robby looked up at him, terrified. Dr. Fix then picked up the tray of shrimp from the table, and threw it onto the deck. The tray went flying, the shrimp hit the deck, and the steward cowered. Dr. Fix stalked out, figuring that was that, and hadn't he shown the culprit up properly!

I reacted with anger when I heard about the squabble. It wasn't fair, an officer throwing food. The enlisted man had no choice but to take it. It was a dirty, unprovoked thing to do. If Fix had wanted fried shrimp that badly, he should have come to lunch on time. Unlike our other doctors, his patients weren't going to miss him for a short period of time. Fix was a large fellow, about my size, 6'2" tall, around 220 pounds. He was filled with self-importance. Not one of my favorite people to begin with, this nasty business caused me to head for his room as soon as I heard what had gone down.

"Fix, what did you think you were doing? Throwing an enlisted man's food on the deck is beneath even you, I would have thought!" Now Fix was four ranks above me so he didn't appreciate being addressed in this combative manner by a lowly Ensign, especially one who wasn't his professional equal, another doctor.

"Just who do you think you're talking to, mister! I don't know what you're talking about, so get out of my room before I put you on report!"

"Put me on report? The hell you say!" We kept jawing at each other for a couple of minutes, then he got real personal.

He poked me, hard, in the chest while yelling, "Get your sorry ass out of my face!" Whoops! That did it. I tried to nail him with a punch, missed, and we then grabbed each other. Pushing and shoving we fell to the deck, rolling up against a bulkhead, then rolling back. Two other officers heard the commotion, looked at the two saps rolling around, and threw a bucket of water over us. I guess they thought that since it worked on dogs it would work on these two idiots. They were right. Fix and I scrambled to our feet, dripping wet.

The XO was called, and he immediately marched us up to see Captain Clark, wet uniforms and all, our shirts hanging out over our belts.

The Captain was disgusted with both of us: with me for having gotten into trouble one more time, and with Fix for behaving so badly. Fix received a letter of reprimand. I was put in hack for seven days. This meant I was confined to my room except for bathroom visits. A Navy Shore Patrol guy, armed, was stationed outside of my room to ensure I stayed in it. Meals were brought to me, and my only reading material was supposed to be the Bible. I cheerfully disobeyed the Bible reading requirement. It wasn't bad duty at all.

Capt. John P. Clark, USNR

Walter "Bud" Stuhldreher

Aftermath

The steward who had been involved came to see me after I was out of hack and requested permission to speak to me. I said sure, what was on his mind? He said that he and the other stewards really appreciated my standing up for him. Now you have to remember that, while President Harry Truman had "integrated" the Armed Services in 1948, the Navy hadn't gotten the word six years later. The forty stewards who reported to me were all black. Their duties had little to do with defending our country. They made up the officers' beds, served us in the wardroom, kept our clothes clean, cleaned our heads (bathrooms), etc. I don't recall if they shined our shoes. If you remember the Pullman porters on trains, either through actual experience or through the movies, then you pretty well know what the stewards did. The Civil Rights Act of 1964 finally changed this, but it was still ten years in the future.

I thanked Robby for thanking me and said I'd do it again. He just stood there, shifting his weight from one foot to the other, not leaving. I asked him if he had something else on his mind. Well, he did, but was obviously unsure how to say it. After some more prompting he finally spoke up, not looking me in the eye. "Mr. Stuhldreher, I don't know what it could be, but if ever you want something special from me, all you have to do is ask."

"Well, Robby, there sure is something you could do for me, which I would really appreciate." He was dumbfounded. I went on, "Robby, do you know how little I understand when you and the other stewards speak to me? I don't understand 90 percent of it and just fake it. But I've overheard you talking with each other and have understood every word. Why do you suppose that is?" Robby just stared at me. He didn't have a clue where this conversation was going. But I did! "I'll tell you what I want: I want you to quit putting that black dialect on me when you stewards speak to me. I know you do it on purpose, and you can talk clearly if you want to, so that's what I want, Robby."

He didn't say a word, obviously uncomfortable that I had uncovered their secret. He mumbled something and took off. I was interested to see what would happen next.

From that day on, for the rest of my tour on the *Haven*, I was delighted to be able to understand everything the stewards said to me. For more than one reason, that fight had been well worth it.

Epilogue

Maybe ten or fifteen years later, long after I had left the Navy, I saw Dr. Fix again. There was a picture in the paper of the president of the West Virginia Tree Growers Association presenting a huge Christmas tree to the President of the United States, the immense tree which the First Lady lights each year at Christmas. Yep, you guessed it, the presenter was none other than my old boxing opponent, Dr. L. Walter Fix. How had a pathologist become a Christmas tree grower? Who knows, I sure don't. And to tell the truth, I don't care.

THE PURPLE ORANGE CAPER

The enmity between Dr. Fix and the Supply Department wasn't over yet. Fix got it into his suspicious head that LCDR Ferrin, my boss and the head of the Supply Department, was up to skullduggery, specifically, selling rotten food to the wardroom. This was absurd since Mr. Ferrin was as honest as the day is long, more honest than Fix could possibly imagine. Here's an example of how honestly Mr. Ferrin operated.

Walter "Bud" Stuhldreher

That's Mr. Ferrin on the left, me in the middle, and Frank Beck, our other Supply Officer, on the right

When we arrived in Hong Kong, the ship was visited by many locals who wanted to do business with the ship, some for ship supplies, others wanting the crew's business. Mr. Ferrin was summoned to the quarterdeck to meet with a Hong Kong businessman. The tradesman wanted an exclusive contract to do all of the crew's dry cleaning. In return he offered to do Mr. Ferrin's dry cleaning free, as well as that of the other supply officers. Mr. Ferrin just stared at him wordlessly. Then he picked up the poor guy and threw him overboard! The OOD was horrified. It was probably 40 feet down to the water and who knew if he could swim? That's if he survived the fall. There were dozens of sampans below hovering around the ladder hoping to sell produce, trinkets, souvenirs, etc.

The Commanding Officer, Captain Clark, was also horrified. He visualized possible public relations repercussions, maybe a lecture from the shore-based Naval establishment on proper vendor relations. Mr. Ferrin, characteristically, was unrepentant.

SOUR M.A.S.H. AT SEA - SECOND WAVE

"He should have known better than to suggest an illegal inducement!" And that was that. Nothing further was heard from anyone on the fateful pitch. But, damn, I wished I'd seen the look on that vendor's face as he went hurtling over the rail!

Mr. Ferrin was looked down on by the ship's medical officers because of his lack of formal education and his rough reputation. (Mr. Ferrin did complete two years at Duke University in order to retain his commission, which he had earned the hard way during WW II. He had started the war as an enlisted man.) The doctors referred to him as the "studly jock and Supply Officer of the Haven Maru." And LCDR L. Walter Fix, MD, the ship's pathologist, was Mr. Ferrin's number one adversary. After the ship visited Hong Kong, Fix thought he had discovered that Mr. Ferrin had served unwashed fruit to the officers and crew. So Fix and his unwilling corpsmen, using little cardboard boxes, collected some 500 samples of fecal matter, one from every man and woman on board, so that he could test for unwanted amoebae in the stools.

Undeterred that no villainous bugs were found, Fix wrote a scathing report on Mr. Ferrin's supposed shortcomings. Mr. Ferrin pointed out that the posted safety regulations in the galley required all fruit to be washed prior to serving it, and that the cooks on duty swore they had followed instructions and had washed the fruit. The Supply Officer in charge of the cooks, Warrant Officer Frank Beck, also stated in a written report that he personally had supervised the washing, since the fruit had come from a foreign port. With no evidence found to support Fix's allegations, especially in the 500 stool samples collected and examined, Mr. Ferrin was declared innocent. Fix was commended by Captain Alexander O. Henry, USN, Commanding Officer of the hospital, for his diligence in protecting the crew. This was simply a reflection of the doctors' dislike of Mr. Ferrin, who knew how they felt about him and didn't give a damn. This episode was the beginning of the Fix/Ferrin vendetta. They truly hated each other's guts. And this set the stage for the purple orange caper.

To prove these findings, Fix clandestinely injected Gentian Violet (a purple dye) into all of the soft oranges which he had just surveyed. At breakfast the next morning Fix cut into the orange he had been served, discovered it was as purple as the sunset over Diamond Head, Hawaii, and shouted: "Now I've got you, you son of a bitch!" He figured Ferrin was caught red-handed, purple-handed if you prefer, and turned him into long-suffering LCDR Clyde L. Ernst, the Executive Officer (XO), who had been refereeing the vendetta for some time. This was a serious accusation, so the XO headed upstairs to bring in the CO.

Rumors were flying around the ship that the enlisted men were eating better fruit than that served in the officers' wardroom. Based strictly on these rumors, Fix formed and headed a secret investigation board. The investigation was conducted, also in secret, and the board declared over-age fruit, vegetables, and other foodstuffs had been found rotten and scheduled for destruction. Then Mr. Ferrin had supposedly sold the mess to the officers' wardroom. This procedure would reduce the cost of feeding the crew, making Mr. Ferrin look better in his reports to the Supply Department ashore.

Captain Clark must have been a Sherlock Holmes fan because he promptly ordered an examination of *all* the oranges on board, both those considered fresh and those ordered to be destroyed. All the fresh oranges were found to be orange; all the surveyed oranges were found to be purple. Most important, none of the other oranges served that morning had been purple, nor were any on the sideboard in the wardroom found to be other than a bright orange. Captain Clark decided one orange, which should have been destroyed, had inadvertently been served to LCDR Fix. The matter was considered closed. Mr. Ferrin and Fix remained steadfast enemies.

As described in the previous story, none of the wardroom stewards had reason to be fond of Fix. Knowing this, and smelling a rat, I questioned the stewards. They admitted Fix had been served the bad fruit on purpose. Further, it wasn't the first he had been served, just the first he had caught, and that I would be well-advised to *never* eat the same food served to Fix. While I empathized with their feelings, hell, I disliked Fix myself, I requested they lay off until things cooled down. They agreed, and I never queried them again on the quality of Fix's food. He was the ship's pathologist, wasn't he, and it was up to him, an expert in such things, to recognize bad food when he ate it. You know what? The poor man did suffer a higher incidence of Montezuma's Revenge than the rest of us. He just kept washing his hands more after every stint in the lab, but to no avail. Probably just a genetic disposition to intestinal flu.

WHERE'S THE CAPTAIN'S GIG?

Reading an earlier story of mine, **The Jeep Sunk? Really, Captain?** *Reminded Dick Ruehlin, my good friend on the Haven, of this incident which happened prior to my reporting on board.*

Walter "Bud" Stuhldreher

The *USS Haven*, had been swinging around her anchor for several weeks. Prohibited by the Geneva Convention to tie up to piers in war zones, she waited in the Kanghwa Bay off Inchon, Korea. When the swift tide went out, she faced the shore. When it came in, she faced the Yellow Sea. When the 700 bed hospital ward filled up, she would leave for Japan to off-load the wounded and the dead. This move usually happened every six weeks, and pretty much told her story. The medical people, the surgeons, nurses, and corpsmen, were busy, but the people who ran the ship were bored out of their skulls. Even the Captain. (This Captain was not John P. Clark but his predecessor.)

Late one Sunday afternoon the Captain, while ashore, used an Army radio to notify the ship's OOD that his gig was missing. Would the OOD please send some of the crew ashore to look for it. The Captain's gig was the boat assigned to the Captain, and only he used it. It was outfitted especially for the Captain and was first-rate in appearance. To be assigned as a crewman on the Captain's gig was a honor. In response to the Captain's request several crewmen were sent ashore and spent hours searching for the gig, without success. Everyone on board, from the XO on down, was nervous about managing to lose the Captain's gig without a trace. Such an occurrence was an unheard-of tragedy aboard a Navy ship. It was bad enough to lose a common ship's boat, an incident which could make the crew the laughing stock of the fleet, but the Captain's gig? How could this have happened? Who was at fault? Who had seen her last? Why didn't her regularly assigned crew know where she was? Sherlock Holmes' presence was sorely needed to unravel this mystery.

There was a good reason why no one was able to find the gig. It was resting quietly on the bottom of the bay. Actually, the Captain himself had sunk the gig. He had been piloting the craft when he took it on a trip to shore and had hit something submerged in the water. The gig had quickly sunk out of sight. On board the gig at the time were two Korean "honeys." He was taking then back to shore after they had spent the weekend with him aboard the *Haven*. He had not wanted the gig's crew to observe this stealth mission.

The Captain might have gotten away with this little mishap even though the gig was worth about $50,000 in 1953 dollars, for the mystery might never have been solved. A Korean fisherman's nets got caught on the sunken gig and were ripped. The fisherman then requested reimbursement from the Navy for the damage, and the story unraveled. Pinocchio's nose couldn't have been any longer than the Captain's when he was caught with his pants in the water, so to speak.

SPAM

In the winter of 1954 the *USS Haven* steamed into the harbor at Pusan, Korea, on our way back from Japan to Inchon. There wasn't much to see, since Pusan had experienced ferocious fighting early in the war. In fact, the farthest North Korean advance was at Pusan in August 1950, and the Allied Forces were almost thrown into the sea. If you look at a map you can see Pusan at the lowest end of Korea, on the southeastern end of the country. My friend Paul Fisher, the ship's navigator, asked me if I wanted to go ashore with him. No, I didn't. It was colder than a seal's butt in Alaska, and besides, my four or five months aboard had taught me that going ashore with Paul was an excellent way to get in trouble. Paul was a rambunctious fellow, very strong, and he liked looking for fights. He insisted I go, making the telling point that Pusan might not be much, but it was sure to be better than Inchon. He had me there, even if it was a specious argument. If asked to name a place in the world

Walter "Bud" Stuhldreher

worse than Inchon right then, I could ponder long and hard but I would have to give up.

LTJG Paul Fisher, ship's navigator and good friend for 50 years, on the pier at Pusan

Situated between Japan, Russia and China, Korea is a very ancient country. It has been a battleground for centuries. Legends say that Korean civilization began about 2300 B.C. Korea developed by itself until five thousand exiles from China settled there in 1122 B.C. Much of the Chinese civilization in Korea was destroyed in the 1200's (A.D.) when the Mongol armies of Genghis Khan and Kublai Khan overran the country. The first Japanese invasion of Korea took place in 1592. After six years of fighting, the Koreans finally drove them out and refused to allow any foreigners to land in their ports for the next three hundred years.

In spite of the intense cold, normal for Korea in the winter and particularly so near the sea, Paul still wanted to go ashore. So we slapped on our Navy-issued foul weather jackets and went ashore to see what, if anything, was up. Paul insisted on calling our jaunt a "walk about," some Australian term he had run across. I was pretty sure this pertained to a lengthy journey in the Australian outback but didn't correct him. Paul didn't take kindly to corrections and was in far better shape than I was. Today I think he would be called a "health nut," but that term hadn't been invented yet. He liked to work out and to box with my boss, LCDR Ferrin, a moose of a man. Paul had given up wrestling with Mr. Ferrin since that was a sure way to get beaten up, but he could last longer at boxing than most of Mr. Ferrin's opponents. Paul, of course, in spite of being ten years younger, lost all bouts with Mr. Ferrin as did everyone else.

Leaving the ship, we learned we were restricted to the port, so we ambled around the immediate area. The city, or what was left of it, was out-of-bounds unless you were in an Army unit stationed there. Now visiting a port in the dead of winter isn't high on my list, but visiting a bombed-out, shot-up port, while freezing every minute wasn't even on the bottom of my list. But Paul, always an enthusiastic fellow, was having the time of his life. He scrambled up every crane he found, peered in ruins of warehouses and pretended to steer the burned-out hulks of the boats we came across.

It was a strange scene, a deserted port, yet not deserted. There were railway sidings but no engines, no freight cars. Evidently the freight trains had not been put back in operation, or more likely, the tracks were not completely serviceable after being shot up by artillery shelling or bombing. American ships of all sizes were tied up to the pier. The workers were unloading the immense quantities of supplies armies needed to survive.

Walter "Bud" Stuhldreher

One scene entranced me. (See picture.) Next to the only remaining wall of a bombed-out building stood about a dozen poles, standing like sentries or pillars for a missing temple. While at one time they must have served a purpose, neither Paul nor I could figure what that could have been. But it was fun to stand there and conjure up possible uses for the solitary, silent sentinels.

Me staring at the mysterious sentinels

Paul and I had been poking around, just killing time, and I was ready to go back to the ship, but Paul wasn't. We had probably covered five percent of the place, and he was ready to keep on exploring for hours. Damn, I hadn't even made it to the Boy Scouts and here we were, boy explorers, playing Indiana Jones, and freezing our asses with no hidden treasure lurking in a nearby cave. No beautiful girls, either. And, strangely, no locals of any sort, men or women. Just swabbies and grunts, sweating in spite of the cold, going about the manly business of unloading ships and loading trucks. And, as we knew, this went on 24 hours a day, 7 days a week, month after month.

"Paul," I asked in frustration, "just what are we doing here?"

SOUR M.A.S.H. AT SEA - SECOND WAVE

"Stu, it's an adventure, a walk-about!"

"Well, when you're ready to go back to the ship, where there's heat and hot coffee, let me know and I'll race you there." Paul just grinned and I knew we weren't leaving.

Me, obviously disgruntled, holding Paul's boxing gloves and freezing my ass

Nearby was a small bar, obviously a local merchant cashing in on the workers' thirst. So we headed there for a quick beer. The bar was crowded with allied forces of many nationalities, and clouded with smoke from cigars and cigarettes. Cursing filled the opaque air. We fitted in perfectly, Paul and I, except neither of us smoked.

"Gee, Stu, isn't this great! Now will you quit your bitching?" Fair enough, I thought, this was the best I had felt in hours. So one beer turned into two, into three, and so on. The juke box, fueled by Korean coins, blared American songs mangled by Korean bands. For background music, the locally popular "coal diggers" song was played endlessly. I was never sure just what it was, a special Korean or Japanese tune, but you

31

heard it all over. To us Americans it sounded like people swaying forward as they moved in a long line, and we pictured coal miners digging in a deep tunnel of coal. Anyway, that's the best I can do in describing it, and every Korean veteran remembers hearing it playing over and over again in Korea and Japan.

Then we heard a loud commotion outside, a racket of yelling and cans being thrown. Paul and I staggered out to see what was up. Two British soldiers were yelling at an emaciated dog whose ribs were showing. Apparently she had been scrounging in the garbage dump behind the bar. The Brits were throwing cans at the poor dog, trying to scare it away. Too hungry to care, the mutt just dodged their missiles and kept digging in the mess. Paul screamed at the Brits to stop, saying the dog wasn't doing them any harm, it was just hungry. The Brits stared nastily at Paul and told him "to bugger off." They didn't want the mutt scattering the trash. Wrong thing to say. Paul didn't take guff from anyone, especially two Brits trying to hurt a defenseless dog. He waded in, throwing punches at the surprised soldiers, ignoring their feeble drunken attempts to fight back. I picked up a golf ball sized rock, made my hand into a fist around it and landed a good one on the nearest Brit. He must have thought I was King Kong. That punch drove all thoughts of fight out of him. He yelled at his friend and they left in a hurry.

"Stu," Paul asked, bending over to get some much-needed oxygen in his beer-loaded lungs, "that was some punch!" I sheepishly opened my fist, showing him the rock which had acted like an accelerator. "Damn, where did you learn that trick?" he asked admiringly.

"Where else? I read it in a book. Mickey Spillane got clobbered that way once, so I thought I'd try it. Worked great.

My knuckles are going to be sore, though." Well worth it, we both thought.

The dog trotted up to Paul, stared up at him with loving brown eyes and rubbed against his legs. Un, oh, Paul, like the rest of us, greatly missed having family pets around, be they cats or dogs, and was returning the dog's pleading look with equal longing. "Stop right there, Paul, nothing doing."

"Why, Stu, whatever you're thinking, you're wrong" he replied, rubbing the emaciated dog's fur as he lied, and I figured he was lying 100 percent.

"Paul, you've got to be out of your mind! There's no way you can smuggle that mutt on board, but even if you did, how can you hide her on the ship? And how can she live — take a crap for instance? Come on, we've done our good deed for the day." And I walked off. Paul didn't move.

"Stu, I just can't leave her here to starve, or be kicked by the next stupid grunt who comes along. Come on, help me figure a way to get her on board the ship. I'll worry about the rest later."

My worst fears realized, I stared at the sap. I could tell that, no matter what I said, Paul was a goner and the dog was coming with us, whether I liked it or not. But how to do it? How to get her out to the ship, anchored in the harbor, and up the gangway past the OOD at the top? And that was just for openers!

Fortunately, or unfortunately, Paul had a small duffel bag with him for his boxing gloves. Why he had brought them, I'll never know. He ditched the gloves and put the dog in the bag. Barely. "Stu, you get on the officers' boat first, and I'll jump on right behind you. If we do it right, the coxswain will never get wise."

"Oh, sure, Paul," I answered sarcastically, "and the pooch knows to keep her muzzle shut and not bark? When did you train her so well?"

"Will you quit dreaming up problems? I'll have my hand around her muzzle when we board, she won't make a sound." Paul was always long on optimism, if not always correct. Sure enough, soon after the boat left the pier the dog barked.

"Mr. Fisher," the coxswain asked, "just what are you trying to pull off?"

"Dave, you've got to help me out here a little. The pooch was starving, and worse, two British soldiers were kicking the crap out of her. Mr. Stuhldreher and I kicked the shit out of them, and I'm not leaving her there for more trouble. Dave, I swear no one will ever know you spotted her." Luckily, unlike some of the officers, Paul was very well liked by all the crew who knew him personally. Dave went along and looked the other way, if a bit reluctantly. He trusted Paul not to rat on him, and besides, Dave missed having a pet around as much as everyone else.

Going up the gangway, Paul kept a firm hand on the dog's muzzle, threw a casual salute to the ship, then the OOD, murmured something, and hurried past. Whew! He, and the dog, had made it! First problem solved, many more to come. As I saluted my way past the OOD he asked what Paul and I had been up to — that the port looked like a lousy place to spend much time in. "Gee, Charlie, you're absolutely right, it was a loser. But it was fun to get off the ship for a while, and we managed to find a bar." Charlie looked a bit worried by my answer. He was my roommate, and had endured enough post-beer smells to last him a lifetime. "Don't sweat it, Charlie, only had one or two." Charlie didn't look convinced. In his experience I, and anyone I had gone out with, had never stopped after only two beers.

Charlie was an interesting fellow, soft-spoken, and, I swear this is true, with absolutely no bad habits. Rumor had it that the Executive Officer had assigned him as my roommate on purpose, hoping osmosis would work, and I would start acting more like Charlie. Didn't work. Of Lebanese extraction, he was from Tennessee, and kept a picture of his fiancee on his desk. I once asked him where he had met her and was flabbergasted by his answer. "Bud, I never have."

"Charlie, what are you talking about, never met her?" Yep, I had heard correctly. Apparently it was still the custom in the Lebanese community for the parents to arrange marriages, at least according to Charlie. "Charlie, you do know it's 1954 and you live in the United States, not Lebanon? No one has arranged marriages anymore." Charlie assured me I was wrong, and that he and the girl were quite happy with the arranged engagement. "How do you know that, Charlie? You've never met her."

"Who do you think I get those perfumed letters from? You know, the ones you're always smelling and making dumb comments about?" Whoops, he had me there. His letters smelled better than any I ever got, which, since I had broken up with my girl in Chicago, were few and far between. My family wasn't much into writing letters, and they wouldn't write perfumed ones anyway.

Leaving Charlie, I hurried down to Paul's cabin. "Down" was the operative word. The *USS Haven*, a big hospital ship, had lots of officers and the junior ones were housed lower than anyone else. One time when the Commanding Officer, Captain

John P. Clark, had stormed down to my room to chew me out, he had to come down so many ladders he was out of breath and had to sit down. I'm not sure if that wasn't the first time he realized how we ensigns lived. Not that he cared much.

Paul had found a pan and the mutt was happily slurping up water. "OK, Paul, so far, so good. But what's next?"

"Stu," Paul answered, ignoring my negative greeting, "I've thought of a great name for her. Spam. It matches her color and I love the stuff."

Paul and I, out of over 500 crew members, were probably the only ones who liked Spam. I still do. Howls of rage would swirl up when it was served for breakfast. Not from Paul and me. We would eat all of ours, and would scrounge off the nearby officers, who were only too happy to give it to us. "Paul, that's a great name, Spam, but how are you going to handle her living on board?"

"Stu, I don't think it's going to be a problem. In the first place, she can sleep and eat here in my room. As far going to the bathroom, I haven't worked that out yet, but am sure there's a solution hanging around waiting to be found." Paul — ever the optimist, I thought. That problem sounded like a "show-stopper" to me. That's what we at IBM called an insurmountable problem, one which stopped a project in its tracks unless it could be solved quickly.

"I'm beginning to believe my first thought, that our (what's this 'our' business, Tonto, you're on your own on this deal) trying to keep her a secret isn't possible. Besides, I don't think it's necessary, except maybe from the CO and XO. Think of how Dave (the coxswain) reacted to her; he actually helped us. I'm positive the crew will like her and help keep her on board."

SOUR M.A.S.H. AT SEA - SECOND WAVE

And that's exactly how it worked out. Spam quickly became a favorite of the crew. The deck apes put their heads together and came up with a solution to the bathroom problem. They rigged a mat made out of a rough covering, sort of like a doormat, a square yard or so in size. Spam was trained, in a remarkably short time, to do her business on the mat, which was kept on the fan tail (rear of the ship). When the mat was soiled, a crew member dropped it over the rail where the salt water cleaned it. It was then pulled back aboard and repositioned. If Spam needed to go, and couldn't find an open door, she would grab the nearest swabbie by the pants leg and pull him towards a door. They loved it, calling it the "DP" duty. DP standing for dog poop.

Spam was also trained never to enter the galley or the crew's mess area. The first rule was for hygienic reasons, the second for Spam's health. The darn sailors would have fed her into oblivion given half the chance. Paul explained how important it was not to feed her for this reason. I mean, one owner giving her a cracker or two was one thing, but if five hundred sailors were doing it the poor dog would have been a blimp.

Our 56 board-certified surgeons — but not Dr. Fix — entered into Spam's care with a vengeance. She was treated with antibiotics immediately after reporting on board. Her ears were examined, eyes were washed out and fleas were eradicated. In short, the displaced orphan received the highest quality medical care any mutt ever received anytime, anywhere. In a couple of weeks, Spam was a beauty. Her coat was shiny and ribs were no longer showing. And one of the doctors decided to test one of Paul's restrictions on Spam: that she not be allowed in the wards. Years ahead of his time, he thought that perhaps her presence would help the patients' recovery, that a reminder of home could possibly pick up their spirits.

Walter "Bud" Stuhldreher

And did it ever! Spam turned out to be a better psychiatrist than our trained one. She would sit quietly by the patients' beds and wait to be petted, never pushing the process. She would moan with happiness from the attention and lick the patients' hands. If they didn't have any hands, double amputees were sometimes present, she would push against their legs. It was a toss-up who had more fun, the patients or Spam. And language problems were nonexistent with Spam. She didn't care if the patient couldn't speak English, she loved him just the same. And he loved her.

Well, you might reasonably ask, do you really expect us to believe that the CO or XO never learned about Spam? I'm not sure, but I do know this for certain: they always pretended they knew nothing about her and that was plenty good enough for Paul and the crew. And for Spam too. Her daily routine was usually far removed from the CO's and XO's haunts. If by chance they came near her, a crew member snatched her up and into hiding until the danger passed. Houdini himself couldn't have performed a better disappearing act. As far as I knew, the CO and XO never saw Spam once.

But, after several months, it was time for Paul to leave the ship. His obligated service time was up, and Rockford, Illinois, his hometown, loomed in his immediate future. And for sure, Spam was going with him. The men were desolate. They had quickly grown to love Spam. She was their tie to their previous life, a life at home with parents, siblings and pets. They thoroughly enjoyed the game of keeping her hidden from the CO and XO. The corpsmen also had the extra joy of seeing her interaction with their patients, the good she had done. In those days kindness towards others aboard Navy ships was pretty scarce, and I think Spam brought out the best in all of the crew.

But everyone had known from day one Spam belonged to Mr. Fisher, so it was a done deal.

The next time we docked in Japan, Paul went up to Senior Officers' country, where the CO and XO lived, to pay his respects prior to leaving the ship, and the Navy. They both knew Paul well, having worked closely with him since he was the ship's navigator. Thanking him for his contributions to the ship, and wishing him well in civilian life, the CO had one last request for Paul. With a twinkle in his eyes the CO asked Paul to let them know how Spam adjusted to life off the ship, a life certain to be far different from the one she had known. Paul was astounded! They had known after all! But he kept a straight face and assured them he would.

Later, Paul wrote me that tears had stung his eyes as he left that final meeting with the CO and XO. Tough, rambunctious, feisty Paul Fisher with tears in his eyes? Their thoughtfulness had really gotten to him.

AROUND THE WORLD IN SIXTY DAYS

In August 1954, I left the USS Haven in Inchon, Korea, to report aboard my next ship which was in the States. At this time the Haven was preparing to return to the States herself, and was scheduled to arrive in September, but I couldn't return with her as I would have preferred. I had to fly back in order to get to my new ship before she left for the Mediterranean. But the Haven didn't get to return to the United States just then after all. Instead, she was, improbably, sent around the world first. This is the story of that epic voyage.

I heard of the voyage several years ago. Boy, did I wish I had been aboard her! Although I wasn't, I wanted to tell the story, but how? Luckily, my good friend, Dick Ruehlin, was the ship's navigator and shared many details of the trip with me. Even more lucky, indeed a coincidence of amazing proportions, I received an order for my first book, Sour M.A.S.H. At Sea - And Other Stories, *from Mary (Shafer) Cermak. She wanted me*

Walter "Bud" Stuhldreher

to call her and I did. It turned out Mary had been on the Haven as a nurse during this long voyage and consented to be interviewed. Mary supplied many of the medical details, plus she had saved a cruise book! Fifty years old, tattered and fading, it was a treasure trove. Finally, I received a long letter from Frank Shemanski, of San Diego, California, who had also read my first book. He, too, had made the epic voyage and supplied many details about operating the ship. Without Mary's, Frank's and Dick's help it would have been impossible to tell this story. I hope you enjoy reading it as much as I enjoyed hearing about it from these participants.

But first, a short look at the history of hospital ships, on one of which I spent a long year in Korea.

Nurse Mary (Shafer) Cermak aboard the Haven at the start of the world cruise

LTJG Dick Ruehlin, my good friend for 50 years, the Haven's navigator on the world cruise

42

Pre-1900

If you're any kind of history buff, you know that for centuries kings, queens, popes and Biblical leaders sent out armies to expand their territories and increase their power. It might surprise you, since they are never mentioned, that hospital ships accompanied many of these armies. In 431 B.C. the ancient Greeks used a ship, *Therapetia,* with three banks of oars on each side to support the Athenian fleet. There are also some early accounts of the Romans using a ship with an equally healing name: *Aesculapius,* the Roman God of healing and medicine.

In support of the Fourth Crusade, Pope Honorius III sent an ambassador to Jerusalem with a ship reported to be equipped to serve as a hospital transport for a large number of patients. In 1588 the Spanish Armada included ships staffed with eighty-five physicians and surgeons. Following the lead of Spain, the British Navy outfitted a sailing vessel, the *Goodwill,* to be used in the Mediterranean as an auxiliary for hospital purposes. In 1741 two British hospital ships were in service; by 1800 the English had seven hospital ships in service.

In 1803 the first American hospital ship, the *USS Intrepid,* was fitted out and commissioned. During the Civil War the hospital ships used by the Union were not under a single command. Some were operated by the Navy and some by the Army, but most were operated under the U.S. Sanitary Commission. Created by President Abraham Lincoln in 1861, the Sanitary Commission was charged to care for the wounded and sick military personnel. The Sanitary Commission outfitted more than twenty riverboats for this purpose, and the Army had five river steamers. The most upscale Army ship was the R.C. *Wood,* which included such amenities as a galley, dispensary, laundry, several bathrooms with hot and cold running water, and rooms for nurses assigned to the ship.

During this period the Navy operated three riverboats which served as hospital ships. The most famous was the *Red Rover*. The steamer had been captured by a union gunboat and promptly sent to St. Louis for conversion to a hospital steamer. She was well-equipped. The *Red Rover* had nine bathrooms with at least two on each deck, a 300-ton capacity icebox, an ice-making machine, an elevator between decks, an operating room, and two galleys — one for the sick and one for well people. Her decks were wide and the cabins roomy. The windows were covered with gauze cloth blinds to keep out flies, mosquitoes, and the smoke and cinders from the ship's stack.

The *Red Rover* was placed in service in 1862 and was sold at public auction in November 1865. During this three year period she handled approximately 2,500 patients. One notable feature: she was the first Navy hospital ship to employ permanently assigned nurses.

U.S. Hospital *Red Rover* 1862-1865

1900

The Geneva Hague Conventions of 1899 and 1907 were the first to detail the restrictions under which hospital ships could be operated, and defined their protection from enemy forces. Essentially, the ships had to be well-marked and were not subject to damage or capture by enemy forces. Today's ships carry the same markings.

During the Spanish-American War the Red Cross placed a total of five hospital ships in service, joined by eight more operated by the Army and Navy.

In World War I over 200 hospital ships of all types and from all nations saw service. The ships varied in size. The gigantic British ship, *Aquitania*, with 4,182 beds, had the largest bed capacity of all the ships. The very small vessels with fewer than 50 beds were used in shallow waters, such as the canals of France and Belgium. The German hospital ships stayed in port serving as base hospitals. During 1914-1917, seven military hospital ships struck mines and either sank or were badly damaged. In 1918, eight hospital ships were torpedoed by the Germans with many casualties. This led the British to repaint their hospital ships in combat colors and place them in convoys with other ships of war.

World War II

At the beginning of WWII, the U.S. Army had no operational hospital ships, the Navy had two. By the end of hostilities the Army had 26 hospital ships and three foreign-flag hospital ships in service. The Navy had twelve hospital ships and three evacuation ships.

Korean War

The only hospital ship operating at the start of the Korean War, the *USS Benevolence*, collided with the freighter *Mary Luckenback* in a fog off San Francisco in August 1950. The freighter's radar was off. She hit the *Benevolence* immediately forward of her forward red cross, one deck below her main deck, then slid down the length of the ship, opening her like a can opener. The *Benevolence* slowly capsized to port. Of her 526 crew members 503 survived, 23 perished. The loss of life might have been less; however, the commanding officer of the *Benevolence*, thinking it had been hit in water only 50 feet deep, yelled incessantly "Don't abandon the ship! Don't abandon the ship!" At that depth the ship would lie on the bottom with some of her upper decks above the water. Unfortunately, the ship had gone down in 70 feet of water and thus sank totally out of sight.

At the outbreak of hostilities in Korea, the *USS Consolation*, *USS Haven* and the *USS Repose* were immediately activated.

The Vietnam War

The *USS Sanctury* and *USS Repose* served in this war.

Operation Desert Storm

Two gigantic new hospital ships, the *USS Comfort*, commissioned in 1986, and the *USS Mercy*, commissioned in 1987, were activated to support this war. The *Comfort* arrived in the Arabian Gulf in September 1990, and for the next six months provided support for the multinational forces. She admitted 690 patients and performed almost 300 surgeries. After treating 21 American and two Italian repatriated prisoners of war, she arrived back in the States in April 1991.

SOUR M.A.S.H. AT SEA - SECOND WAVE

Gigantic is the proper description for these two hospital ships. Prior to the Iraq War, they were on Reduced Operating Status, meaning they could transition to Full Operating Status in five days. Both are designed to receive 200 patients a day, with a capacity of 1,000. They are three football fields long (894 feet) and are ten stories high from the water line to the mast. They each have twelve operating rooms and nine elevators. Each elevator can carry 25 ambulatory or six patients on stretchers. *(My ship, the USS Haven, was only 520 feet long, with two operating rooms and two small elevators.)*

Inchon, Korea

Enough history; back to Inchon, Korea during August 1954. The Commanding Officer of the *Haven*, Captain John P. Clark, was surprised to receive a radiogram directing the ship to immediately proceed to Yokosuka, Japan. There the ship was to off-load any wounded and load supplies in preparation for a long trip which would start in Saigon, French Indochina. The French had been fighting the communist Democratic Republic of Vietnam, led by Ho Chi Minh, since 1946. The fighting had continued until recently, when the Communist Vietnamese decisively defeated the French at Dien Bien Phu, in western Tonkin. The 55 day siege of this fortress cost the French about 16,000 casualties; the Vietnamese lost about 20,000. This defeat ended the rule of France, Viet Nam was partitioned, and the entire French army was withdrawn. The *Haven* was to pick up over 700 French Legionnaires who were wounded in this last battle.

To say the radiogram was a blow to the crew would be a major understatement. From September 1950, until August 1954, the *Haven* had been 100 percent involved in the Korean War. She had served four tours, admitting over 18,000 patients and treating over 35,000 outpatients. Over 700 helicopter landings had brought in upwards of 800 patients. (I was the helicopter landing officer during her fourth tour.) Fifty-four percent of those treated on the *Haven* returned to duty. (*Haven* nurse Mary Cermack says seeing the patients return to the front lines was one of the toughest things she had to handle.) The *Haven* had an extremely low death rate of one half of one percent. This was a result of the fine care the wounded received from the doctors, nurses, and corpsmen aboard the well-equipped *Haven*, the immediate availability of plasma, and the quick attention the wounded received, both at the front, at M.A.S.H. units, and on board the hospital ships. (The *Haven's* record was getting a wounded soldier into the operating room within 17 minutes of being wounded.) With the tension in Korea abating, this was to be the *Haven's* final tour, and the return home was eagerly anticipated by the crew. She had left Long Beach for this tour in January 1954, eight long months earlier, so not going home now was bad news.

Captain Clark called my best friend, LTJG Dick Ruehlin, the ship's navigator, to his cabin and showed him the radiogram. "Dick, you're the only navigator on board. This is going to be a grueling trip sailing west from Siagon to California. We'll sail through the Indian Ocean, the Suez Canal, France, the Atlantic, the Panama Canal — maybe 35,000 nautical miles before we reach our home port. Can you do it?"

Dick, true to form, answered with a smart-ass remark: "Sure, as long as we keep heading west we'll get there!" This was definitely not the answer the Captain was looking for.

"Dick, I'm not asking you about the condition of the ship, the condition of her power plant, the condition of the doctors or the crew. That's not your responsibility. What I want to know is, do you feel confident in your ability to navigate us around the world without a back-up? You're pretty young for such an assignment, but you've had a great deal of experience for someone your age and, if you feel you can do it, I'm inclined to accept your assessment. Otherwise I'll ask to have a higher ranking officer flown in for this trip."

Dick, by now understanding this was a serious business, replied, "Captain, I'm sure I can do it with two conditions."

"What are they?"

"First, that Chief Lovinggood be with us the whole trip. He's my right-hand man when it comes to navigation matters, and I wouldn't feel comfortable trying this deal without him. Second, I must have the most up-to-date navigation charts available. We don't have any on board for those waters." There was no GPS or LORAN to assist in navigating 50 years ago. Dick would have to rely on his sextant to determine the position of the ship and use navigation charts to determine the correct course the ship should take. An extremely difficult assignment.

"Dick, I can guarantee Chief Lovinggood is yours for the duration. I'll get the XO cracking on obtaining the charts you require. And, Dick, this thoughtful answer, unlike your initial response, tells me you'll do okay."

Yokosuka, Japan

"This is the Captain speaking ..." started the first of many conflicting messages. Dispatches, commands, and counter-commands flew around the *Haven* at such a furious clip that the ship's office finally gave up in disgust, locked the door and posted a sign that read: "Don't ask us ... we don't know either!" Apparently the higher-ups were arguing among themselves about the wisdom of helping France, help which required such a long trip by a US vessel. The reservists hungered to go home.

Walter "Bud" Stuhldreher

The regulars were torn between seeing their families once again and making an important voyage first. Countless messages later, on September 1, 1954, with a reduced medical complement aboard, the *Haven* left Pier 2, Yokosuka Naval Station, and headed for the week-long passage to Saigon, Viet Nam's "Paris of the East."

The Haven pulling away from the Yokosuka pier

The 56 doctors had been reduced to 9. Not a single dispatch had been received from the French regarding the condition of the wounded, just that over 700 needed transport. Based on the assumption that the wounded would have been operated on before the *Haven* arrived, the reservist doctors had been released from the ship to return home. On board were 24 ship's company officers, 9 doctors, 28 nurses, three dentists, one pharmacist officer and 464 enlisted men, including a couple hundred corpsmen.

Saigon, Viet Nam

Arriving on September 8, the ship had a five-hour trip up the Riviere de Saigon prior to docking. The *Haven* was greeted by a military band and several hundred soldiers standing at attention. But no wounded. The French had received notification of the *Haven's* pending arrival too late to begin loading today. Tomorrow would be the best they could do. So, at 0200 (2 a.m.), the crew was awakened, had breakfast and was ready to accept what turned out to be 721 patients at 0600. As far as the eye could see, French ambulances of varying sizes stretched out in an orderly row along the broad, tree-lined boulevard.

Walter "Bud" Stuhldreher

The ambulatory patients were assisted aboard and the first words spoken were "Ou est la head?" The rest were either carried up the ship's ladders by the corpsmen or winched up on litters. It was a slow process with many French military and civilians signing many documents. Red tape, of course. Four French officers also came aboard for the trip. Pay Officer Gaillaid, Chaplain Simon, Dr. Arrighi and Dr. Reydy were to assist the *Haven's* crew, interpreting when necessary, otherwise handling administrative duties.

The wounded were a disparate bunch — 420 enlisted French Foreign Legionnaires plus 300 regular French Army, French Navy and Legionnaire officers. Among the enlisted Legionnaires were two Americans.

Filled almost to capacity with patients, the *Haven* started its voyage down the Saigon River shortly before noon the next day, enroute to her refueling destination at Port Said, Egypt, via the Suez Canal. The ship left the expensive town of Siagon with local children happily chomping down on popcorn donated by the crew, crowds of well-wishers lining the quay, and the inevitable French military band playing the French National Anthem. As the soldiers on shore held their salutes, they were probably wishing they were going home to France themselves in the air conditioned comfort of the *Haven*.

SOUR M.A.S.H. AT SEA - SECOND WAVE

The *Haven* would transport the wounded enlisted Legionnaires to Oran, Algeria, then proceed to Marseilles, France, to off-load the wounded officers. (Enlisted members of the French Foreign Legion weren't allowed in France. Talk about snobbery! I think the French have elevated it to an art form.) The regular French Army and Navy wounded would also be off-loaded in Marseilles.

Enroute to the Suez Canal

Captain Clark was concerned about the crew's morale and the readiness of the ship to endure this long and difficult voyage. Nevertheless, these were his orders, and he intended to fulfill them as best he could. Trouble only waited until the next morning to rear its ugly head.

"Captain," the French Chaplain informed Captain Clark, "the Muslim patients wish to have an area designated for their prayer services, which as you know (Captain Clark didn't) occur six times a day. They face the east, remove their shoes and kneel down. Prayer then starts with the cry 'La ilaha illa-liauhu, Muhammad rasul aliahi.' This means, 'There is no God but Allah, and Mohammed is his prophet.' The prayers last about twenty minutes." Captain Clark was dumbfounded. The Navy takes religious services seriously, and, since time immemorial, the loudspeakers had blared every Sunday morning: "Now hear this: Catholic (or Protestant) religious services will commence at 1000 hours. The smoking lamp is out until further notice."

With cigarettes selling for only a dollar a carton, and with few other relaxing activities aboard, almost every swabbie smoked. You can probably remember seeing sailors in their dress whites or blues, both bell bottomed. No zippers, only 13 buttons, the same as the number of original colonies. No pockets either. When wearing white tee shirts, the sailors rolled the sleeves up over the pack of cigarettes. Wearing blues, with long sleeves which had to stay down, the sailors put their smokes inside their socks. No way Captain Clark wanted to eliminate smoking six times a day during this trip! He sent for the senior American chaplain, CDR Roy L. Bonner, for some advice. Chaplains Bonner and Simon conferred.

"Captain," Chaplain Bonner announced, "there appear to be about 20 ambulatory Muslim patients who wish to be accommodated. The helicopter landing deck will do nicely for the prayer area and won't interfere too much with regular ship activities. We can put a portable record player up and the Imam's recorded call to prayers can be heard by those assembled there. Chaplain Simon is agreeable to this if you are."

"OK, Chaplain, sounds like a reasonable solution. Make it happen. But remember, no 'No Smoking' announcements over the loudspeaker system six times a day." Everything seemed to be in place until the first Muslim service commenced. The working sailors gawked at the kneeling patients, chanting prayers loudly in a foreign language. The Muslim patients complained bitterly. The helicopter landing deck might not be a mosque, but it was a sacred place six times a day, and such rude behavior by the Americans would not be tolerated! So the sailors were instructed to stay away from that deck during prayer services. If their duties required them to be there, or pass by, they were to keep their mouths shut and eyes averted. This order was not what they wanted to hear, but was obeyed.

Perhaps the first Muslim prayer service aboard a US Navy ship in the 20th century

This fracas set the tone for the entire voyage. The French seemed to have forgotten, or didn't care, that they were guests of the American Navy, who were going to great lengths to transport them home safely, and in comfort, something their government was apparently unable, or unwilling, to do. They never asked, they *demanded* that their requests be met promptly, no questions permitted. They tried the Americans' patience and the crew was soon tired of their company. Captain Clark, the officers, and leading enlisted men held the ship's crew together. Their attitude was that it was only for 60 days, and if they had to, they could make this trip standing on their heads. So the crew groused incessantly, but did their jobs. Meanwhile, more trouble was brewing in the medical wards.

While the medics had treated many nationalities in the Allied Forces in Korea, including the intractable Turks, the French Foreign Legionnaires were setting new records in behaving badly. They were a tough bunch, consisting entirely of volunteers, mostly from countries other than France. Some had joined to escape political imprisonment, others to escape punishment for crimes, and still others to seek adventure. Discipline in the Legion was harsh, the pay was low, and the Legion served in unpleasant areas. While they had put up a final heroic resistance at Dien Bien Phu, nevertheless, they had been soundly whipped and were leaving the battlefield in disgrace. But they had survived the terrible fighting and were now living in undreamed-of comfort. They were attended by pretty young women while lying in comfortable beds in air-conditioned wards. You would think they would have been happy. Well, you would be wrong.

By nature, and custom, the Legionnaires were bitchers. By virtue of simply being in the Legion they were tougher than hell, eager to provoke trouble. Fights were their normal solution to all problems. Most had little or no education. Few could write, but all could curse with every breath. In short, according to the nurses, they were a handful. The word "thanks" apparently wasn't one of the few English words they knew. Their number-one complaint was the loss of their daily wine ration. As in the British navy, a daily serving of alcohol helped the Legionnaires put up with substandard living conditions. Forget that they were now living better than they ever had in their entire lives! No, by god, they were entitled to their wine and where was it? Well, not aboard a US Navy ship, that's for sure. No booze aboard was a strict Navy regulation, rigidly enforced. So the Legionnaires were out of luck for the duration of the trip, but they never quit bitching about their missing wine.

A bigger problem was the Legionnaires from Senegal, the westernmost country in Africa. Volunteers from the six main tribal groups, the Senegalese Legionnaires, were huge fellows with ebony skin and white teeth filed to sharp points. Scary customers, indeed. And, according to Mary Cermak, quite insistent in pressing their unwanted affections on the nurses, grabbing them as they went past, touching them, etc. It got so bad in Ward D, the lowest ward in the ship, that the nurses were not allowed to enter unescorted.

The *Haven's* food was another problem. Because the deployment had happened so fast, no special effort had been made to ascertain, or provide, the Legionnaires' normal rations. It would have been a tough project in any case since so many nationalities were represented, but, plainly, hot dogs, baked beans, etc., didn't sell. Rice and fish became mainstays on the menu. Baked potatoes, not mashed, were OK also. But bitching over the food was a constant. Truth to tell, the French wore out their welcome long before reaching Algeria and France.

In comparing the difficulties the nurses had with these patients with those aboard the *Haven* back in Korea, Mary Cermak tells an interesting story. Because some of the other nurses were reluctant to tend an enemy soldier, Mary ended up the chief caregiver to a North Korean soldier with a gaping chest wound. Nothing could be done for him, it was just a question of time before he died. But Mary tended to him, mostly holding compresses against his chest. What made it difficult to continue this thankless task was the soldier's habit, every time he gained consciousness, of spitting at her, his sworn enemy. The Senegalese Legionnaires weren't so different from him.

So, with over 700 unruly patients and a crew of over 500 who were wishing they were going home instead of heading away from the "good ol' USA," the *Haven* plowed doggedly on. Like the fabled *Flying Dutchman*, maybe they too, were doomed to sail forever. And crossing the equator was next on their itinerary.

Walter "Bud" Stuhldreher

Crossing the Equator

Crossing the equator is a big deal in the Navy requiring extensive preparations. Part of this involved the "Shellbacks," any sailors who have already crossed the equator, warning the "Pollywogs" what dire things were being planned for their initiation. The official records were checked, and all Pollywogs had a "W" painted on their foreheads the day before the dreaded ceremony. During WW II, the equator ceremony had gotten out of hand several times, and serious injuries had resulted. On this occasion the presence of 28 women on board probably had a restraining effect, and so the *Haven's* ceremony proceeded without any injuries, but with a lot of embarrassment, as was the intention.

Two *Haven* sailors tried to escape the impending ordeal by wearing borrowed French Foreign Legion uniforms. Since they hadn't been completely successful in eradicating the "W's" on their foreheads, they were caught standing on the tank deck, enjoying the initiation rites like the rest of the French patients. A bunch of newly converted Shellbacks grabbed them. They were tried by a quickly convened court, found guilty, stripped naked and put through their initiation. The culmination of the rites, which include a lot of paddling, plus immersion in unmentionable smelly unknowns, was the traditional kissing of the fat-smeared belly of "King Neptune," a Shellback chosen for having the biggest belly on ship.

SOUR M.A.S.H. AT SEA - SECOND WAVE

For LCDR Ferrin, in spite of his being a Shellback of long standing, the crew pulled off a special rite. A couple of Korean tours earlier Mr. Ferrin had, according to the crew, cornered the market in Westpac (the Western Pacific Naval Command) for grape-flavored ice cream, only to discover that the sailors would not eat it. Even the Marines who visited the ship, and were desperate for some ice cream wouldn't eat it. Mr. Ferrin finally had to throw it overboard. Prior to this trip he had cornered the Westpac market for Quaker Puffed Wheat and Quaker Puffed Rice, his all-time favorite cereals, only to discover that the crew disliked both of them. The crew even threatened to riot for Cheerios, Wheaties, and Sugar Frosted Flakes. Since the ship was underway, and unable to procure other cereals, the ship was stuck with great quantities of the puffed rice and wheat, which were served every morning. Consequently, the crew decided crossing the equator would give them an opportunity for a double-header: insult Mr. Ferrin and get rid of a lot of the hated cereal. (A wider latitude was permitted sailors during crossing-the-equator ceremonies. Physical encounters between officers and enlisted personnel were OK, as long as they didn't cross certain boundaries.)

With great glee the Shellbacks sweet-talked the "Snipes" (the engine room gang) out of a huge vat normally used to circulate used oil through cleaning agents so it could be used again. Getting the vat topside, in the dead of the night, was a monumental achievement. It was filled with barrels of Quaker Puffed Wheat and Rice, hosed down with sea water, then topped off with some dead fish saved for the occasion. A curtain was rigged around it to keep it hidden.

When all the Pollywogs had been turned into Shellbacks, a ceremony followed by everyone on board except the luckless crew members on watch duty, eight of the biggest, toughest sailors grabbed the unsuspecting Mr. Ferrin. The curtain was ripped open, and the sailors threw Mr. Ferrin, clothes, shoes, watch and all into the vat. This was accompanied by some well-rehearsed Shellbacks yelling: "Now you can eat all of the damn stuff you want! We don't want it!" When Mr. Ferrin tried to climb up the slippery sides of the vat they pushed him back into the noxious brew. Finally King Neptune relented, and after getting Mr. Ferrin to swear he would never order the damn cereals again, let him escape. It was easily the highlight of the equator crossing ceremony, and Mr. Ferrin took it with good grace. After all, he had been an enlisted man once himself and understood that the rough nature of the joke was not done in malice. In truth, all Mustangs (Navy slang for officers who had started out as enlisted men) were admired by the enlisted personnel. They knew the Mustangs had earned their rank, unlike us college boys.

Leaving the equator behind, the *Haven* proceeded through the Indian Ocean enroute to the Red Sea, an arm of the Indian Ocean that separates the Arabian Peninsula from northeastern

Africa. Some of the crew who were familiar with the Bible knew this was the location where Moses commanded the sea to part. The waters divided, permitting the Jews to escape to the other side. Then, as the Pharaoh's army followed, the sea closed on the army, drowning everyone. The Red Sea gets its name from the hot winds blowing clouds of desert sand that settle on the sea's brown surface in great reddish streaks. Some members of the crew put this coloration to good use by heaving overboard the remaining supply of the hated Puffed Wheat and Puffed Rice. It blended in quite nicely and was greatly enjoyed by the seagulls who noisily gathered it up in low, swooping dives.

Next up, the dangerous screw-up at the Suez Canal.

The Suez Canal Debacle

The first of the crew who saw the canal said: "That's a big ditch surrounded by acres of sand." That observation wasn't far off the mark. The *Haven* was approaching the southern end of the canal from the Red Sea. The canal, a narrow man-made waterway extends a hundred miles, connecting the Red Sea and the Mediterranean Sea. To handle larger ships, it has been widened and deepened a number of times since it was opened in November 1869. When the *Haven* went through, it was 46 feet deep, had a bottom width of 118 feet and a surface width of 390 feet. Most of the canal can handle only single-lane traffic, and dredges operate at all times to remove the sand blown in from the desert. Although scheduled to turn the canal over to Egypt in two years, Great Britain was still operating the canal at the time.

The Suez Canal runs north and south across the Isthmus of Suez, between the cities of Suez, at the southern end, and Port Said at the northern end. As you proceed north, the *Haven's* direction, you encounter Little Bitter Lake first, then Great Bitter

Lake, and finally Lake Timsah. It normally takes less than 15 hours to pass through the canal; however, the *Haven's* passage was a bit longer. Arriving the morning of September 26, the *Haven* did not exit at Port Said until the evening of September 27, 32 hours later.

It's not clear if the *Haven* had instructions for entering the canal. It probably did, but if so, the instructions were misunderstood. In any event, the *Haven* proceeded very slowly, blinking the canal headquarters — with no reply. Captain Clark turned to no one in particular and asked, "What's the matter with these people?"

Ruehlin remembers saying, "Let's just sit here."

The Captain replied, "We'll proceed very slowly. By the time we get to the canal's entrance, we should have the pilot aboard."

At that point the *Haven* received blinks (flashing light signals) from canal headquarters advising that the pilot would arrive "in due course." That's all the communication said. Obviously it meant something different to both parties, and, Ruehlin believes, that was the cause of the screw-up. The ship entered the canal without a pilot. Remember, the canal handled single-lane traffic only. A southern bound convoy was exiting the canal at the same time the *Haven* was going north! (This was the same as a car going in the wrong direction on a one-way street during rush hour. But cars have brakes and can be stopped in a few seconds. These leviathans are hundreds of feet long, at least 70 feet wide, and take miles to stop.)

It was a scene straight out of Dante's *Inferno*. The large white ship, the *Haven*, faced squarely into the oncoming convoy of ships. She looked like a deer caught in a car's headlights at

SOUR M.A.S.H. AT SEA - SECOND WAVE

night, frozen in fear and unsure of where to run. The officers on the bridge of the *Haven* didn't know what to do next. They had never been in a mess like this before.

Neither had the southbound convoy. As the ships milled about in the narrow passageway which was less than 400 feet wide, they began to blow their deep fog horns, sounding the international call of danger: seven blasts, then an interval, then seven more blasts. All the ships were doing this at the same time, creating a continuous blast of horns loud enough to wake the Pharaohs. Since some ships were 10 to 15 stories high and were close together, the sounds of the deep fog horns echoed off the other ships. The cacophony was deafening.

By now the water, normally brown and placid, was forced into small areas between the ships and was frothing like white water in a rapid. The *Haven* looked like a VERY LARGE salmon swimming in a raceway upstream to spawn. The danger was very terrifying. If one ship bounced off another, it would then be thrown sideways into yet another ship. Soon the southern end of the Suez Canal would look like a 70 car pileup on a Los Angeles freeway.

The small boat carrying the forgotten pilot threaded its way desperately through the melee so that he could board the *Haven*. In his hurry the pilot hadn't stopped to dress and boarded the Haven in his underwear! The pilot, an Egyptian, hurriedly took charge. The people on the *Haven's* bridge, stunned with the tumult they had caused, were glad to let him. A captain isn't always happy to turn things over to a pilot. The captain still remained responsible for the ship and was often reluctant to relinquish control to a pilot. Both large canals, the Suez and Panama, give you no choice. But there, due to the highly specialized knowledge required, the captains are glad to step back. Often entrances into ports require that a pilot take over, but the knowledge of the local pilots doesn't necessarily exceed that of the captain, particularly when the ship's steering foibles are taken into account.

The pilot quickly steered the *Haven* over to the side of the canal, where some of the southbound ships missed her by four or five feet. When you consider that the ships were over 70 feet wide, and couldn't stop, it was a very narrow miss. The airways were filled with nervous voices of the other, bewildered pilots. The *Haven's* pilot screamed for radio silence; he instructed the other pilots to stay on the port side of the canal, as far as practicable, thus trying to slant the herd away from the *Haven*. To the surprise and overwhelming relief of the other pilots and the canal authorities, no mishaps occurred. No bashes, no wrecked ships, nothing but a bunch of shattered nerves.

When the pilot saw the danger was past, he pulled a bottle out of his oversized brief case and took a mighty swig.

"Hey, what do you think you're doing?" shouted the OOD. "Liquor isn't allowed on US Navy ships!"

"I'll have a drink if I want to!" replied the unrepentant pilot. "You people are incredibly lucky I pulled this chestnut out of the fire. In twenty years I've never seen a bigger mess. Now we're going to sit here until the Brits arrive and figure out what to do with you. My nerves are shot, so I'm drinking whether you like it or not." And he did.

The British authorities arrived immediately and were livid. The valuable canal, the busiest in the world, had come mighty close to being shut down by this bunch of landlubbers. Not a seaman among them, in their estimation. And they were just getting warmed up! It was not pleasant for Captain Clark and his crew on the bridge.

The first decision was to turn the culprits back and force the *Haven* to take the long way around Africa and the Cape of Good Hope which would add another 4,000 miles to their journey. But after a couple of hours cooler heads prevailed when they learned that while the *Haven* was guilty of negligence of the highest order, her crew had never navigated the canal before. The skippers of the merchant ships had done it hundreds of times and were familiar with procedures. Also noted was the purpose of the *Haven's* journey, one of mercy and compassion. Finally, the Brits were interested in maintaining good relations with their greatest ally in WW II, knowing that the U.S., although belatedly in their opinion, had saved the free world at great price, both in casualties and materials. So the Brits relented, but with severe restrictions.

First, the *Haven* was to wait until the canal was virtually free of other traffic. Second, command of the ship was not to be returned to her crew until the ship had cleared Port Said. Any questions? Any disagreements? Didn't think so.

So the normal 15 hours required for the passage through the canal took 32 hours for the *Haven*. With not a single murmur arising from the CO, XO, or anyone else in the *Haven's* crew. They had been damn lucky, and had many miles of waters they had never sailed before in front of them. The *Haven* had never previously been out of the Pacific Ocean, and had never gone through either the Suez or the Panama Canal before. This incident alerted them to the disturbing fact that they had a lot to learn and no school to attend. They were truly on their own.

Meanwhile, the pilot and Ruehlin hit it off well and he told Ruehlin how "out of it the British were." What had just happened to the *Haven* was bound to have happened some day. Ruehlin took this to mean that the Brits were having tea and/or asleep as the *Haven* approached. No one will ever know. Later in the day the pilot explained to Ruehlin that where Moses led his flock across the water was no big deal. "It was the narrowest part of the Red Sea!" Maybe a little Egyptian bias there!

The Brits and the American consul made a big issue out of the screw-up. The Brits blamed the *Haven* for not being more prudent. Ruehlin continues to believe that some employee of the canal company was asleep at his post. In any event the *Haven* was assessed 100 percent of the blame, and Captain Clark received "a letter of caution" from the Chief of Naval Operations, i.e., the top gun in the US Navy. Ruehlin received nothing. Years after he left the Navy, Ruehlin drove down to New York City and had a nice chat with Captain Clark who was then in charge of recruiting for the Navy in the Northeast United States. Ruehlin asked the Captain if his promotion possibilities had been damaged by the canal incident and he replied no, he didn't think so.

But the *Haven's* troubles going through the canal weren't over just yet. The Captain was asked to anchor in the Great Bitter Lake, midway through the canal, in order to pick up some special equipment not put aboard when it should have been, back at the entrance. To top the ship's humiliation, the anchor windlass which was used to lower and raise the anchor failed, and the ship was unable to stop. The other ships transiting the canal, who knew all about the debacle at the southern entrance, sent the ship flashing light signals saying "Still in a hurry?" At least they had enjoyed the *Haven's* problems!

Next on the agenda was a short stop at Port Said, Egypt, for refueling. While there the enterprising local merchants encircled the ship in small boats (called "canoes" by the *Haven's* crew), offering trinkets, shoes, rugs and almost anything else. The desired goods were brought up to the main deck by the crew throwing down "heaving" lines to the waiting vendors below, and hauling the purchased goods up the 40 feet from the water. Truly a "bargain basement!" The crew bought more of the stuff than perhaps they should have. The "leather" bags soon began to reek of some indescribable odor, and most of the zippers were defective. The Egyptian slippers, which the crew thought were loafers, didn't look nearly as good when worn with their "civvies," and the "hand loomed" rugs turned out to be machine made. At least none of the crew's hard-earned money went on booze and women; they hadn't gotten any liberty.

Next up, Oran, Algeria, in five days. Then, at least, the unruly enlisted Legionnaires would be gone. It couldn't happen soon enough!

Oran, Algeria

On October 2, early in the morning, the *Haven* arrived at Mers El Kebir, the closest port to Sidi-bel-Abbes, headquarters of the French Foreign Legion. The dirty little city looked damn good to the crew, who had been promised a two-hour liberty. It would be the first solid ground they had touched in 22 days. After receiving official callers who were accompanied by a military band and a drum & bugle corps, the debarkation began. The 420 enlisted Legionnaires either walked down the gangway or were carried on litters to the waiting ambulances. They were eager to lay claim to their long-absent wine ration!

While topside to watch the patients leave the ship, LCDR Ferrin and LTJG Ruehlin saw a small US Navy warship anchored off in the distance. Mr. Ferrin took a look through his binoculars and handed them to Dick. "Take a look, Dick. Unless I'm mistaken, that's Stu's ship, the *Kleinsmith*." Dick, incredulous they could be in the same port as my ship, had to agree with Mr. Ferrin. They signaled over with flashing lights and asked, "Is Ensign Stuhldreher aboard?" I was called up to the deck and was dumbfounded to see the *Haven* sitting there in this godforsaken port. When I left her at Inchon, she had been preparing to return to the States. What was she doing here? I took a ship's boat over to the *Haven* and had a nice mini-reunion with my friends whom I had never expected to see again. No one could believe the coincidence. What a nice surprise, and what a small world! I have never seen Ruehlin or Mr. Ferrin since. We have corresponded all these years, however.

Transportation time to downtown Oran turned out to be a half-hour ride each way. Many of the crew, divided into port and starboard two-hour liberty parties, decided to stay in Mers

SOUR M.A.S.H. AT SEA - SECOND WAVE

El Kebir. The horny crew found the only whorehouse in town and brought back exotic venereal diseases of various kinds. Some defeated the best efforts of the *Haven's* doctors, who were quite expert in the subject of sexually transmitted diseases. Dick's impression of Mers El Kebir was the same as mine: "The end of the line. An absolutely huge cultural difference."

By early afternoon everyone was back aboard and the gangway had almost been pulled away when word was passed for the mail working party to report to the quarter deck. Morale suddenly zoomed about 1,000 percent. After months of no mail, the twelve sacks of Air Mail letters were a wonderful sight. But not for Ira, a seaman. Ira's girl wrote, "I love you more than I can ever explain, but two extra months is too long to wait..." Ira pulled out his address book, unconcernedly crossed off her name and said, "Now about this first liberty in Marseilles..." But first, an unexpected problem.

Man Overboard

Early in the morning the *Haven* left Oran, bound for Marseilles. Soon after the ship sailed, the dreaded message sounded over the loud speakers. "Man overboard! Man overboard!" It turned out a sailor, drunk out of his skull, had jumped overboard to swim back to Oran to visit his "friends." The ship immediately initiated "man overboard" procedures.

It's not an easy task to find a person in the vast expanse of the ocean. Very much like finding the proverbial needle in a haystack. First the spot is marked with a buoy. Secondly, the ship begins a "lazy eight" turn. This maneuver is the best chance the ship has of returning to the closest spot to where the man had gone overboard. Just visualize an "8" on its side and that's the course the ship took. Finally you man the rails with every sailor available, equipping as many of them as you can

Walter "Bud" Stuhldreher

with binoculars. And you start looking, an almost hopeless task. According to Dick, Captain Clark did a masterful job in directing the search and the sailor was found shortly before nightfall. Sobered by the cold water, he had made a life jacket out of his pants. To do that you slip them off, tie each leg with a knot, and fill the trouser legs with air. Then you keep the trousers wet so the air won't escape as fast as otherwise. It sounds simpler than it is. He was one supremely lucky fellow, but his luck ran out soon after the rescue. He was killed in a motorcycle accident a few weeks after the *Haven* returned to Long Beach, California.

Marseilles, France

On October 4 the *Haven* arrived in Marseilles for a four-day stay. For the third time since the *Haven* had left Korea, a French band down on the dock greeted the ship with an American medley. Unfortunately, this medley included *"Sherman's March Through Georgia"* and the rebels in the crew had to be restrained from making some sort of demonstration. The whole ship, especially the corpsmen and commissary men, breathed a sigh of relief as the last patient was carried off the gangway at 11:05 a.m., ending the *Haven's* care and movement of the 721 French Army, Navy and Legionnaire patients embarked at Saigon. It had been a difficult trip with a difficult bunch of patients, few of whom thanked anyone as they left the ship.

70

SOUR M.A.S.H. AT SEA - SECOND WAVE

Now, the crew thought, Wine, Women and the Eiffel Tower, as promised! Alas, it was not to be. The promised 48-hour liberties failed to materialize, for reasons never made clear to the crew, so they had to satisfy themselves with the dubious pleasures of Marseilles. My ship later went to Marseilles, and since I hadn't lived in Cleveland or Houston yet, Marseilles was easily the worst city I had ever been in. It was the home port for the French Navy, much like Norfolk, Virginia, is for our Atlantic fleet, and consisted mainly of bars, cheap restaurants and whorehouses. I'm sure there was a nicer part of town, but I never saw it. And the local police, while unarmed, were all too quick to use their billy clubs on sailors, be they French or American.

Hey, I better clear one thing up. A couple of years ago Bettie and I were on a cruise ship which stopped in Norfolk. I had no intention of getting off; I had seen all I wanted of Norfolk in my Navy days, but Bettie insisted. Well, I gotta tell you, Norfolk is a changed town. The locals have done a wonderful job of transforming the city into a beautiful town, one that is a pleasure to visit. Norfolk, I salute you!

The crew was certain Marseilles was well-stocked with French wine and beautiful mademoiselles. Well, half-right isn't all that bad. What a sorry excuse of a town. The crew was glad to see it over the fantail as the *Haven* left, but scared, since the French newspapers had mistakenly reported their next destination as Saigon. So they were mighty relieved to see the Rock of Gibraltar on their starboard side as they left the Mediterranean Sea. Now they were dead certain their destination was really Long Beach.

Next up, the Panama Canal but, first, an unexpected adventure.

Walter "Bud" Stuhldreher

Rescue at Sea

Eight days after leaving Marseilles the ship changed course in order to rendezvous with a Swedish oiler, the *Soya Maria*. Five hours later, a crew member on the *Soya Maria* who had been stricken with acute appendicitis was transferred to the *Haven* and an emergency lifesaving operation was performed. The 27 year old seaman was placed in the Canal Zone's Immigration Station at Corozal six days later when the *Haven* arrived in Panama. How fortunate for him that a fully equipped hospital ship with surgeons aboard was in the vicinity.

Panama Canal

The two-day transit through this canal, unlike the debacle at Suez, was completed without incident and the ship headed for Long Beach, California. A poem, author unknown, was posted in the crew's mess hall:

>She worked us days, she worked us nights,
>>She kept us on the run,
>She took us clear around the world-
>>To get her mission done.
>
>We griped and groaned a time or two,
>>Our crew was always ravin',
>But as the cruise came to an end,
>>We ALL were proud of ... la belle HAVEN!

Long Beach, California

On November 1, 60 days and approximately 30,000 miles after leaving Yokosuka, Japan, the *Haven* approached Long Beach. The Captain's voice came over the loudspeaker system. This time the words didn't concern orders or ship's movement but were offered in appreciation for the individual effort put forth by each crew member during their world cruise. The *Haven's* arrival wasn't front-page news, but to the crew, their friends and their relatives waiting on Long Beach Municipal Pier it possibly was the event of the year. True, the Navy's enthusiasm was nonexistent; it had sent the Long Beach Junior High School Band instead of a Navy band to greet them, but that's the shore establishment for you. Without a doubt, it was the only Navy ship to return from an around-the-world cruise that year, yet the shore establishment didn't bother to send a single representative. Guess what? It didn't matter to the crew: they were home.

Mail and relatives were received aboard, followed by a mass migration to the Navy Receiving Station by a sizable percentage of the crew. Either discharge or a transfer to another ship was their immediate future. The rest of the crew tried to adjust to the fact that the *Haven* was home, that they were through world cruising, and that stateside leave and liberty were more than a dream. Fifty years later I want to say, in the time-honored brief Navy fashion, a heartfelt "Well Done."

Walter "Bud" Stuhldreher

The author and Mary (Shafer) Cermak in 2003 holding Mary's World Cruise book

USS KLEINSMITH

STORIES FROM THE USS KLEINSMITH (APD-134)

What do converted Destroyer-Escorts (APDs) do? They roll and they plunge. They buck and they twist. They shutter and they fall through space. Their sailors say they should have flight pay and submarine pay both — they are in the air half the time, under the water half the time.

Ernie Pyle from Okinawa, April 1945

HONEY, WHERE'S MY CAR?

Perhaps you thought some of these stories were bizarre, even untrue. This one is surely the most bizarre of the lot. If you doubt its authenticity, and have access to the archives of the Norfolk, Virginia newspapers, look up June 1956. It's all in there. Front page stuff.

In February 1956, the *USS Kleinsmith*, got a new Captain. He was my third skipper and easily the strangest. A very weird fellow, he kept to himself, rarely joining us for meals. He preferred eating alone in his cabin even though it was small and didn't have a table.

But that was OK; it was his choice. What was strange was his demeanor. He never reacted to anything — good or bad. Nothing seemed to make any difference to the skipper. And he was nonchalant about things he should have cared about. For example, if we were in our assigned position in a convoy he might say, "Mr. Casey, let's try the other side of the convoy. Make a starboard turn and go over there." LTJG John P. Casey, OOD and my best friend on that ship, would gently point out that wouldn't go over too well with the convoy's Commodore. The Captain would answer, "Oh, that's all right, Mr. Casey, just a thought."

If we had a deadline, he could care less if it was met. Required reports, radio messages to superiors, even getting the ship somewhere at a certain time, were all approached with equal indifference. It was almost impossible to carry on a conversation with him. If he opened a conversation and we responded, his next tack would be toward an entirely different subject, and always, always, with no expression. His face never changed. By far his worst habit was quietly instructing the helmsman to do something contrary to the OOD's wishes. The OOD was normally following orders received earlier from higher up, and obeying the skipper's new instructions would have meant trouble of some sort, sometimes putting us in danger. This happened so often that the sailors on the bridge had a tacit agreement to ignore the Captain's orders unless the OOD said otherwise. Not a good situation, but livable. Luckily, we were rarely at sea when this new skipper took over.

The ship had just returned from seven months in the Mediterranean. The ship needed repairs due to damage suffered in a terrible storm off Greece. So we had gone into the Norfolk Navy Yard for repairs, and it was there that this new skipper assumed command. After leaving the yard, we went to sea infrequently until we sailed to Cuba and Puerto Rico for six weeks. On this cruise the skipper's aberrant behavior when observed on a daily basis was much more noticeable. Luckily he was never aggressive about it. He was too laid back to be aggressive about anything. Nevertheless, we stayed away from him as much as possible. Also, luckily, we four department

SOUR M.A.S.H. AT SEA - SECOND WAVE

heads were experienced, knew our jobs cold, and had the confidence of the crew. So we squeaked through the six week cruise OK, with one notable exception.

We were leaving the port of San Juan one sunny Sunday morning. Because the passageway was very narrow, we were forced to back out — a difficult task for any ship. (If you have ever tried to back up a car while towing a trailer, you'll know what I mean.) The Captain was on the bridge quietly issuing nonsensical orders which no one was heeding. As usual, the skipper didn't mind being ignored. After a while, for reasons known only to him, the Captain climbed on top of the flat roof of the bridge. He stood on it looking around with interest, then fell over and just lay there.

As we continued to slowly back out, we passed close by two American cruise ships. There were far fewer cruise ships in those long-ago days, and simply seeing an American warship was quite a thrill for the passengers. They gathered at the rails, waving and yelling as they looked down on us. What did they think about the guy wearing nothing but bright blue pants (no shoes or shirt), that was spread-eagled on top of the bridge? He was, of course, our skipper who had returned from shore leave wearing only that. A strange duck.

When we returned to Little Creek, Virginia, our home port, it became obvious from the cruise that the ship had suffered greater damage in the storm than anyone realized during our first time in the yard. Once again the *Kleinsmith* was ordered back for repairs. This time it would be for a major overhaul, one which would require several months. During this time my obligated service time ended, and I left the Navy. But before my departure, I discussed the Captain's strange behavior with a doctor with whom I played golf occasionally. His diagnosis surprised me. "He's a bottle baby."

Walter "Bud" Stuhldreher

"A what?"

"A bottle baby, a lush, a drunk."

"What are you talking about?"

"Gee, do I have to put it in writing? Your skipper's behavior is a classic description of one type of drunk."

"Doc, are you sure? He sure doesn't behave like any drunk I've ever been around."

"Where he probably faked you out was his behaving so quietly, and always in the same manner. Never up, never down. Rather placid at all times. You probably would have guessed, but for one other symptom: he's drunk all the time. He's never sober, so you couldn't tell the difference. This type of drunk often goes a long time before anyone guesses the truth."

Well, that sure explained a lot. To think the skipper was never sober was a scary thought. I was more glad than ever I was getting off the *Kleinsmith*.

Obviously, I wasn't aboard the Kleinsmith when it left the yard the second time. My good buddy, John Casey, kept me up to speed on the happenings by letters and newspaper clippings. I am positive the following is an accurate description of what happened.

The *Kleinsmith* was released from the yard after 30 days of repair work. To get to the Atlantic from the yard, she had to first navigate a narrow river, the James. The ship left the yard later in the day than planned, and it was dusk as the ship approached the river. The skipper was on the bridge issuing

80

stupid orders. (The officers now knew he was always drunk.) His orders were ignored by the OOD, my buddy, LTJG John P. Casey. Then the Captain did something he had never done before in similar situations. He spoke the fateful words: "Mr. Casey, you are relieved. I have the conn."

Legally the Captain was in command now, and his orders had to be obeyed by the engine room and the helmsman. No more ignoring him now. No one ever understood why he chose to take over at that moment.

"Full speed ahead."

This meant 22 ½ knots, around twenty-five miles per hour. Casey and the XO argued with the Captain that this was way too fast in the river. Unperturbed, the skipper didn't seem to hear them. The engine room had no choice but to increase speed. The lights from the houses on the banks of the river flashed by at an increasing rate. You could see headlights of cars on a road parallel to the river; the ship was actually keeping up with them. All too soon, a 90 degree bend in the river was approaching, a turn impossible for the ship to handle at that speed. Casey, who had studied the charts prior to leaving the yard, warned the Captain about the approaching bend in the river. The drunken Captain uncharacteristically told Casey to shut his mouth, that he was in charge. He had navigated this river many times, and it was as straight as a razor blade. Horrified, Casey and the others on the bridge prepared for the inevitable. A sailor on the bridge with a telephone headset warned the rest of the crew to brace themselves: a crash looked imminent!

WHAM! BOOM! CRACK! The *Kleinsmith*, all 1,450 tons of her, traveling at 25 miles per hour, hit the river bank that was soft from spring rains. She grounded with a horrific impact at a cut in the bank, a natural ditch which allowed run-off from the street above to flow downward into the river. She plowed up a slight incline, slipping over mud and snapping off trees. Branches whacked the ship as she forged ahead. A rusting, abandoned car was obliterated. Reaching a side street located too close to the river, she snapped off streetlights and crushed two cars. The asphalt helped grind her to a stop. The noises she made as she traversed the ground waked the sleeping neighborhood. Lights came on in nearby houses. She was hopelessly aground and so far ashore that her propeller was sticking out in the air. The entire length of the ship had made it ashore. With most of her mired in dirt, and the screws out of water, there was no way to get her off simply by putting her in reverse.

The Captain, thrown to the deck by the impact, got to his feet and looked around, bemused. The remaining streetlights cast a glow over the bridge. "Gee, I wonder what street this is," murmured the skipper, apparently undisturbed by the fact the *Kleinsmith* was on the ground — actually a street — rather than in the water where she belonged. "How did we get here?"

"You stupid bastard, you ran us aground," yelled the XO at the Captain. The XO, as the ship's navigator, knew this mishap would end his naval career. The Captain got to his feet, looked at the street lights visible in the darkness, staggered off the bridge and passed out on the floor of the wardroom. The angry officers and stewards left him there.

Can't you just imagine some nearby homeowner going out on his front porch the next morning and asking his wife, "Honey, where's my car?"

"Why just where you left it on the street, dear, but now it's under that ship, I should imagine."

"Oh my God! Where did that come from? It's huge! What's a ship doing on our street?"

"I'm sure I don't know, dear. Maybe it's some sort of publicity stunt the Navy thought up."

The next day Navy tugs pulled the *Kleinsmith* off the shore. The immense impact had bent the main shaft. Since the ship was without power the tugs had to return the *Kleinsmith* for repairs. In disgrace, she was towed back to the same yard she had left less than 24 hours before. The yard was not happy. The Navy was upset. The local papers had pictures of the ship sitting on the street, and ran some unflattering columns about the danger to life and limb this unnatural shore excursion could have caused. As details of her crazy speed emerged, the publicity got worse. The mayor of Norfolk insisted on a public apology and payment from the Navy for all the damage. The owners of the three crushed cars asked for new cars. The Navy was in no position to argue with anybody, but they could take their anger out on the jerks responsible — the Captain, the ship's Navigator and the OOD.

The usual, lengthy process involved before formal court-martial proceedings could be initiated was omitted. All three officers were immediately relieved of their duties and restricted to their quarters. And I don't mean off the base. No, they were confined to the base with armed Marines standing guard outside their doors. They were notified that court-martial proceedings would start the next Monday, and legal defense would be provided. A fat lot of good that would do, they knew, and they were right. The Captain and the XO were found guilty of numerous offenses and kicked out of the Navy with no pensions. Casey, as OOD, would have received the same punishment but for mitigating circumstances. Witnesses testified that the Captain had legally relieved Casey, that Casey had warned the

Walter "Bud" Stuhldreher

Captain to slow down, and that Casey had warned the Captain the bend in the river was coming up. But the Navy, with a huge publicity mess on its hands, in a city where the townspeople suffered the presence of the Navy solely due to its economic impact, had to offer up as many scapegoats as it could muster. So Casey was judged guilty and issued a Letter of Reprimand. This would have been a career-breaker if Casey had been planning to stay in the Navy, but his obligated time was up, and he didn't really care. He was just happy to get out.

The Captain (who had left the Navy after WW II, had struck out as a civilian and reentered the service) returned to the job he had prior to rejoining the Navy — selling hot dogs on the streets of New York City. The XO was never heard from again. Casey returned to Massachusetts and enjoyed a long and successful career with the General Electric Company. We still correspond. The ship was repaired and returned to active duty. Some years later she was sold to Taiwan who renamed her the *Tian Shan*. When last heard of, a couple of years ago, she was patrolling the Taiwan Strait between China and Taiwan. God speed, *Tian Shan*.

A MONKEY NAMED LAZARUS

I'll bet a lot of you have wanted a pet monkey. As a boy, I sure did. They looked so cute in the movies, and unlike a dog or cat, would be a pet not everyone would have. Yes sir, a monkey was the way to go. But my parents didn't think much of the idea. In fact, too often, they didn't think much of me, either. Did any of you have a family in the neighborhood with whom you were always unfavorably compared? We did, the Mooney family. My mother had gone to grade school and high school with Mrs. Mooney. There was a group of about six or seven girls who had gone through school together, and they remained friends their entire lives. They were all Irish so we called them the "Irish Mafia." I grew up with the battle cry ringing in my ears: "Why can't you be more like Bill Mooney?" Fragging was invented in Vietnam when angry soldiers would throw grenades into their officers' tents. It is probably good that fragging wasn't practiced in those pre-WW II days or I swear Bill Mooney would never have made it.

When the youngest Mooney kid, Mike, went into the seminary to become a priest it was all over for me. My Mother, like all Irish Catholic mothers in those days, desperately wanted one of her boys in the priesthood. Why she selected me, instead of one of my two brothers, was never clear. To be truthful, I sorta leaned in that direction myself — at least until I discovered girls. That was the end of that! But to this day I can't think of the Mooney boys with equanimity. Man, was I tired of failing to live up to Mrs. Mooney's standards. I'll bet that unknown to Mother the Mooney boys were too.

So I had to wait to get a monkey until I left the proverbial coop. And I did. For $12 I bought a monkey while on my first midshipman cruise in the Panama Canal Zone. It was 1950. I was stationed on the battleship *USS Missouri*, nineteen years old, and drunk. The fact that I made $50 a month shows you just how important that monkey was to me. The $12 price left a huge hole in my pocket. My buddy also bought one. We staggered back to the dock and the ladder leading to the ship, where a Marine guard rudely informed us that we had a decision to make. "I ain't letting you on the ship with them. That's against Navy regulations. Either keep the monkeys and go AWOL, or get rid of them and come on board." Even in our drunken state Frank and I recognized we were between a rock and a hard place. Going AWOL was an unacceptable option, so the monkeys had to go. We slipped the leashes off their skinny necks and saw them scamper off. Good-bye $12. They probably returned to their original owner who sold them to the next guys who came along.

So the next time I was in the Canal Zone, six years later, I bought another monkey and named him Sambo. I was a junior officer serving on the *USS Kleinsmith*. And I was drunk again. Returning to the ship, I was able to sneak Sambo past the guard,

SOUR M.A.S.H. AT SEA - SECOND WAVE

but I was worried about the reception he was going to receive on board ship. (I know, Sambo isn't a politically correct name for a small brown monkey, but this was long before the P.C. police started interfering in our lives.) I needn't have worried. Our skipper, LCDR Pounders, was a great guy and welcomed Sambo with open arms. Let me tell you about Jerry Pounders, my all-time favorite skipper.

Captain Pounders was a Mustang, Navy slang for an enlisted man who had been promoted to officer rank. Very unusual, and a person had to be outstanding to accomplish this. He was a little rough around the edges, extremely profane, tall and lanky. Kinda looked like the movie actor Sam Sheppard, except uglier. He golfed with us, drank with us, and shot the shit with us. But one thing we didn't do with him was women. Did you ever hear about Navy guys "having a girl in every port?" That was a huge lie, except for Jerry Pounders. I swear he had at least one in every port we ever visited. That wasn't the problem. The problem was that he invited them to live aboard the ship while we were in port! And finding them having breakfast in the wardroom, with the two of them eating in their pajamas, was unsettling to say the least. We got used to this situation, at least until we went on a summer cruise carrying a contingent of midshipmen.

It was the Captain's custom to invite two different midshipmen to eat in the officers' mess at every meal. This way they could observe how officers lived. But eating at the officers' table with the Captain's woman, obviously not his wife, who was safely back in Norfolk, Virginia, was somewhat outside of the midshipmen's sheltered experience. Particularly so when the Captain's friend looked more like a hooker than anything else, or when she — and he — were helplessly drunk. Word got back to the officers that the midshipmen were pretty upset and intended to complain when we got them back home.

Walter "Bud" Stuhldreher

The Executive Officer (XO) was a gross, incompetent fellow, so as the next senior officer, I was deputized by my fellow officers to speak to the Captain about this possible problem.

Reluctantly I approached the Captain in his cabin after we were underway and his latest paramour was safely left back on shore. Luckily, he thought the whole thing was funny as hell, and agreed to keep his women out of sight during the rest of the cruise. Another crisis averted!

On a small ship you hope and pray for a skipper who is a decent ship handler. On a small ship, even small mistakes can get the crew killed in a hurry. So whatever shortcomings Captain Pounders had, and there were many, they didn't count for much with us because he was a superb ship handler. The best any of us had seen. He endeared himself to the crew and us officers because of his unbelievable skills. We would have loved him for that even if he had otherwise been a bastard, which, of course, he wasn't. He was a simple, decent fellow by anyone's standards. He trusted others to try to do their best, and expected the same honesty from others that he showed them. Who cared if he drank like a fish, scored women of all ages (and looks) with remarkable ease, and liked a fight now and then? We sure didn't care, not when he could handle the ship as well as he did. I'll give you an example.

Approaching a dock, particularly in any kind of wind, is a tricky operation. The other three skippers in our squadron always used tugs to help them approach the pier. Not Captain Pounders! Coming in last, because he was the junior captain, he disdained the tugs. Rather, he would have the ship approach at full speed, an unheard-of dangerous procedure. Waiting calmly until the last possible moment, knowing the other jealous skippers were watching with envy, he would quietly command: "Reverse the engines. Full speed astern."

SOUR M.A.S.H. AT SEA - SECOND WAVE

The Navy didn't approve of any of this. A speeding ship could wreak havoc on a pier. And going from full speed ahead to full speed astern was the same as speeding down a street, then suddenly slamming a car into reverse. It wouldn't do your car's transmission much good, and the same applied to a ship's huge main shaft. You think Captain Pounders gave a damn? Hardly. He was more intent on showing how good a seaman he was.

Every time, without fail, we would shudder to a stop, maybe one foot, two feet, or three at the most, from the pier. Then the Captain would quietly say, "Stop all engines," as we drew abreast of the pier. The Commodore and the other captains just shook their heads. Pounders had done it again. The crew would throw the lines over to the waiting swabbies on the pier, proudly knowing that everyone topside had, once again, witnessed the most amazing ship handling they would ever see. The crew loved the Captain. He was truly a man among men. He was their skipper.

So Captain Pounders wasn't bothered by my bringing Sambo on board. In fact, he liked the little fellow and fed him all the time. Sambo proved to be one hell of an eater. Sitting at the wardroom table with us, he daintily ate bits of apples, grapes, curried dishes and, his favorite, fried plantain. I doubt many monkeys liked curried dishes, but Sambo did, perhaps because our black cooks didn't have the slightest idea how to cook them. Are you surprised that we let a monkey eat with us? The truth is, his table manners were better than those of most of us, particularly Ray Brown, the Executive Officer (XO). The XO, a short, squat fellow, with a porcine face, ate like a pig. Didn't like to shower either. His worst habit was cleaning his fingernails with a table knife, then scraping it clean on the tablecloth. Gross! You don't think Sambo looked better than that? Hell, yes, a lot better! And he was brighter, too.

The crew also enjoyed playing with Sambo. They gave him so much food that the little bugger got fat and couldn't scamper about as easily as he had when he first came on board. His lousy BMI (Body Mass Index) rating led to his downfall.

While at sea we would let Sambo run loose. He loved to scurry to the top of the ship, one of his favorite spots. He would chase around, jumping from one cable to another, screeching as he went. His agility was amazing. He could jump 20 feet from one cable to another. Sometimes he would slide down, and sometimes continue on to another line. He even learned to detach signal flags from their lines, then throw them at the sailors far below who enjoyed these antics even more than Sambo did. It confused the hell out of the other ships in the task force, however. They would signal over "Can't understand your flag message. Repeat signal." Word soon got around the squadron who the culprit was. Disliking Navy regulations about no pets on board as much as we did, the other crews kept our secret.

Then one day his increased bulk led to Sambo's early demise. Jumping from one line to another, he missed his target and grabbed hold of a different cable, one which he instinctively knew was a no-no and had always avoided. Charged with electricity, Sambo was cooked instantly, and, hanging from the cable, looked pretty much like the fried plantains he liked so much.

Was this an insensitive way to describe our dead friend? Well, you have to understand we existed in a tough environment, an environment which made us less sensitive than those who lived in a normal society. For example, this was my seventh straight year of going for months with absolutely no women around, the fairer sex which originally brought man out

SOUR M.A.S.H. AT SEA - SECOND WAVE

of caves. And that was pretty much par for many of the swabbies. We had women in port but they were not the kind you brought home to meet your mother. It was a rough, callous existence, where cursing was the norm, and if you didn't get into a fight now and then, your shipmates shied away from you. And drinking was perfected to an art form. Serious, falling-down drinking. A hangover was a badge of honor in our twisted society. Injuries were sniffed at, "Dear John" letters a normal occurrence. A "love 'em and leave 'em" attitude was encouraged. Certain subjects were taboo, such as religion, politics, and your female relatives. Captain Pounders was particularly against any reference to religion. In his lexicon a Bible was "Pap, crappy pap, bullshit" and he never allowed one to be displayed or carried in plain sight. He went berserk when he saw a Bible. On Sundays, when the Navy was serious about conducting religious services on board, he kept to his cabin.

Sambo didn't go quietly. His body short-circuited an important part of the ship, the radio room. Messages between the *Kleinsmith* and the other ships were temporarily unavailable. This rare condition was quickly noticed by the task force Commander's ship and it asked us, by flashing light signals, what happened? We responded that an animal had shorted out the radio and repairs were under way. What kind of animal? Not sure, was our lying response. Notify us when you're back on line. And that was that. Or so we thought.

At the next Caribbean port the crew contributed to a fund, and a Sambo II was procured. Things seemed back to normal. But a storm cloud was brewing, one we didn't know about. Unfortunately one of the Admiral's aides, a brown-noser, overheard some sailors talking about Sambo's accident. He quickly, and gleefully, reported to the Admiral that, contrary to Navy regulations, the *Kleinsmith* had let a monkey live aboard her. Even worse, when the pet's death had disabled radio communications, they *had lied* about the cause. Whew! We now had one pissed-off Admiral to deal with. We didn't know he knew about Sambo, and we were sure he definitely did not know about Sambo II.

Not until his barge was just off the side of our ship — on very short notice — did we learn we were going to be visited by the Task Force Commander, Vice-Admiral "Spike" Fahrion. An admiral visiting a ship in his command was virtually unheard-of. If that august personage wished to speak with someone on another ship, that person went to the admiral, not the other way around. And here we were, anchored off a small, uninhabited island, minding our own business. (We later found out the admiral had wanted to go fishing off his barge and used the trip to the *Kleinsmith* as cover for his use of a Navy boat for unofficial business.)

The Admiral summoned Captain Pounders to the deck and quickly got to the point. "Captain, it has been brought to my attention that you, contrary to regulations, permitted a pet monkey aboard. A monkey whose death caused a breakdown in communications between your ship and the task force, which you then lied about. This condition could have resulted in a dangerous situation. What do you have to say about this?"

Well, poor Captain Pounders was floored. He couldn't have imagined a worse nightmare. The Admiral pretty well knew the whole story. What could he do except fall on his sword? "Admiral, that pretty much describes what happened. It was an unfortunate business all around, but you have my solemn word it will never happen again."

That's when Sambo II decided to swing over the Admiral's head, snatching his heavily gold embossed Admiral's hat off his head. A pregnant silence ensued — but not for long. "WHAT

IN HELL WAS THAT? Where's my hat? What kind of rum-bucket are you running here?" The Captain was stupefied, rooted speechless in his tracks, as were the rest of us. "DAMN IT, THAT WAS A MONKEY, WASN'T IT! Next you're going to tell me you don't know where it came from, that his name must be Lazarus!"

Captain Pounder's eyes bulged out, he was red-faced and sweating, completely flummoxed by the sight of the angry Admiral glaring at him, not a foot away. A baldheaded Admiral. And the poor, Bible-hating Captain hadn't the slightest idea what the Admiral was talking about. Scared out of his wits he blurted: "Yes, sir, that's right. I don't know where he came from, and his name must be Lazarus all right." Standing inconspicuously behind the Captain, I almost passed out. A bad situation had just become a major debacle. Where was a Bible when you needed one?

And that's what the Captain needed all right, a Bible, because the next 20 minutes weren't pretty, or forgettable, even 50 years later. The Admiral went crazy, reaming the Captain out, cursing him inventively, describing how many Navy rules the Captain had broken, and how he, the Admiral, intended to deal with the Captain's career prospects, which weren't much. It was pitiful. And I knew who was to blame for this unholy mess. Yours truly. I decided to fess up and started to speak. "DON'T OPEN YOUR MOUTH! Shut the hell up! I damn well don't need a junior officer, trained by this imbecile, telling me anything! ALL OF YOU, GET THE HELL OUT OF HERE!"

And we did. While the severely chastened Captain never did share with us the rest of the dressing down, he did have one question for me. "Stuhldreher, who in the hell was Lazarus?"

RANK HATH ITS PRIVY

If you were to visit the oldest cemetery in your town and head to the oldest section in it, you would probably find some tombstones, or markers, engraved with the initials RIP. They stand for "Rest In Peace." That meaning changed during WW II when the envious dog soldiers observed how much better the senior officers lived. They changed RIP into "RHIP" meaning "Rank Hath Its Privileges." During my last year on active duty in the Navy I found a new meaning for those well known initials.

My small ship, the *USS Kleinsmith*, was sailing along in the Caribbean one sunny day. Sailing, of course, is a figure of speech. We were steaming under power and rocking crazily as we always did. Up and down, rolling from port to starboard, our violent movements never changed. If the sea became rough, our movements simply were rougher. One would never use the word "placid" to describe any of our passages. And the ship

Walter "Bud" Stuhldreher

wasn't the only thing acting crazily. Our skipper, on his good days, was as jumpy as a bedbug. Exaggerating am I? You be the judge.

For some time I had been trying to get our Captain to perform an important ceremony, a ceremony necessary for me to get out of the Navy, so it was damn important. Believe it or not, we really didn't have many ceremonies in those peacetime days. Promotions didn't merit much attention. Transfers of people to and from a ship happened so often they, too, went practically unnoticed. A change of command, one Captain replacing another, was about the only real ceremony we participated in. I saw only two of those during my four years as a midshipman and three years on active duty as a junior naval officer. But, oh boy! a ceremony starring me was much needed, and I was having trouble making it happen.

The ceremony involved me being sworn out of the Navy as a *regular* officer and then immediately being sworn back in as a *reserve* officer. The Navy wasn't discharging officers holding a regular commission. My three years of obligatory service would soon be up, so I was damn interested in obtaining that reserve status and leaving. When I received my commission as an Ensign, I signed up for *two* years active duty, not three years. We always called the extra year we had been stuck with "the Truman year" since President Truman had added an extra year on our forced servitude. He didn't ask our opinion about it, either. So I figured I had already served one more year than my country might have expected of me, and I intended to get out as soon as my crazy Captain would let me. As usual, he was being difficult about it.

I say "as usual" because *nothing* was usual, or normal, about this guy. He was a weirdo. With a normal Captain, if you screwed up, you would hear about it. If you or your department or the ship did well at something, maybe you would be congratulated. If the Task Force Commander ordered your ship to go somewhere at a designated speed and get there by a certain time, you obeyed. If your Captain issued an order to jump, you said, "How high and how far?" and promptly did it. But not this skipper. No sir, he existed in a parallel universe, one not touched by orders, either given or received, or by the actions of others. It was amazing - we could be talking to him about oranges, and with no change of expression he might respond about apples. If his superiors ordered us to maintain a course of 180 degrees, he would suggest a different course. The Officer of the Deck (OOD) would gently remind him we had no choice but to follow orders and maintain a heading of 180. He would then merely smile. He apparently didn't care if we followed his orders, or if he followed his superiors' orders. Luckily, we four department heads were experienced, knew our jobs, and managed to run the ship without any input — useful input that is — from the Captain.

Quite by accident, several months later, I learned that he was a drunk. We didn't know this because *he was drunk all the time*. How can you tell when a fellow is drunk if you have never seen him sober, thus having a point of reference? Our beloved Captain was a true bottle baby, a souse, a lush, and we didn't know it.

Realizing that our Captain just sailed along in his own world, I was nonplussed about how I was going to get him to perform the regular officer/reserve officer ceremony. I finally figured out a strategy. The ship's yeoman, the sailor who acted as a secretary, and I would corner the Captain in the wardroom with the necessary documents and with the format of the ceremony all laid out. All the Captain had to do was to walk through the ceremony, with not a thought passing through his head. We would lead him by his nose, so to speak.

Walter "Bud" Stuhldreher

This routine was often successful with him, but it sure didn't work this time. He actually came to life and said in no way would he assist me in such a stupid move. The yeoman and I stared at the skipper. Had we heard right? Was he actually reacting to a situation? Unheard of! And, to our amazement, the Captain actually continued the conversation. "Stuhldreher, you have done so many stupid things in the Navy, I can't even remember them all. It beats me how you have managed to survive this long. I have never met an officer who managed to insult every Admiral he could. An officer who challenged so many of the Navy's rules, regulations and traditions. In spite of all this, you've actually received honors and have even been decorated. It beats all. Even so, I'm not going to let you make an ass of yourself in this case. Kicking your regular commission overboard on my watch ain't going to happen!" And he stalked off.

The yeoman and I almost fell over. It was the longest speech we had ever heard the Captain make, and to top it off, it was on the subject we had introduced. Gee! What was that all about?

It turned out that the yeoman knew something about our curious Captain that shed some much needed light on his mysterious actions. There was a strong bond between our ship's yeoman and the yeomen on the other ships in our squadron. They swapped tales, studied new regulations to help them understand the probable meaning, discussed promotion vacancies, and, in general, worked together for their immediate gain and their ship's success. Through this process our yeoman had learned some history about our Captain which the other yeomen had heard from their captains. Stuff we officers were in no position to learn.

SOUR M.A.S.H. AT SEA - SECOND WAVE

It seems our Captain had been a regular commissioned officer in WW II. He quit the Navy after the war, failed miserably in civilian life, and applied to get back in the Navy. Since he had been a hero in WW II, with several decorations, the Navy agreed to take him back, but as a reserve officer. With the war over, Congress was continually reducing the military's appropriations, making jobs in the Navy hard to come by. Naturally, the Navy favored the retention of officers holding regular commissions rather than the reservists. So our skipper, according to the other squadron captains, was very bitter over this situation, and felt losing his regular officer status was the biggest career mistake he had ever made. Hearing this from our yeoman, I now understood my Captain's strange behavior. While he didn't think much of me as an officer, he still didn't want me to make the same mistake he had made.

Understanding where the Captain was coming from didn't solve my problem. I *needed* to make the move, and the Captain was standing between me and a happy ending — defined as my getting out of the Navy. What could I do to move things along? I had no idea. But providence, in the person of the yeoman, provided for me. Unknown to me, a new regulation had been promulgated to commanding officers. Translated from the normal Navy gobbledygook, it told the captains to *encourage* officers to leave the service. The more officers who left voluntarily would reduce the number the Navy would have to involuntarily separate from the service. This regulation was supposed to be read only by commanding officers for obvious reasons. But the yeoman, who worked closely with me on matters affecting pay decisions, particularly payments to reimburse travel expenses, had come to respect me as an officer who tried to be fair towards enlisted men, an outlook he thought of as rare. So he shared the information contained in this new, secret regulation with me. Hot damn! I now had some leverage to get the Captain off the dime.

"Captain," I said, feigning ignorance of the regulation, "I'm surprised the Navy isn't encouraging guys like me to leave regular duty. After all, if more of us leave the service, it makes it that much easier for the Navy to hit their numbers for a reduction in officer strength." Unspoken, of course, was the thought that this happy occurrence had a direct impact on the skipper's chances to remain on active duty. He glared at me. Probably, lurking somewhere in his booze-rattled mind was a suspicion that I just might know something about the new regulation. He skirted away from my statement, unsure what his next move might be — and promptly left the room.

I had expected that reaction. Getting decisions out of the Captain was a time-consuming business, but if there was one thing I had plenty of, it was time. Bouncing around in the Caribbean was lonely. Our ship was a metal bucket floating in a very large body of water. Our isolation gave us a feeling that nothing else existed beyond the hull. Sure, we saw the occasional whale, many flying fish, some playful dolphins and, if close to an island, birds. That was about it. A strange way to live, but that was our lot and we made the best of it. There was no Internet in those days, and no satellite shipboard TV, so we were pretty much cut off from shore-based events, friends and family. Now I was counting on this strange way of living to make my ceremony happen. Sooner or later I would wear the Captain down. And so I kept after him. Relentlessly. Every chance I got I reminded him about my desire to get out.

I was like a "Chinese water torturer." During the "Chinese water torture" the prisoner is held in an immovable position and a drop of water falls on his forehead every few seconds. At first it isn't a problem, just a minor annoyance, but it will drive the prisoner crazy after a day or two. The Captain was relatively confined aboard the ship and I played torturer. I was hell bent on making him give in and perform the regular/reserve ceremony. So one morning I wasn't totally surprised when he relented and agreed to do it. I was, however, surprised by his plan.

"All right, you stupid bastard, I'm tired of having to listen to you bitch about this. It's a move you'll come to regret, a move that's just about as dumb as anything you pulled off in this man's Navy, but I'll do it. And when you fall on your ass while trying to make a living outside of the Navy, where someone else does your thinking for you, you'll remember this day!"

How could I explain to a guy who had failed outside the Navy (unless you consider selling hot dogs on the streets on New York City a success), that the chance to do that was exactly what I wanted, a chance to think, a chance to get ahead on my own efforts. He continued, "But it's such a crappy idea that that's where we'll do it."

What did he mean by that? "Yes sir, it's such a crappy idea, that's where we're going to have it — in the crapper!" And off he went, calling for Roland, the yeoman, to join us in the privy. I told you this Captain was crazy, but this move looked like a topper, even for him.

Space on a small ship is always at a premium for essentials and nonexistent for nonessentials. I remember President Clinton was appalled at the lack of space on an aircraft carrier he once visited. Hell, the overstuffed buffoon couldn't even have gotten into the officers' head on the *Kleinsmith*. In order to use the facilities, we had to slip sideways into a small room containing one stall and one stainless steel urinal. The one minuscule shower had a canvas shower curtain which was always, always rotten with mildew. That was it for the six to eight officers, and we had it better than the enlisted men! The three of us squeezed into the privy: the paunchy Captain, a yeoman who bulged out of his tee shirts and pants and I. (The yeoman claimed the water we used in the ship's laundry was too hot and shrunk his clothes. Since the rest of the crew didn't have that problem, I figured the food he was always bumming out of the galley was his real problem.)

The yeoman sat on the toilet, the Captain stood in the shower, and I leaned against the urinal after first checking to be sure it was dry. The Captain then hurriedly proceeded to swear me out of the United States Navy. Next he loudly swore me back in but, as a shit-faced reservist. "Satisfied, you sorry piece of shit?" he asked.

Well, we sure were in the right compartment to talk about shit, not that I wanted to. "Yes, Captain, I'm satisfied, and look forward to serving the Navy as a reserve officer."

He replied, "Damn you, I hope that won't be for long." Then he squeezed by me, leaving the yeoman on the toilet and me in the urinal.

I looked over at Roland. "Hey, you always did want to use the "luxurious" officers' head, didn't you? Now's your chance." I figured I owed Roland one for tipping me off about that new, secret regulation. I left a happy Roland to his business; he sure didn't have to move very far.

COLONEL BO PEEP HAS LOST HIS JEEP

It was the summer of 1955, and the *USS Kleinsmith* had been ricocheting around the Mediterranean for several months. The sea was the rich, deep blue that it saved for special days, and the sky overhead was cloudless. The bright disk of the rising sun reflected off the wave tops in a shining path to the east. Our bow wave showed crisp and white against the water as she cut a path through the open ocean. How could any of us imagine that a day with such a perfect start would end in a mess? Not me.

This event occurred in Sardinia, a strange place to visit, even for us. Have you ever been there? Have you ever wanted to go? I thought not. We had been to Algeria, Crete, Turkey, Greece, France, Italy, Spain, Sicily, Corsica, Portugal and Gibraltar, visiting many ports twice, some several times. If we missed an island — or country — I don't remember it. Sardinia and Corsica didn't have much going for them. Just one attribute: deserted beaches, which were good for practicing amphibious landings. Of course, being deserted meant they were lousy liberty ports.

We had just participated in a practice amphibious landing in Corsica. Now we were going to do one in Sardinia, then we would return to Corsica for another. We carried frogmen aboard the *Kleinsmith* who participated in the landings with the three thousand Marines aboard other ships in the task force. And that's where the trouble started, at Corsica. Knowing our schedule, a Marine Colonel who was temporarily assigned to the task force, had requested that we ferry his beloved jeep on the trip to Sardinia and back to Corsica. He would then retrieve it. At that time, law and order was pretty much nonexistent in Corsica, and he was afraid to leave it there unguarded during the three weeks he would be gone. It would either be stolen or stripped — take your choice. Since he outranked our Captain by a mile, we didn't have much choice but to bring his jeep on board. The Colonel, of course, would travel on one of the larger ships in the task force, where he would have more room and be more comfortable. When the jeep was secured to the deck, the Colonel made sure we had it well covered with a tarp to protect it from the salt water spray. Little did he know that since we rolled so crazily, it also needed protection from the ocean waves, which were sure to wash over it at least several times during this three-week exercise. What none of us knew was that the jeep was also going to need protection from our Executive Officer (XO), Lt. Ray Brown.

SOUR M.A.S.H. AT SEA - SECOND WAVE

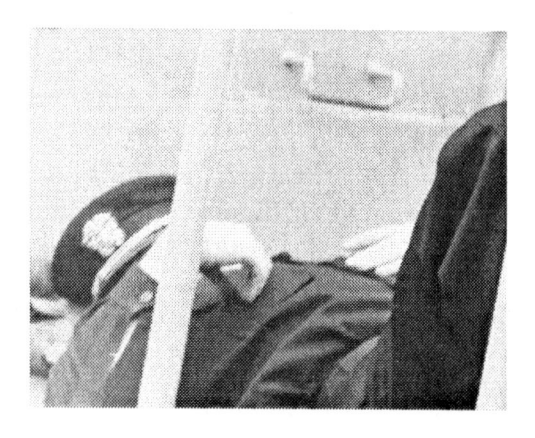

The XO hard at work

The XO was a piece of work. A sorry excuse for an officer. He was stupid and lazy with terrible manners, but mostly he was stupid. If he had a measurable IQ, it wasn't readily apparent. Against strict orders from the Captain, he decided to go joy riding in the jeep while we were in Sardinia. He had to wait until the Captain was called away to a conference aboard one of the bigger ships. (They were all bigger than we were.) Now, as the ranking officer on board, the XO ordered the jeep to be off-loaded to the pier, and off he went. You have to understand this was 1955, and the only roads in our area of Sardinia were dirt ones. Where was he going to go? There weren't any cities or resorts around, just hills, wild animals, and a few peasants who were remarkably uninterested in us.

But away he went, happy in his ignorance, traveling from one scene of nothing to another of the same. Crazy.

Several hours later he returned — walking. No jeep. Earlier, the Captain had returned from the conference, and was furious to discover the jeep was missing. His fury turned up a notch when he learned the culprit was the XO, who was not safe with a roll of toilet paper, much less a jeep belonging to a Marine Colonel

— a Marine Colonel who was tougher than our entire crew put together. And here came Lt. Hapless, sans jeep.

"Ray," asked the Captain, speaking deliberately, much as you would do with a four-year old child, (it didn't pay to go too fast with the XO), "where's the jeep? Later we'll talk about why you disobeyed my order for no one to touch the jeep, but first things first. Where's the jeep?" The XO stood there, his small eyes squinting as he tried to think of an answer that would get him off the hot spot. We bystanders were very interested and hugely amused as we watched this latest screw-up by the XO unfold. We knew, as did the Captain, that the XO was too dumb to lie well, and this explanation should be a doozy. "Well, Ray?"

The XO's eyes blinked rapidly in desperation, sweat poured down his porcine face. Damn! This was going to be a good one. "Captain, I'm not sure where to start."

"Ray, take your time, we're not going anywhere until tomorrow morning. Just tell me as best you can." The Captain was proving remarkably calm. This missing jeep could put a large crimp in his career.

The XO started over, "Well, I don't know where the jeep is," and then he stopped, as if this simple non-answer was enough. He shifted weight, obviously intending to flee this unpleasant interrogation.

"Stop right there, mister! You're not going anywhere until I get some answers from you!" The Captain was no longer calm, and was no longer playing the good cop routine. He had been upset long before the XO had returned to the ship, and this charade wasn't making him any calmer. "Dammit, Ray, where in hell is the jeep? Speak up!"

And the XO did, with a long rambling, disjointed tale which made no sense at all. About all we and the smoldering Captain could make out was that the XO had driven someplace — where, he wasn't sure — and had done something with the jeep, something he couldn't, or wouldn't, remember. All he knew was that the jeep had disappeared; so he did the only thing any reasonable person would have done, which was to walk back to the ship. And he was thirsty. Would it be all right if he got a drink of water? Oh, wow, we snickered, this was going from bad to worse. The XO would have been better advised to ask for a drink of hemlock.

"No, it's not all right to get a drink of water! I need a better answer than that, and time's running out on us. We have to find that damn jeep and you're the only one who can help us!" The Captain was right about one thing, the afternoon wasn't getting any younger, and we needed daylight to search for the jeep. But he was wrong about the second part; based on past experiences with the XO, we seriously doubted he was going to be much help. The Captain was whistling in the graveyard on that hope. And a graveyard was where his career was headed at the moment. The Captain finally understood this meeting wasn't helping. "Stuhldreher, get a search party organized. Have Ray show you the last place he saw the jeep, and start scouring the area. Meanwhile, I'll have Hamilton (another officer) take a search party and look around here. There's no telling where it might turn up."

So we did. The XO retraced his steps, as best he could. Twenty enlisted men and I trudged along in the dusty hills. And if you think we were in shape to take a hot hike, you're sadly mistaken. Woefully out of shape, we found this visit to an ugly part of Sardinia turning into an all time loser. Finally the XO stopped, looked around dubiously, and said he thought this was the last place he had seen the jeep. I looked at him incredulously. "Mr. Brown, there's absolutely no place around here where the jeep could be. It's nothing but flat ground with hills in the distance. Are you sure this is where you left it?"

The XO avoided looking at me. It became painfully obvious he didn't have a clue where he had last seen the jeep or what he had done with it. I couldn't understand that: how could a man, even one as dumb as the XO, lose a jeep in broad daylight in the midst of nowhere? There had to be more to this than the XO was letting on.

I decided to take a different tack. I sent the guys out to make a useless fan-like search, and Mr. Brown and I sat down for a man-to-man talk. "Ray, you can level with me. If we don't find that frigging jeep you'll be in such hot water you'll think hell would be cooler! We have to find the jeep. The wheres and whys you managed to lose it can be settled later." The poor devil sagged; I was right. There was something more to tell. "Ray, spill it. We haven't got much time. What happened?"

"Well, Stu, this isn't going to look too good on my record," he began. What record I thought sourly, but I kept silent. "All I wanted to do was take a little ride, it's been so long since I've driven a car!" Join the parade, mister. The rest of us miss driving too, but none of us stole a Marine Colonel's jeep, just you. "So I decided no one would even know if I went for a short spin. I was going to have it back on board before the Captain got back." I was amazed. Did he really think no one was going to turn him in? Didn't he have a clue how poorly the crew and officers thought of him?

"Well, everything was going great guns, and I was really enjoying myself, driving around and seeing how fast a jeep could go. I had never driven one before, you know." Well, I hadn't known this but who cares? Would he ever get to the point? "So I stopped somewhere — I really don't remember where; this whole place looks the same to me, and that's when the kids came up."

Aha! We were finally getting somewhere! "What kids?" I asked softly.

"I don't know! Just some kids," he responded angrily.

"Go on, Ray, we're getting off the track."

"They wanted to climb on the jeep. They were only ten or twelve years old, and I didn't see anything wrong, so I let them." The XO stopped his recitation; he was having trouble telling what happened next. "Then they drove off, laughing like hell. I ran after them but couldn't catch them." Jeez! Why hadn't the numskull told this to the Captain earlier? It would have made a huge difference in how we conducted the search. Too late now. I called the men back in, and we returned to the ship.

I told the Captain what the XO had told me, and he looked at me helplessly. "God, the fat's in the fire!" he exclaimed. "Without any kind of vehicle, we don't have a prayer of finding them. What am I going to tell that Marine Colonel when he comes looking for his damn jeep? What in hell am I going to say?" We called in the other search party and sat down to a silent dinner. I can't remember the wardroom ever being so quiet.

The next morning we did our part in the amphibious landing. Shoving off early, we dropped the frogmen over the side so they could reconnoiter the beach where the landing would take place. We took our position offshore where, as guard/overseer, we would lead a succession of landing craft filled with Marines into the beach. We then returned to the huge troop transport ship, waited for the circling landing craft, and repeated this procedure until all the Marines going ashore were in place. Then we waited in the hot, sunny Sardinian morning while the top officers ashore conducted post-landing briefings. Once they were satisfied all the mistakes had been discussed, and changes for tomorrow's exercise were in place, the Marines were transported back to their troop transports. After cleaning up and dinner, it was early to bed for them because they were going to repeat today's exercise tomorrow. But our routine was somewhat different.

While waiting for the "after battle" discussion to end, we had a visitor. A certain Marine Colonel had boated over to check on his jeep, and was mighty upset to see that it was missing. Murderously upset. The Captain finally convinced him that yelling wouldn't get his jeep back. After finding out approximately where we had tied up, he went ashore, gathered his troops and invented an impromptu bush exercise for them. They marched off toward the area that the Captain had said was the best place to search for the jeep.

Now this wasn't a bunch of Boy Scouts on an overnight hike. No sir, this was a large-scale Marine exercise involving a couple of hundred Marines who would have much preferred to return to their bunks and a night's sleep. A couple of hundred! That was twice as many as the crew on the *Kleinsmith*! A bigger force than that which invaded Grenada or Panama many years later. But Marines do as they are told, and split off as ordered to find the jeep. (Remember when Senator Proxmire was giving "Golden Fleece" Awards for stupid military expenditures? This one would have been a winner!) Just before dusk they found it. Out of gas but otherwise OK.

SOUR M.A.S.H. AT SEA - SECOND WAVE

They now had to march back to the landing beach where they were picked up and boated back to a late dinner. They had only a few hours sleep before they had to practice another landing the next morning. Two Marines were left to guard the jeep. The Colonel called the *Kleinsmith*, told the Captain where the jeep could be found, and ordered that the jeep be picked up. He also told the Captain, in short, profane words, what would happen if all didn't go well.

So around noon, after the next morning's exercise, the *Kleinsmith*, now enroute back to Corsica, made an unscheduled stop at the scene of the crime — the same crummy pier which we had just left the day before. We found the jeep and the two bored and disgruntled Marines guarding it. The night, apparently, had not gone well. One Marine, from northern Michigan, reported that Sardinian mosquitoes put the infamous northern Michigan mosquitoes, known for their size and ravenous appetites, to shame. The crew put some gas in the jeep, and drove it and the Marines back to the ship. We loaded the Marines and the jeep on board, and proceeded to Corsica. Where the Colonel was waiting for us.

He thanked his Marines for their efforts, damned the officers and crew of the *Kleinsmith*, and drove off in a huff. We weren't sorry to see him go. And his threat — or promise — to never let his jeep near us again was greeted with smiles. We hoped he meant it. The Captain then had a private meeting with the XO. Due to the thin steel bulkhead we heard most of it. I believe "moron" was the kindest expletive hurled at the XO during the twenty minute dressing-down conducted by a tired and thoroughly enraged Captain.

There was a small bar near our anchorage at Corsica. A bunch of Marines were overheard discussing the strange beach exercise one of their units had done. Apparently the troops

Walter "Bud" Stuhldreher

involved had kept their mouths shut in order to protect their Colonel, who could have gotten in trouble for using his troops in such a manner. And you better believe the crew of the *Kleinsmith* didn't enlighten them. After all, we were used to covering up for the XO. So the case of the missing jeep was solved.

By now you're wondering how the XO stayed in the Navy. I often wondered about that myself. But his luck was soon to run out. Within 18 months he was thrown out of the Navy, courtesy of a well deserved court-martial. I missed seeing that happen by a couple of months, having left the Navy as soon as my obligated service time was up. I've always regretted missing it. It would have been nice to see justice served.

As for the Marine Colonel and his damn jeep, our paths never crossed again. Just as well; we understood he was a man who held a grudge a long time.

HOW BACHELORS LIVE

My wife says men would still be living in caves if it were not for women. That's probably true.

Returning in the Fall of 1955 from a long deployment to Europe, the *USS Kleinsmith* entered the yard for repairs. These needed repairs were the result of a terrible storm we lived through off Greece. After the ship was patched up, we went to sea a couple of times for exercises, then shoved off for six weeks in Cuba and Puerto Rico. It soon became obvious that the ship had suffered even greater damage in the storm than was realized when the ship was first repaired. We limped home and once again entered the yard. But not for band-aids this time. This was going to be a major overhaul to repair structural damage and would require several months. The power was going to be shut off on the ship, thus making her uninhabitable.

Walter "Bud" Stuhldreher

Several in the crew were sent to various naval schools across the country; many went on extended leaves; the rest were housed ashore. The married officers happily lived in their homes. We four bachelors were faced with living in the Bachelor Officers' Quarters (BOQ) on the base. That was an unappealing option. The quarters were of decrepit WW II vintage with small, bare rooms and bathroom facilities down the hall. Ugh! We decided to rent a house and furnish it with Goodwill stuff, and not much of that. We found an old wooden two-story house on the wrong side of town. Not much was available to sailors in those days in Norfolk, Virginia. Some homes had signs in their front yards: Dogs, cats and sailors keep off. While the Navy was the main economic support for Norfolk, that didn't mean the townspeople had to associate with sailors. And they damn well didn't.

The Kleinsmith's junior officers, including the UDT officers aboard, posing for an official Navy photograph. I'm the third from the right in the back row.

We four were a disparate bunch. At twenty-five, I was the oldest, senior in rank, and had been in the Navy the longest. John P. Casey was a redhead LTJG from Massachusetts and my fellow conspirator in many shenanigans especially those against the Executive Officer. For example, we once put insulation in the bunk of the XO. The dockyard worker who gave it to us had warned us to be very careful handling it. "If you get it on your skin it'll work its way in, and you'll end up in the hospital for sure." We saved the insulation until the next time we were once again at sea and it was hotter than hell. With no A/C in those days, we would wake up covered with sweat. We put the insulation in the XO's bunk, fully expecting to enjoy his stint in the hospital. Wouldn't you know, he showed up for breakfast the next morning, chipper as ever! We guessed his skin was so tough he never felt the stuff.

The XO was despised by the crew and officers. Even the Captain didn't have any use for him. A short, squat fellow, he had a barely discernible IQ, no common sense, and no social graces. He wasn't too fond of showers, either.

Our all-time winner was a deal involving the XO's safe. All the officers' cabins had safes in them, small, cheap ones attached to the bulkhead at about eye level. I kept my sidearm and wallet in mine. The safes had simple combination locks. With the door open the combination could be changed by rotating three rings located on the inside of the door. The XO, in addition to his personal stuff, kept the ship's papers in his. And the XO had a bad habit of forgetting to close his safe after using it.

Observing this, Casey and I came up with a brilliant scheme. The next time the XO left the door to his safe open I engaged him in conversation while Casey slipped into his cabin, changed his combination, and left the door open. Sure enough, shortly after, the XO entered his room, saw the safe door open and slammed it shut, which is what he always did, thinking he had simply forgotten to shut it the last time he used it. That afternoon all the officers were gathered in the wardroom, summoned there by the Captain to go over the orders for the next exercise, orders which were in the XO's safe.

Mr. Brown's cabin was next to the wardroom, only two or three feet away. We clearly heard him work the combination, curse, repeat the process, and curse again. After several unsuccessful attempts, with the cursing becoming louder and more inventive, the Captain called out to the XO, "Ray, are you having some kind of trouble in there?"

The XO replied, "Hell, no, Captain. I'll be with you in a jiffy." But, of course, he wasn't. And the Captain started to get warm, not understanding why we were all having to sit around, waiting.

"XO, what is going on? We don't have all day!"

Pretty soon the XO stormed out, red-faced and sweating. He grabbed a fire ax hanging on the bulkhead, returned to his room, and started flailing away at the safe. The ax made loud, whacking sounds which were accompanied by the XO's snarls. Casey and I had all we could to not burst out laughing.

The XO finally got the door smashed in and yelled, "Damn it, somebody changed the combination!" He then returned to the wardroom, ax in hand, also with the ship's orders, which he slammed on the table, glaring at all of us.

Captain: "Ray, do I understand you couldn't get into your safe because someone changed your combination?"

Oh, boy, the XO was between a rock and a hard place. If he admitted that, it meant he had left his safe open, a big no-no. "No, Captain, I guess I forgot I changed the combination and the old one wouldn't work."

SOUR M.A.S.H. AT SEA - SECOND WAVE

The Captain knew damn well what had really happened, but had enjoyed the whole deal so much he shut up. But the XO never did give up trying to find the culprits. I was at the head of his list, with Casey a close second, but the safe-combination caper went unsolved.

Casey and I followed the same daily routine while in port at Little Creek, Virginia. We left the ship at quitting time, usually 4 p.m., and walked to a small bar at the end of the pier. Splitting a case of beer, we then stumbled back to the ship and collapsed on our bunks. And we did the same thing the next day. Were we drinking too much? Of course, but we had plenty of company. Looking back on those days, there just wasn't a lot a sailor could do in Norfolk or Little Creek. I played golf when I could, but Casey wasn't a golfer.

Ensign Norm Feldpush was another bachelor. A slender fellow, he stayed a long way from the troubles Casey and I went hunting for, although he immensely enjoyed hearing about them. He was a pleasant guy and a nice companion, very young and new to the Navy and the ship. He was bright, but with a lot to learn. His one claim to fame was an incident at the Officers' Club (O club) at our last Captain's going-away party. He got hopelessly drunk, threw an easy chair out of a second floor window and inadvertently followed it out himself. We rushed down to the ground, thinking we would find Norm hurt. Incredibly, he had landed in the chair and was fine. Luckiest thing I ever saw.

Ensign Philip Plack was the fourth bachelor. Phil was very thin and short with small hands. If any of you watch the hit TV show *Frasier*, he looked and acted much like Niles, the brother. He stayed away from rough people and dirt. Not cut out for the Navy, he clearly had come from a wealthy background. He was a gourmet, and even knew how wines differed. Not only was Phil non-athletic, he actively disliked such useless activities.

One scary thing happened to Phil and me that spring. Although not a golfer, he enjoyed the outdoors and walking a golf course, so he sometimes followed me during a round. At the very far end of the course I accidentally hit a low slice off the tee and caught Phil in the temple. (He had walked off the previous green and decided to wait for me there instead of walking back with me to the next tee.) He went down as if shot. I was horrified, knowing the temple was a terrible place to be hit by a fast-moving golf ball. And there we were, at the farthest end of the course with no telephones at hand. I ran back to the caddy shack and screamed for them to call an ambulance and get to the eleventh tee as soon as possible. Phil was unconscious for several hours and in the hospital for two days with a slight concussion. We were damn lucky. I have been nervous about hitting another golfer ever since, and I never swing with someone in front of me, even if the person is over to the side. Once was enough. I felt terrible about it.

So we four bachelors rented a house with only two rules. One: if a bedroom was being used for purposes other than sleeping, a pair of briefs was to be hung over the door knob, and no one was to enter under penalty of death. Two: no empty beer cans were to be thrown out. The empties were to be stacked in front of the fireplace. I'm not sure why we installed the second rule, but we soon enjoyed the sight of the rapidly growing collection.

Our normal routine was cereal for breakfast, then driving to the ship's office located in the shipyard. There really wasn't much for us to do. We would show up, review any paperwork we needed to, and shove off, usually by ten o'clock. Mostly we would go our separate ways. I headed to the golf course if the weather was OK, or sometimes I'd play tennis or swim with the Underwater Demolition Team (UDT) guys. Can't remember what Casey and Norm did, but I can remember what Phil did. He would head to a museum or a college campus to see what was going on. Often he went to his stockbroker's office to see what he could learn there or to check up on his stocks.

Most days we ended up back at the house by 4 p.m. when the sun was over the yardarm and it was time for drinking to commence.

None of us knew how to cook, so dinners were simple things like hot dogs or hamburgers, which Phil and I could manage. No fast-food joints in those days, unfortunately. If we had a dinner date it would be at someplace cheap, where we didn't have to dress up. The O Club would do nicely, especially when it had a dance night. Cheap for us, and very appealing to the girls we dated, mostly nurses. The college girls were off limits to sailors, even officers. They knew we were only going to be there for a short time and marriage wasn't in our plans. Nor would the few professional girls date sailors. Job choices were few for women in those days: teaching, flight attendants, and doing entry level jobs as secretaries or typists were about it. But there were plenty of nurses around. They usually lived in dormitories or apartments. Best yet, they always knew plenty of other single nurses looking for dates. Our social calendar was full.

So there you are. That's how we usually lived. But with Easter Sunday approaching, Phil and I decided a big-time dinner was the way to go. We asked four nurses for dinner. Six showed up. A couple of the guys asked two to ensure at least one would come. They all came! And let me tell you, that was a bummer. More girls than guys. We soon realized there would be no hankey-pankey later in the evening. Those six girls insisted it be "pal" night with no pairing off, or the two left-out girls would be uncomfortable.

Phil and I had decided a ham was appropriate for Easter Sunday, so we bought one. We stared at it Sunday morning, not having a clue how to cook it. That wasn't strange in those days; most girls didn't know how to cook, either. My sister, Marge, had gotten married a couple of years earlier and only knew how to make fudge and cook bacon. I'm not so sure about the bacon, come to think of it. So Phil and I weren't any dumber than any other guys our age, just inexperienced. What were we going to do with the darn thing?

Guys didn't call their mothers for help back then, particularly long distance. And if Betty Crocker's famous cookbook was around then we sure didn't know about it. There were no TV cooking shows, either. We were on our own. Then a dim memory from the past floated in: "Phil, I remember Amanda (our cook back home) drawing diamonds on the ham, then pushing cloves in at the intersections."

"Walt, that sounds like a plan to me, but what about this junk on the outside of the ham?"

"Beats me, Phil. I don't think anyone wants to eat that crap (the skin and fat)." He didn't think so either, so we scraped it off.

I then cut shallow lines on the ham and we pushed cloves in where the lines met. Then I remembered Amanda putting some stuff on the outside of the ham, some sort of sweet stuff. "Darn it, Walt, can't you remember what she used?" Phil asked. (Phil was very mild mannered; he didn't cuss like the rest of us.)

"Well, no, but maybe it was brown sugar." So we patted brown sugar on the ham. It fell off in big clumps, looking like golf divots.

"Gee, Walt, that isn't going to work." Duh, Phil, I could see that!

"OK, she must have used something to make it like a paste. Look in the icebox for a Coke. They're sweet." Phil took a look and saw nothing but beer cans. "Hell, Phil, beer ought to do. It's wet, anyway." So beer it was, and into the old oven it went. Phil intended to serve baked sweet potatoes and peas with the ham, so I left him in the kitchen.

Later, while we were sitting at the dining room table Phil proudly brought the ham in for all to admire. "What in the world is that?" one guest asked. Why a ham, of course. "A ham? Why is it gray?"

Phil was getting defensive by now. I sure wasn't volunteering that I had helped cook the damn thing; it truly looked terrible. "Well," Phil replied, "that must be the stuff we put on the outside, brown sugar and beer."

"Are you crazy?" another girl exclaimed. And she promptly got up, grabbed the ham and headed for the kitchen. Phil followed her into the kitchen, and was astonished to see her put it in the sink and pour water over it.

"Stop it, you're going to ruin it!" Phil yelled at her.

"Listen, no one could ruin this ham any more than you already have. Who in the world ever thought a Virginia ham should have something sweet put on it?"

Phil and I were both from the Midwest. I was from Indiana and Phil was from Missouri. We didn't know Virginia hams were supposed to be salty. Who would have thought? But the dinner went OK after that bad start. All of us enjoyed the ham. The girls were used to the salty taste, and we guys learned something new.

The rest of the evening was extremely chaste. I swear we could have been in a seminary, someplace my mother always wanted me to go. Live and learn. Never again have more girls than guys. More men than women was OK, it seemed. Some strange tribal custom I guess.

Next, my going-away party. My service time was almost up. Going-away parties were given for officers being transferred to another post or, in my case, leaving the Navy. This didn't happen in every instance. In fact, probably less than half of the time. It wasn't often done on large ships. But the boys were planning a wing-dinger for me.

First, who to invite? Naturally, all the nurses would come. And the Captain, who would not be bringing his wife. She was in the process of divorcing him and, indeed, had obtained a restraining order to keep him out of her life. The XO and his wife would not be invited, for reasons previously mentioned. We also had friends on the three other ships in our squadron, so they and their wives were invited, plus the bachelor officers and their guests.

That left the married officers aboard our ship, and we were undecided about them. Each morning at the 8 a.m. meeting in the office they had eagerly asked for details about the previous night's escapades. If it had been a quiet evening we often invented wild tales — stories which made them quite envious of our bachelor lifestyle, a lifestyle they had left behind. These

SOUR M.A.S.H. AT SEA - SECOND WAVE

made-up tales, along with the true ones, were unwisely shared with their wives. The wives were disgusted and let their husbands know their feelings. So we weren't sure what to do. We knew it would be a huge mistake to invite only the men. Their wives probably wouldn't let them get within a hundred miles of us by themselves.

Although in short supply, wisdom prevailed, and we asked the guys what their wives thought about attending the party. It turned out, in spite of their disgust, that they were anxious to see the place, particularly the pictures of the nudes. (We had stapled pictures of nudes all over the place, walls and ceilings included. There was even one strategically placed in the bathroom.) Remember, this was 1956 and such things simply weren't done in polite society. The wives were intrigued to think that we had pictures of nudes everywhere, hundreds of beer cans stacked to the ceiling, and dozens of women coming and going. It was beyond their wildest imagination, so nothing was going to stop them from coming! They were properly horrified to find out the stories their husbands had eagerly reported to them about our house were true. In fact, it was worse than they had imagined.

We had also stapled up pennants of all the local women's colleges. Just in case one of us ever managed a date with a coed, we thought seeing their college represented in the house would impress them. We didn't stop to think that having their college pennant stuck between nudes wouldn't be considered much of an honor. Didn't matter as it turned out. A coed never graced our doorstep. There was also a nice bright blue pennant containing three white stars stapled on a wall. Once, after playing tennis with my sometimes doubles partner, Vice-Admiral "Spike" Fahrion, the top gun in the Atlantic Amphibious Forces, I had snitched it off his official car. It was a bit the worse for wear, full of holes and small tears. The guys had used it for dart throwing. The wives of men who held regular commissions and planned to be career Navy officers, were struck speechless by this display. We were thumbing our noses at a flag rank representation. I was convinced, however, by their shining eyes that they secretly enjoyed seeing how stupid unmarried officers could be. No way their husbands were going to live like that!

We had laid in soft drinks, potato chips, cheese, pretzels and two large bags of popcorn purchased from the local movie house. Big band songs were playing on the record player. The normal denizens entered into the spirit of the evening in a hurry; the more uptight ones took a bit longer. But eventually everyone was having a big old time, particularly the squadron Commodore and his wife. Did I forget to mention we had invited them also? It was their first ship's party for an officer lower than Captain and they were going great guns. I had always liked the Commodore's wife, a tall, earthy, bright woman, and had always danced with her at official functions, so I had invited her and the Commodore, and was surprised when they accepted. Too bad the Commodore, a quiet fellow, hadn't been more like her; he probably would have made Admiral. Instead, later that year, he was passed over for the third time and was forced to leave the Navy as a Commander.

"Hey, where can we dance?" cried out one inebriated girl a couple of hours into the party.

"Right here!" Casey yelled back, promptly tearing up the cheap, worn-out carpet, ignoring the shocked looks from the uptight wives. They were as young as the rest of us, and were gradually moving from the few still uptight to loose as a goose. We threw the furniture out the door. The hardwood floor made dancing much easier, and the music was changed to faster numbers. Damn, what a party!

The highlight of the evening for me was an honor given to me as the departing officer. I got to throw the first empty can against our impressive collection of empty beer cans. More than three deep, they were stacked to the ceiling. We had decided to end the party with all the guests throwing cans at the stack until they had all come tumbling down, and there were literally hundreds of empties. What a racket! Even the Commodore's wife entered into the fray with enthusiasm, yelling with pleasure when a well-aimed can brought down a bunch. It was a fitting end to my Navy career, I thought. We four house mates enjoyed hearing everyone pronounce ours the best party ever. We then poured them into their cars and headed for bed.

The next morning, with a massive hangover, I viewed the shambles through red eyes. The bare floor was littered with empty beer cans, and the furniture was outside in the rain. What a party! The wrecked scene reflected my Navy career, I thought. Unknown to me at the time, my present Captain had summed up my career in the Navy's last official report on me:

"He has demonstrated an excellent ability to administer his department, but too often, his personal attitude has interfered with his proper performance of duty. He is not particularly receptive to suggestions or criticism, and his open criticism of policies and regulations of the Navy is tiresome. He has a pleasing personality and generally acceptable appearance."

Right on, Captain! Couldn't have said it better myself.

THE VIRGIN MARY

The two young Naval officers were drunk — helplessly, falling-down drunk. Not only were they out of their senses drunk, they were out of their minds to be in Tiguabos, Cuba at 2:00 in the morning. As an American, you could hardly find a more dangerous place to be in August 1955 than in Fulgencio Batista's Cuba. Batista, who had become Dictator of Cuba three years earlier, would be replaced by Fidel Castro four years later, in February 1959. Neither dictator had much use for Americans, but thanks to a 1903 treaty which gave the United States the right to a permanent naval base at Guantanamo Bay, they were both stuck with us.

Cuba, discovered by Columbus in 1492, is the largest island in the West Indies and is about 760 miles long with an average width of approximately 60 miles. At its most westerly point, Cuba is only 90 miles from Key West.

Walter "Bud" Stuhldreher

Guantanamo Bay was first known as Cumberland Bay when British Admiral Vernon sailed into the harbor in 1785 to lick his wounds after his failure to capture Cartagena. In the days of the Spanish Main, it was the hideout for pirates such as Mau and Sores who raided ships traveling through the Windward Passage. On June 10, 1898, 600 Marines from the transport *Panther* landed on the eastern shore of the bay and undertook to secure the outer harbor for the use of American vessels. In 1901 the U.S. chose the site for a naval station, and in 1903 the land on both sides of the entrance was leased. The island in the bay, conspicuous by its round tower, is Hospital Cay, so called because long ago an English squadron sent its yellow fever patients there.

Guantanamo Bay is on the southern side of Cuba, facing Jamaica and Haiti across the Windward Passage. The Caribbean Sea doesn't offer a prettier passage than the Windward Passage. The naval base includes the large, protected bay with McCalla airfield on the left as you enter the bay. It was never called by its formal name, but was "GITMO" to the many U.S. sailors who spent some time there in those years. After President Kennedy's 1961 Bay of Pigs debacle, Castro tried to throw the US out, but the 1903 treaty stopped him. It stated it could be nullified only by the mutual consent of both countries. But all this doesn't explain what the two officers were doing in a small town ten miles from GITMO at 2:00 in an August morning in 1955.

My ship had been involved in numerous practice landings in the Caribbean, principally at Vieques Island. The *Kleinsmith* had been commissioned in 1945 at New Orleans. She operated in and out of the Japanese home islands from 1945 until 1946, when she returned to the U.S. From 1947 until the time of this incident, the *Kleinsmith* had participated in nearly every amphibious operation scheduled in the Atlantic from Labrador and on south to Vieques Island. Each summer she had taken part in amphibious training of midshipmen or had gone on midshipman cruises. In 1949 she became a movie star when the motion picture *"The Frogmen,"* featuring Dana Andrews and Richard Widmark, was filmed primarily on board, telling the story of the Under Demolition Team (UDT) personnel and their duties.

Prior to this 1955 midshipman cruise, the commanding officers of the ten ships in the task force had been required to have their pictures taken for the cruise book. Our skipper, LCDR Jerry K. Pounders, in addition to being a superb ship handler, for which we adored him, was a man of many idiosyncrasies. Besides those I have already mentioned in other stories, Captain Pounders hated having his picture taken. This explains his dour expression in the picture. Told to wear his ribbons in the picture, something no other officer ever had to be told to do, Captain Pounders grabbed three of his many medals, pinned them on haphazardly, and faced the incredulous Navy photographer. The photographer managed to get one shot off before Pounders stormed out of the studio. "Assholes!" he snarled to me as we headed off to the golf course, "Can't they find something better to do!"

LCDR Jerry K. Pounders, USN

Walter "Bud" Stuhldreher

Captain Pounders was one of a kind: profane to a fault, but damn! could he handle a ship! And on a small ship that was vitally important. The sea is an unforgiving place at best, and a small ship is particularly vulnerable. Our crew of 100 sailors and eight officers felt safe with our lives, literally, in his hands.

The task force of Midshipman Cruise "Charlie" had left Norfolk, Virginia, on July 18, visiting the Panama Canal Zone, then Havana. We had entered GITMO the previous Friday, August 22 for the weekend. The huge base, in addition to the normal operational facilities common to all naval bases, was loaded with recreational facilities. The base had eight clubs, divided between Officers, Chief Petty Officers, Petty Officers and Enlisted Men. Wow! Talk about a strict hierarchy. There was even one, The Private's Club, for Marines only. GITMO also had three restaurants, three exchanges, a slew of athletic facilities, two swimming pools (one for officers, another for enlisted men), picnic and beach facilities, sail boats, and an eighteen hole golf course. Thankfully, the course was open to both officers and enlisted men. I say "thankfully" because my regular ship's foursome consisted of LTJG Don Joyce, LTJG Jerry Hamilton, myself and Chief Petty Officer Sam Thornton, an enlisted man and the ship's chief electrician. We always loaned "Sparky," our nickname for Thornton, officer's insignia to get around the normal "For Officers Only" signs.

There were riding stables, bicycles to use, tennis and basketball courts, a roller skating rink, baseball and softball diamonds, and two bowling alleys, one for officers, one for enlisted men. Plus a hobby shop, photo lab and a library. With all this, why did two of our officers choose to go looking for trouble in Tiguabos at 2:00 in the morning? Easy. You may have noticed there was one thing missing from GITMO: women. None. Nada. Zero. Zip.

SOUR M.A.S.H. AT SEA - SECOND WAVE

There was absolutely nothing outside the base unless you were interested in jungle plants. Some unappetizing bars, nothing more than shacks, had sprung up, manned by locals intent on separating young American sailors from their money. They rimmed the entrance to the base and had only one redeeming feature: Hatuey beer. A Cuban beer with an oval label, Hatuey was sold in a brown bottle with the word "Havana" embossed on the bottom. It was easily the best beer in the Caribbean. Really good. Cheap, too. But it became expensive when U.S. sailors, passed-out drunk from Hatuey beer, were rolled by the locals who waited for such opportunities. The sailors would come to and discover their watches, cigarettes, sunglasses and wallets were missing. And no cops in sight. The Cuban police were notorious for protecting the local citizens, so even if a victim spotted a policeman he was still out of luck.

The two Ensigns had drunk their share of Hatuey and were interested in bigger game. Women. They knew none were near the base; the Shore Patrol kept them away. But the Ensigns figured a taxi driver would know where to go. Sure enough, the first driver they hailed said, in pidgin English, "Women? You bet! Get in, I show you."

Yes, they had been warned not to use local transportation. Being taken somewhere and robbed was a common occurrence, but the officers were reasonably short of common sense by now. They jumped in the cab and off they went down a dusty dirt road lit only by moonlight. The taxi's headlights didn't work, but that didn't disturb the intrepid driver who thought he was driving in a NASCAR race. Bouncing merrily along the rutted road, missing trees by the depth of the taxi's paint job, hurtling around curves they were sure they weren't going to handle, it was enough to sober one up. But not them. They had brought a supply of Hatuey with them which they charitably shared with the taxi driver.

"Where in hell are we going?" one Ensign asked the other.

"Don't know," replied the second Ensign, "but he seems to want to get there in a hurry." And that's how they found themselves in the small town of Tiguabos, which was ten miles from the U.S. Naval base and light years from safety.

The driver pulled up in front of a wooden ramshackle house that was more like a two story cottage than a house. A red light glowed over the front door. The driver indicated they should get out; this was the place with women. One officer, upset with the wild ride, snarled at him and asked, "Yellow cards, no?"

"Si, si, yellow cards!" It was the practice in Cuba in those days for whores to be examined periodically by government doctors for venereal disease. If clean, they were issued yellow cards. It wasn't much protection, but something.

They stumbled up the three rotting stairs, and not seeing a doorbell, knocked loudly. An older Cuban woman answered the door, saw two officers and waved them in. Didn't have to ask what they wanted, not at 2:00 in the morning. Her English wasn't much, but enough to tell them the price, and should she bring the girls down? They nodded yes, she yelled upstairs, and down came around six or eight women in various stages of undress. They lined up for the cursory inspection, all clutching their yellow cards. It was obvious they had done this hundreds of times before. And then it happened.

As the two officers looked the women over, they both saw a small table with a lamp on it. Resting on the table was a statue of Mary, the Blessed Virgin. Both practicing Catholics, this stressed them. After all, they were there on a mission Mary would hardly approve of. Trying to avoid seeing her didn't work. Their eyes were invariably drawn back to the serene statue. Guilt washed over them like a tropical monsoon. Catholicism is a guilt religion, and these two young officers were consumed by it at this point. No matter how hard they tried, even in their drunken state, the statue and the guilt would not go away. Without any words passing between them, they knew what the other was thinking. They gave up, and leaving the angry madam and women, lurched out to the waiting taxi.

"Back to the base and don't be in such a hurry!"

The driver sped off and yelled, "Din take you long in there, Mon!"

"Shut up and drive!" they responded.

The two officers returned to the *Kleinsmith* safely and were greeted by a sleepy OOD. "Didn't get into trouble, did you?" he asked.

"Hell no, but how did you know?"

Somewhere, the Holy Mother smiled.

THE UNHAPPY ADMIRAL

Have you ever seen a dog come in out of the rain and shake himself all over, eagerly flipping the water off his coat in all directions? Well, the *Kleinsmith*, was — figuratively — doing the same thing as she prepared for a long cruise to the Mediterranean during the summer of 1956. She had endured a string of unhappy disasters earlier that year. In early spring she had returned from a seven-month Mediterranean cruise with damages from a terrible storm encountered off Greece. She entered a Navy shipyard for repairs. Then a six week cruise to the Caribbean, complete with many breakdowns, showed that the repair work was either flawed or lacking in scope, whereupon the *Kleinsmith* returned for additional repair work. Shortly after leaving the second time, her drunken skipper had run her hard aground in the James river, which necessitated her being towed back to the yard once again.

Walter "Bud" Stuhldreher

Getting the same ship back for the third time that spring was a little too much for the yard workers. They were tired of the *Kleinsmith*. Would they ever see the last of that damn ship? One thing was for sure however; they wouldn't see the Commanding Officer or the Executive Officer again. They were long gone, thrown out of the Navy after a quick court martial. Wouldn't see the Supply Officer (me), again either. Escaping a court martial of my own, for different reasons other than running a Navy ship aground, I had completed my required Navy service and had happily departed for civilian life.

So the crew of the *Kleinsmith*, with a new CO, XO and Supply Officer, tried to shake off their recent troubles and redeem the ship's reputation during the upcoming Med cruise. Alas, apparently dogged by the *Kleinsmith's* own version of *Moby Dick*, the cruise did nothing to regain the crew's rightful place in the squadron, i.e., to be considered to be the number one ship, first by any standard the Navy cared to use. Hard to believe but that's exactly where the *Kleinsmith* had been ranked prior to unluckily getting an incompetent drunk for a skipper. And if the crew hoped this deployment was to be the turning point, well, that hope was soon done in.

After entering the Mediterranean, the *Kleinsmith* improbably ended up off Lebanon while the rest of the task force rendezvoused off the island of Corfu, Greece, many miles away. You don't have to look at a map to realize this was a horrendous mistake; I mean we're talking *many, many* miles from where they were supposed to be. This happened when, during an impenetrable fog, the *Kleinsmith* had somehow committed an unforgivable error. They missed a radio message from the Task Force Commander, Vice-Admiral Fahrion, directing the task force to Corfu. Now staring at the coast of Lebanon, the new CO and XO knew they weren't off to a good start. The *Kleinsmith* was back in the Navy's dog house once again.

SOUR M.A.S.H. AT SEA - SECOND WAVE

For punishment, Vice-Admiral Fahrion directed the *Kleinsmith* to function as the task force's mail ship. This meant the ship had to go to lousy Navy ports like Reggio Calabria, La Spezia, the Isle of Rhodes and Salonica, Greece, to pick up the mail. Meanwhile, the rest of the ships got to go to great liberty ports like Barcelona, Naples, Cannes and Nice. Later they would meet up with the *Kleinsmith* to get their mail. It was a dirty duty, much despised by the crew. And it didn't help that they knew the other crews were reveling in the *Kleinsmith's* misfortunes. Even they couldn't understand how they had ended up by their lonesome off Lebanon while the other ships, *all eleven of them*, correctly met at Corfu. Was this damn ship doomed forever? Requests for transfers began to pour in to the ship's office. All were refused. The CO and XO weren't about to let unhappy swabbies transfer to other ships and tell how great it was to be off such a terrible tub!

Finally the Task Force Commander relented and began to rotate the despised mail run among the other ships. But not for long. Only until the task force entered Genoa, Italy.

As the ship with the most junior skipper, the *Kleinsmith* entered port last; thus the rest of the ships had a good view of the ensuing debacle. Particularly Vice-Admiral Fahrion.

The CO and XO hadn't known they were going to be required to tie up in a peculiar fashion know as "the Med moor." In 1956 this procedure was used only in the Med. It required the ship to back in and tie up to the pier with the rear end of the ship next to the pier and to do this while avoiding the other ships tied up in a similar fashion close by. Imagine several cigars almost touching each other with their ends up against a ruler. Substitute large ships backed up perpendicular to a pier and you've got the picture. It's difficult enough to simply back a ship up; after all, it's designed to go forward, not backwards. That's why the bow is pointed and the rear isn't. Now try this difficult procedure while slipping by other ships maybe only ten feet away plus stopping before whamming into the pier. Don't forget: YOU AIN'T GOT ANY BRAKES TO HELP YOU STOP!

It proved to be way too much for the crew. None of them had ever done this before. The first attempt was going OK. They backed in, managing to miss the ships on either side, but failed to reverse engines in time. The rear end of the *Kleinsmith* plowed into the pier, its 1,450 tons doing considerable damage. Going forward a bit, putting several yards between the ship and the damaged pier, they tried again. With the same pitiful results. SLAM! BAM! BOOM! But this time, repelled by the pier, they bounced off one ship next to them, then the other. Both ships were seen busily securing additional fenders over their sides as this crazy ship backed in to try again.

No better luck. The only difference this time was the absence of the previous loud whacks as they crushed the pier. By now it was in tatters, with softened timbers hanging loosely, its concave appearance replacing its previously straight lines. It was too much for the Italian Port Director. He ordered the *Kleinsmith* to stop any further attempts. He sent a mooring team over to do the job for the thoroughly embarrassed crew. After apologizing profusely and agreeing to pay for the repairs, the Task Force Commander ordered the *Kleinsmith* back on the mail run. The recruiting posters promising you would "See the World" were but a memory. For the rest of the cruise the crew of the *Kleinsmith* would see only the lousy Navy mail ports once again.

But Vice-Admiral Fahrion wasn't done with the *Kleinsmith* yet. He "volunteered" the ship to be the plane guard for the aircraft carrier *Saratoga* the rest of the trip. This duty was normally rotated since riding in the huge carrier's wake, while ready to pick up any pilots who had been forced to ditch, was a mighty rough, uncomfortable ride. The *Saratoga* normally had flight operations three times a day for one or two hours each time. Even in mild seas the *Kleinsmith* was a terrible sailer. Modified to transport UDT teams, she was top-heavy and always rolled like a drunken sailor. Following in the carrier's wake made things much worse. I suppose it gave the Admiral great satisfaction to see her roll and pitch violently while the rest of the task force steamed smoothly on. The crew of the *Kleinsmith* could only hang on, pitching their guts out over the rails, while cursing their fate for serving on such a luckless ship.

And that's how the rest of the cruise went until they returned, months later, to their home port in Little Creek, Virginia. The Admiral's last message, congratulating and thanking the ships' crews for a successful deployment, was the final nail in their weary hides. Of the twelve ships in the task force only the *Kleinsmith's* name was omitted from the addressees in the message. At least, the crew told themselves, they didn't have to go back in the hated yard. No, the dog house they were in would do just fine. God help them; they were getting used to it.

STORIES FROM THE STATES

SERGEANT STUHLDREHER OF THE PINKERTONS

After completing my required three years of Navy service, I entered graduate school at Indiana University (IU) in Bloomington, Indiana for the summer semester in June 1956. Since I hadn't been able to figure out how to get a job interview while continuously at sea, graduate school on the GI Bill, plus a teaching assistantship and a small amount of savings would see me through my MBA. That was the plan, anyway.

I'll never forget the first day of class. I had been assigned to Professor Thornton as his teaching assistant for a Freshman class "Introduction to Personal Finance." A "crip" course, the students called it, as well they should have. A remarkably easy one, to me it was a joke. Imagine getting college credits for learning how to maintain a checkbook, for instance. But even so, some managed to fail the darn course!

Just walking around the campus had shown me I was in for a huge culture shock. Women everywhere! Good looking young women! Man, I thought I had gone to heaven and couldn't even remember dying. You have to understand, it had been a long thirteen years since I had gone to school with girls. Our Catholic grade school had separated the girls from the boys after sixth grade. So I spent two years there, four more at a Catholic boys high school, four more at Notre Dame (which didn't go coed until 1972), then three years in the Navy, all at sea. No sir, it was quite a sight to see girls everywhere I looked. Nevertheless that first day in class threw me for a loop.

It was one of those auditorium classes, with 250 students, mostly girls, who just took notes as the professor droned on — no questions possible due to the huge class size. Not that anyone would have wanted to ask one. It was knitting that had the girls' undivided attention. Can you imagine the racket 250 girls make while knitting angora socks? It was deafening. Click, click, click from all sides, their multiple short knitting needles flashing. It was the year angora socks were "in" and they were making them for their brothers (I hoped!) or, more probably, their boyfriends.

After class I asked Professor Thornton why he permitted it, and he looked at me mournfully. "Oh, yes, you haven't been around a public school for some time, have you?" Well, never, to be truthful, but what did that have to do with the price of eggs? "Since IU is a taxpayer funded institution, we can't enforce discipline as strenuously as a private school. They can knit away, and there's nothing I can do about it."

And that was my introduction to public education at the tender age of 25 — with 250 students knitting industriously away, drowning out the teacher's voice. The damnedest thing I had ever seen or heard. So the dumb course continued on its boring way that summer with me taking attendance at the start of each class. I did this by the numbers on the seats. The students had been assigned a numbered seat for the semester, and if that seat was vacant, I recorded that student as absent. The students quickly learned that I always started at the top of the auditorium and worked my way down to the bottom row, or the one closest to the professor. So the game was on. After I had recorded the empty seats in the top rows I could hear and see the students scampering down to occupy empty seats below me. This way, one student, if agile, could fill in for several missing friends. Sorta like playing leap-frog. You think I cared? If a few wanted to knit elsewhere that was OK by me. I got paid for recording empty seat numbers and recording empty seat numbers was what I did. Besides, it couldn't hurt for a young teaching assistant to make friends with some good-looking freshmen girls, could it?

As usual in my dumb younger years I went overboard, dating every coed I could. For a while, I was dating five Barbaras at the same time. My grades suffered and I lost my assistantship for my final semester Luckily I had started tutoring football players during the previous semester, so I just increased the hours I did that and started studying in earnest myself. I managed to slip out of IU by the skin of my teeth, clutching my MBA.

But back to the end of that first summer semester. My brother Bill, who was also attending IU, and I were faced with a three-week hiatus and needed jobs. But who wanted to hire us for three weeks? No one. Earlier, a former girlfriend's uncle had gotten me a job at the Indiana State Fair in the publicity department. (I can still remember the thrill of seeing my first words in print: "109 Blessed Events in the Swine Barn." It was an account of the many piglets being born during the nine days of the Fair. Imagine: pigs being born called a "blessed event." Simpler times then, that's for sure.) So out to the fair we went and got hired on as Pinkerton guards. Pinkerton had been hired by the Fair for the first time that year. It's job was to keep the nonpaying customers out and collect the cash from the paying customers.

Have you ever been in Indiana in late summer? Not too different from Hades. Sweltering hot, so humid you thought it was raining but it was only your sweat. I sweated buckets at the fair that year. And standing around for twelve hours a day, collecting cash from the cars as they drove in, looked like a bitch. With nothing to lose, I confronted the boss of the Pinkertons the day before the fair opened.

"Sir, as an ex-Navy Supply Officer, who is trained to handle cash (a big lie), I want to tell you that the handling procedures for your cash collectors stink. You are going to be out a lot of cash and never know it." Indeed, their so-called procedures were a joke. They used the two-man station procedure. The first guy counted the number of adults and children in the car. He then sold the appropriate number of tickets and collected the cash. The car would then drive on to the next guy who would collect the tickets, count the number of visitors in the car, and if the tickets and visitors were correct, would signal the car to pass on through the gate. Simple, huh? Too simple.

The Indianapolis 500 used the same procedure in those days for the cars entering the infield the day of the race, typically around 4 a.m. My high school friends, who worked there, made hundreds of dollars each the day of the race by cheating the 500. It was simple. The first guy would correctly count the people and charge the correct amount. He would then hand over the tickets. The second guy would collect them. There were two ways to scam the race track. Either resell tickets given back by the second guy, pocketing the cash, or by the first guy charging the right amount but giving fewer tickets than paid for. It only

SOUR M.A.S.H. AT SEA - SECOND WAVE

took two guys at each entrance to operate the scam. With crowds of over 400,000 the day of the race, and mostly in the infield, thousands of dollars were skimmed off the top and there was no way for the race officials to catch it. Illegal? Sure. Immoral? Sure. But easy big dough translates into mighty loose morals in a hurry. Just ask the guys at Enron if you don't believe me.

So I stared at the Pinkerton boss, confident that the same scam was a sure bet to be in the works at the Fair. Hell, some of the same guys who worked at the previous 500 were working at the Fair. The boss looked at me and said, "Well, son, assuming you're correct, why should I care?"

Now my time in the Publicity Department of the State Fair came in handy. I knew the administration had a hot button: the number of visitors was vital. The higher the better. Their jobs and bonuses were tied to the number of visitors. So I reminded the head of the Pinkertons of this and stated he probably could, with the right cash procedures, improve the official head count by 10 percent. Now I had his undivided attention. Mine too, since I had no idea on how to improve cash collection procedures whatsoever! But I also knew the ten percent figure could never be proved or disproved.

He next said, "Sergeant Stuhldreher, the job is yours! But we open tomorrow; can you handle it?" (I later learned the record for making sergeant in the Indiana section of the Pinkertons was twelve years. And I had made it in eight hours! What a success story!) I told the boss I was sure I could pull it off (truly a whopper, but what the hell, in for a penny, etc.), but needed another guy, a vehicle assigned to me, and authority to make such changes as I thought necessary. He readily agreed, but could I find a guy with the right credentials? Yeah, I answered, it just so happened I knew another Pinkerton who

Walter "Bud" Stuhldreher

would do. So twin brother Bill made sergeant in a record eight hours also! (Mother proudly sewed our new stripes on our uniforms that night, reveling in our promotions. I didn't tell her that going from LTJG, an officer position, to sergeant, an enlisted position, would not be considered going in the correct direction by knowledgeable people, but, thankfully, Mother always did have trouble getting the various ranks sorted out.)

Brother Bill, while happy to be out of the sun (we had been assigned desks), was not nearly as confident as I was about our ability to do our new jobs.

"Do you have any idea how we're going to pull this off?" he worriedly asked me.

"Sure, Bill, it's a snap." I replayed my conversation with the boss, stressing there was no way to actually find out if we really had improved the cash take. The important thing was to be active, visible, officious, and run around in a hurry, like we had important things to do. I hadn't spent three years in the Navy without learning how to get ahead! And, actually, believe it or not, I had figured out a course of action which just possibly might improve the take.

We held a meeting with the ticket takers, our new employees. I told them I knew all about how they had screwed the Indianapolis 500 out of thousands of dollars every year and it damn well wasn't going to happen at the Fair this year. Their eyes bugged out: did this bastard sergeant actually know how they had done that? Bill's eyes bugged out too; I had forgotten to tell him I was privy to the 500 scam, a scam he had known nothing about. Although twins, we were as different as night and day. He was bookish and a good son; I hated being indoors and doing what my parents told me to do. So we pretty well took different paths growing up and had different sets of friends.

SOUR M.A.S.H. AT SEA - SECOND WAVE

I knew about a lot of scams which he would have been shocked to discover. Strangely though, I was never kicked out of school and he was — for smoking in the rest room. (I didn't smoke because athletes weren't supposed to. My whole family smoked — parents, brothers and sister, aunts and uncles — the whole lot, but I never have. Some of them would tell you it was my single redeeming feature.)

I put in some simple accountability rules. A cash box for each money changer, with cash counted in and out for each shift. Numbered tickets, also. Now, if you understood the 500 scam correctly, this deal wasn't going to stop the scam. But it was different and showed I meant business. Next I told them a whopper. I claimed I had hired a number of people to go through their ticket stations who, randomly, would test the cash collection process to see if it was being handled properly. Anyone caught doing differently would be fired on the spot and prosecuted. With twelve entrances to the Fairgrounds I told them I hadn't had to hire as many as they might think, that all of them would be tested at least three times an hour with the testers going through different entrances each time. They left the meeting muttering to themselves; it was clear they weren't going to make as much dough as they had counted on. Just their salaries! What a concept!

Oh, yes, that whopper I had referred to? I hadn't hired any testers, not one! I deduced, correctly, they would never figure that out, so how could they learn the truth? Even Bill, and for sure the boss, thought I had come up with a remarkably clever scheme. How clever they never knew! So Bill and I went from brain-dead jobs, standing around in the hot Indiana summer sun, to speeding around in our jeep looking important. And sitting in an air-conditioned office reading trashy novels and listening to the radio. And, let us not forget, wearing our sergeants' stripes with pride. The Pinkertons were truly on the job!

Walter "Bud" Stuhldreher

The Fair opened on time and did a brisk business all nine days. The Fair officials couldn't figure out where the crowds were; the official attendance was up 17 per cent, yet the crowds in the barns, stands and at the exhibits looked the same as last year. But the Pinkertons were quick to take credit, insisting the improved cash collection procedures were responsible for the increase in the official numbers! And you know what? I believe, in all honesty, that we had cut down on the amount of money stolen by the ticket takers, and had truly earned our pay. Maybe that's not why I had started my particular scam in the beginning. All I had wanted was to get out of the sun and make a little more money in the bargain, but, gee, isn't it amazing how it turned out? Now to collect my just rewards.

I went in to see the big boss, who was basking in all the favorable attention his outfit was receiving from his bosses, the Indiana State Fair officials. He about fell out of his chair when I requested bonuses for Bill and myself.

"Are you crazy? I made you sergeants, with increased pay, and you simply did what we told you to do! Get the hell out of here!" And that was the last whopper told in the Indiana State Fair Pinkerton office that year.

I should have known when I was well off, that is, out of my Pinkerton uniform, but like a fool, I agreed to a one-night assignment the next week when they called me. The $25 was too good to pass up, That was big pay in 1956 for eight hours work, and that's how I found myself bouncing around in a cheap Pinkerton car with no shocks heading for southern Indiana the next Saturday night. (And to make it worse, I had canceled a date, who informed me it would be a waste of time to ever call her again.)

"Where to?" I asked Tim, who had picked me up at 6 p.m. Tim named a small southern town I had never heard of, Beanblossom.

"What's the job?"

"Oh," Tim replied, "just a guard job. You see, they want a couple of uniforms added to their regular bouncers. And I thought you, a big guy like me, would do OK."

I was beginning to get worried. Maybe Tim and I were the same size, but I was pretty sure our IQ's weren't. "Tim, level with me. Why does this place, whatever it is, need some 'uniforms' in addition to their regular bouncers?"

"Sarge, it's like this: it's a C & W joint and they just feel they need some extra security for awhile."

Since that didn't answer my question I pressed on. "Tim, come clean with me. That's an order." Holy God, had I just thrown my weight around? Tim, a veteran with several years with the Pinkertons, knew a hell of a lot more about guarding doors than I ever would. "Just what kind of a place is this, and why do they need any bouncers at all? It doesn't seem reasonable that a root beer place would need bouncers."

Tim's reply cleared the air somewhat. "Sarge, I don't know where you got the idea it was a root beer place. It's a country and western roadside joint. Saturday night is their big night, and sometimes the cowboys get a little out of hand."

Ah, I thought he had said "A & W," a well known root beer chain at the time. Instead, he had said "C & W," rural shorthand for "Country & Western." I always had trouble understanding Tim due to his impossibly large, ever-present cud of chewing tobacco. It would travel from side to side in his mouth, staining all his teeth in the process. And, of course, staining whatever was within spitting distance, which was a considerable distance in Tim's case. You had to be careful to never get downwind of Tim.

My Uncle Gerald, the only hunter in the family, had often spoken of the importance of being downwind when hunting. I never paid much attention to hunting stuff, but during the previous nine days at the Fair had learned a lot about being downwind. Tim was mighty careless when spitting and, all too often, if you were nearby, you took a shot of his mammoth wad of expectorated tobacco. I well remember the time when Tim and I were returning to the Pinkerton office in my jeep with Bill in the back seat. Tim let loose, and the air rushing by the moving car pushed his wad into the back seat, and Bill's uniform looked like he had sergeant's stripes all over him. We stopped, and Bill, while holding the damaged areas taut, tried to scrape the crap off himself with a pop sickle stick. With little success. It didn't help that I was laughing so hard Fair visitors stopped to see what was going on. So staying on the right side of Tim was a good idea.

But now at least I had the story straight. We were going to beef up the bouncers at a C & W roadside joint. OK, but the $64 question hadn't been answered. "Tim, this is the last time I'm going to ask you: why do they need help?"

"Sarge" Tim slowly replied, "things got out of hand last Saturday night and a fellow got killed."

I couldn't believe what I heard — a fellow killed? And Tim and I were going to make a difference tonight? And for putting my life out on a thin limb I was going to make the magnificent sum of $25?

"Tim, you may be crazy, but I'm not! There's no way I'm going somewhere to keep the peace where a guy was killed last week! I'm not trained to do this and I bet you aren't either. What was the office thinking of when they accepted this job?"

For the first time Tim looked a bit uneasy, it was clear he hadn't thought this deal through. But then he cheered up. "Sarge, I guess I forgot to tell you. If you'll look in the back seat you'll see two belts with billy clubs and holsters. The office decided we might need them so I guess they do understand this job might be a little dangerous."

I looked, and sure enough, there they were. "Tim, I don't know about you but I don't know how to handle a gun, never could."

"Godwhompit, Sarge, you don't have to, the holsters are empty! But the bad guys won't know that. They'll just see us in our uniforms with those big belts and holsters and behave themselves. There's nothing to worry about!"

"You idiot! There's one thing worse than toting a gun, and that's toting an empty holster! The bad guys will figure they better draw theirs first to keep ahead of us. No one in their right mind would ever carry an empty holster! Pull the damn car over, I'm getting out right now!"

Tim was baffled, his careful explanation had just made me feel worse than ever over this all-time stupid assignment. It was turning into a full-fledged screw-up. I was furious, mostly at being so dumb as to have blithely accepted this job without asking the particulars. I knew better than to blindly trust the Pinkertons on anything more difficult than replacing toilet paper rolls. Jeez, was this a mess or what?

"Sarge, you gotta understand there was no way the office was going to issue us guns. In the state of Indiana only licensed, trained professionals are allowed to carry weapons while in a police type uniform, and we Pinkertons aren't either one." For once I agreed with Tim: we weren't trained and we weren't professionals. We were a couple of hicks in way over our heads and I had to try to convince Tim of this.

"Tim, listen to me. This job stinks and you and I are in big trouble. If any shooting starts, guess who they're going to be aiming at first: you and me. Do you understand that?"

"Gee, I guess I hadn't thought about it as well as you have. What are we gonna do?"

"Tim, I'll tell you exactly what we're gonna do. Make a U-turn and get this heap back to Indianapolis as fast as it will go."

I won't bore you with Tim's sad recital over the next ten minutes. Basically it boiled down to his being down on his luck, no education, and a family to support when the Pinkertons came along. This was the best job he had ever had, would probably be the best one he could ever get, and wasn't there a way we could pull it off? If we returned now, when it was too late for the office to get someone else to replace us, he would be fired. I thought it over, and against my better judgment, decided I couldn't be responsible for getting Tim fired.

"OK, Tim, we'll go on down but with these conditions: 1. No holsters. I'll be damned if I'll let those yahoos think we're armed. 2. If bad trouble erupts, I'm out of there. If you can beat me to the door, more power to you. We ain't getting paid enough to get shot at. 3. If you know how to use a billy club, fine. If you don't, I'll show you before we get there. 4. We don't swagger around like we're looking for trouble. We keep a low profile, stand against the wall as much as we can, and smile at everyone in sight, especially anyone who tries to give us a bad time. You think you can do that?" It was pathetic; Tim couldn't agree with my rules fast enough. He was desperate to keep that lousy job. But what about the billy club thing?

He pulled over and I showed him the proper way to use a billy club. Unlike the wide sweeps you see on TV or in the movies, moves which leave you wide open for a punch before you can whack your opponent, you jab with the club. Faster and much more deadly. The force is concentrated in a small place, with your weight behind the end of the club. You catch the other guy in the crotch or eye, and he tends to quit real quick. And you can get in many more blows, since the club isn't going back and forth as far as when you swing it. Tim was excited with his new skill and wanted to know where I had learned this.

"Tim, the important thing is I don't want to be backed into a situation where we have to use the damn things. Remember, we're going to keep a low profile, and at the first sign of trouble, we're out of there. Now, repeat that back to me. I want to be sure you understand. But, if we do end up being screwed and have to fight, I want you to be as good as you can be." Tim repeated the rules back to me and we got back into the jalopy and continued our trip to perdition. (I never did tell Tim where I had learned to fight with a billy club and I'm not going to tell you either. Some things are best left unsaid.)

We arrived at the honky-tonk shack an hour later. The dirt parking lot was empty except for a few cars parked at the end. I figured they belonged to the help. We went in and found the band tuning up, the bartenders getting ready, and the waitresses setting the chairs up. A couple of huge surly guys warily watched us approach. Tim had cowboy boots on and I wished I did, they would have made me look taller. I sucked my gut in and tried to look tough, but calm, in control. (I kept my gut sucked in the rest of the night, the longest I ever did that. It actually hurt by the end of the night.)

"You the hired help for tonight?"

"Yeah, I guess so" I replied, "But let's get one thing straight between us. You guys are in charge and we'll take our lead from you. As we see it, our job is to stay inconspicuous and only back you up if we have to. And from what we hear that's probably not going to happen. OK?"

That thawed the room up considerably. Obviously, they hadn't thought we were needed, worse, we'd probably come in and throw our weight around. Instead, we were buds!

The crowd started coming in soon after. Some couples but mostly singles. The guys in casual street clothes, some in half-assed western stuff, the gals in jeans and western shirts. Many, of both sexes, had cowboy hats on. And I swear every last one smoked like a chimney. Pretty soon the room was so clogged with smoke that if one of them had twirled a lariat I couldn't have seen it. The noise was a low uproar and the dancing fierce. I soon figured out where the trouble would come from, if it did. Some of the boys resented being cut in on, but the women loved it. A nice recipe for trouble. And there were more guys than gals. Not many, but enough.

Tim was enjoying the scene immensely. We leaned up against the wall, watching the couples twirl endlessly around. Tim especially enjoyed the girls spinning so their cute skirts flared out exposing their cute thighs. And his spitting habit sure didn't bother anybody; most of the men and some of the women were chewing, too. Dumb me: when we arrived I had thought all those metal pails around the dance floor and walls were for a fire. Different strokes for different folks.

Tim, bored, started slapping his club into the palm of his other hand, you know, like cops do when they want you to know how tough they are. I stared murderously at him, hard enough to stop a skunk in midair.

"Tim, for god's sake, put a sock in it!" I whispered. "We're supposed to be keeping a low profile, remember."

"Ah, gee, Sarge, why do we have to pretend we're softer than them?"

"Because we are, that's why. You promised to obey my rules, so I came along. I want to get out of here in one piece. Put it away, make sure you don't stare at any one girl too long and smile until your mouth falls off!" So we stayed in place, Tim spitting and smiling, me smiling and ducking. Then trouble swaggered through the front door.

Four liquored-up guys came in the door walking unsteadily, and carelessly bumped into a couple of dancers. I knew easy times were over. But the bouncers seamlessly maneuvered in between them and the rest of the crowd and herded them over to the bar. Gave them a free pop and escorted them out the door. It was neatly done. The owners had spent useless dough on Tim and me, the bouncers knew their jobs and were damn good at it.

And that was it. Lights out at 2 a.m., drunks pushed out the door, handshakes all around, and Tim and I hit the road. Whew! Was I glad I got out of there in the same shape as when I went in. I almost asked the bouncers to escort us to our car but thought better of it. Didn't want to ruin our Pinkerton image. Tim was full of himself.

"See, Sarge, I told you it would go down slick as hog slop in a trough. You got all worked up over nothing. Damn, that was great music! I don't see why you wouldn't let me dance some."

"Well, Tim, just because there were more guys than gals, and we were getting paid to keep the peace, and I was scared out of my britches most of the time, I don't know why either." I shouldn't have been so subtle with Tim. He kept bitching about it all the way back to Indianapolis, and all I wanted to do was snooze.

That was my last job with the Pinkertons. Good thing, too. About a month later I read about that same roadhouse in the Bloomington newspaper — another shooting and the place got closed down. Brother Bill read the same article and asked, "Hey, Bud, wasn't that the same place you guarded one Saturday night about a month ago?"

"Hell, no. What kind of an idiot do you think I am? I wouldn't go near a place like that!"

THE STING

In 1973 a wonderful movie was released, *The Sting*, starring Paul Newman, Robert Redford, Robert Shaw and featuring the music of Scott Joplin. A great, great movie and I loved it. Still do. And, for the first time, I realized a caper I had planned, directed, and pulled off four years earlier had a name. It was a sting operation, in fact, a double-sting operation. This is the story of that caper.

In 1969, along with 2,300 other employees, I was working in the space program for IBM in Huntsville, Alabama. In those days, but no longer, IBM was a paternal type of company, as were many others. In addition to other aspects in keeping with the culture of such a company, IBM annually held a dinner dance for their employees. Even paid for the baby sitters. It was a very nice affair, always well attended, and it gave me the opportunity to pull off one of my better escapades.

The first player in this drama was a manager named Don. He was an average manager, nothing special. That's not important. What was important was that his wife had left Don, their two children, and their home *for a woman*. Remember, this was over thirty years ago. Such goings on were virtually unknown. It was a big-time scandal in our IBM community. Don, in addition to feeling bad about what this did to his kids and himself, had to suffer the knowledge that his IBM cohorts knew about it and felt sorry for him. Indeed, some even scorned him. After all, what kind of man could lose his wife to a *woman*? Not much of one, in their estimation. Now Don was a nice guy and normally fun to be around. Feeling sorry for him, I resolved to help rebuild his confidence and improve his image in the IBM community. This dinner dance was going to do it.

The second player was Jeannie, my wife Barbara's hair dresser. Jeannie was about twenty-five, and a knockout. A stunner. She had an unbelievable curvy figure, green eyes, and masses of gorgeous black hair, set off by an unblemished fair complexion. A former Miss Alabama first runner-up, she stopped traffic everywhere. Just as important for my plans, she was not stuck on herself; rather, she was very unassuming, a regular church goer, and friendly to everyone. And single. Perfect!

The third and fourth players were a married couple. Badly married. The wife, Maureen, for several reasons was convinced she had married below her station. She was a college graduate; her husband, Ken, was not. She came from a wealthy family; Ken did not. An IBM programmer, Maureen was smart, aggressive, and intent on advancement; qualities she was sure Ken did not possess. Loving her Mom and Dad more than Ken, she forced him to build their house next to her parents. And it didn't help that her parents paid for it. Maureen's father, a self-made man, doted on Maureen and his granddaughter. At best, he tolerated Ken. Ken was not good at business, either. There had been several failures in succession. At the time of the dinner dance Ken was laying carpets for his father-in-law.

Why had Maureen married Ken? None of us knew. It had happened while she was attending Auburn University. After a big wedding in Huntsville, she had returned to school, leaving Ken back in Huntsville. No, it wasn't what you're thinking. The baby didn't come along until Maureen graduated. So, who knows; we sure didn't.

What I did know, however, was that I was disgusted by how Maureen treated Ken. She could have kept her disdain for Ken private, but no, she was very public about it, constantly belittling him in front of others. She treated him like dirt, ordering him to do this, do that — and he took it. She hugely enjoyed making fun of him and pointing out his many failures. To top it all off, Maureen flirted shamelessly with every pair of pants that came near her, married or not. She simply enjoyed the game. If Ken was with her, even better. Unfortunately, Ken was a doormat where Maureen was concerned. A perfect Mr. Milquetoast. I felt he didn't deserve this treatment. Maureen was not bad-looking and had managed to invoke fear and loathing from most of the wives. I decided it was time for Mr. Doormat to assert himself and bring Maureen down a peg at the same time. So the stage was set.

Part One

For the dinner dance I reserved a table for six. Barbara wanted to know who the other four would be. "Hey, you like Jeannie. I thought we could fix her up with Don. He's looking for a date."

Barbara wasn't sure this was a good idea. "Are you sure his divorce is final? Jeannie won't date a married man."

I replied, "Yeah, it just happened, and Don is feeling pretty low about it. You know he's a nice guy and didn't deserve this mess. I thought taking a pretty girl would be good for him. (Careful boy, don't get too effusive about how gorgeous Jeannie is. You need a date for the dance yourself!) Also, I think Jeannie would enjoy a nice dinner date, especially going with you, someone she really likes." Well, the idea was looking better to Barbara so she called Jeannie who accepted.

Part Two

Don, of course, didn't know I was out scouting a date for him, but I was confidant he couldn't get one on his own, and would appreciate my efforts. Damn! I misjudged the situation. Yeah, he hadn't gotten a date, but he wasn't sure he wanted any part of a blind date, particularly at a large IBM affair where everyone would see him. "You're positive she's a good looker?"

"Don, you won't believe how good looking Jeannie is! A former Miss Alabama (notice how I had promoted her) and nice as she can be. Barbara's hair dresser. She's looking forward to the chance to get dressed up."

Don, suspiciously, "If she's so good looking how come she's willing to go on a blind date?"

I had assumed that question would be asked and was prepared. "Don, you're right. She normally doesn't accept blind dates, but Barbara did the asking. She likes and trusts Barbara, so she was agreeable. She's really looking forward to the occasion. She rarely gets an invitation like that."

Whew! Was Don going to keep giving me a hard time on this? After I have managed to fix him up with a former Miss Alabama? Is he nuts? Don was finally convinced I had done a good job for him and accepted. Right on! This caper was shaping up.

Part Three

Over Barbara's stern — and loud — protests I invited Maureen and Ken to fill out our table. Naturally, I hadn't told Barbara about my nefarious plans, and my wanting to spend any time around Maureen was news to Barbara. I just told her I liked Ken and felt we could put up with Maureen for once. "Besides, you don't even have to talk with her. You'll be with Jeannie most of the time." She still didn't understand my wanting to invite them to be at our table, but she went along.

Maureen, intent on advancing with IBM, must have concluded being seen sitting at a table with me might help her career, and accepted with enthusiasm. "Don't you want to call Ken first?" I asked innocently.

"Of course not. He does what I tell him to do." As if I didn't know.

Part Four

I immediately started passing the word about the plant that I had pulled a fast one on Don, that I had fixed him up with a real bowser. And that I had told him a huge lie, that his date was a dream boat, a former Miss Alabama. The others were all too willing to believe Don was being victimized, and he was going to show up at the dance with a walking disaster. I mean, after all, what kind of a date could a guy get whose wife had left him for another woman? A dog, that's what. So they believed me. But, I told them, all would be lost if they talked. If Don found out, he would obviously back out. They were to keep their mouths shut! And they did. Almost. Word did filter back to Don that I had fixed him up with a bow-wow, and he came to me about it. "Don, do you trust me? Do you really believe I would pull a dirty trick like that on you?"

"Well, why are the troops saying this?"

"Don, I don't have any idea, but they're probably just pulling your chain, trying to get your goat. DON'T BELIEVE THEM! TRUST ME!" And, thankfully, he did.

Part Five

This step was critical for the double-sting caper to have a chance of success, and it was the one I felt most nervous about pulling off. I had met Jeannie once or twice, but I didn't really know her. Now I had no choice but to call her. "Jeannie, this is Walt Stuhldreher. I'm really pleased you agreed to go to the dance with Barbara and me as Don's date, and I'm sure you're going to have a great time."

"Well, I'm looking forward to it and thanks for thinking of me."

"Jeannie, there is a favor I'd like to ask of you."

"Oh, what is it?"

Starting to sweat now, I plunged ahead. "Jeannie, there's going to be another couple at our table and I want to play a small joke on him. It's really no big deal and it's just in fun. I want you to make a play for him. Ask him to dance, stare into his eyes, you know, that sort of thing." Whew, I had said it!

"Gee, Walt, I don't have a problem with that, but what will Don think?"

Oh boy, she was going to do it! That's a big hurdle behind me. "Hey, Don won't have a problem with it. He's so excited about going to the dance with such a beautiful date he won't mind a bit." Maybe, maybe not, I wasn't sure about that, but the caper was shaping up exactly as planned. Now if I could only keep everything in place.

The First Sting

On the big night Don came over to our house and we three drove to Jeannie's apartment. Barbara and Don went up to get her. (Barbara later told me what happened.) Jeannie opened the door, a vision of loveliness in a clinging black dress. It was obvious that the dress, and some perfume, were all that Jeannie was wearing. Don almost sagged to his knees in wonder. He was relieved I had been telling the truth all along, and this dream boat was going out with him!

Damn, I'd like to have seen that scene, particularly when Barbara told me what happened next. After entering the apartment, it was evident to Barbara that an adjustment in Jeannie's attire was required. She took Jeannie into the bedroom where Barbara convinced Jeannie that the dress, while wonderful and didn't Jeannie look good in it, was a little revealing. She suggested Jeannie put two band aids on her nipples to tame down the effect. Jeannie agreed that maybe that was a good idea and made the necessary repairs. Don never noticed the change. He was besotted with his overwhelming good luck in landing this goddess as his date. I, of course, didn't know any of this until later in the evening. All I knew was that Jeannie was one fine-looking woman, particularly getting into our car with her gown riding up her thigh. Barbara punched my leg, a signal to behave myself, and off we went. I couldn't wait.

We entered the ballroom filled with couples happily dancing away to the music the band was playing. Soft, slow music. As luck would have it, our table was across the room, so we started across the dance floor. I held Barbara back, eager to see what happened next. Do you remember Cecil B. DeMille's great movie, *The Ten Commandments?* Charlton Heston played Moses, and in one epic scene he parted the Red Sea. He stood majestically on the bluff overlooking the water and commanded the sea to part, to roll back, thus making a path for the fleeing Jews to escape their pursuers. Well, that's *exactly* what happened on that dance floor. As Jeannie and Don walked through the crowd, the dancers parted on each side. The men stared openly. What was Don doing with this beauty on his arm when his date was supposed to be a dog? And, omygod, was she good looking! A true knockout! They couldn't stop staring. Their dance partners were not pleased. After all, they didn't care *how good looking* that girl was, the guys were supposed to be paying attention to *them*, not *her!* More than a few left the dance floor, dragging their unwilling partners after them. The rest just stood there, drinking in this amazing — and unexpected — couple. Jeannie, knowing full well the effect she was having on the male population in the room, stopped and invited Don to dance with her. The table could wait. And so could I. My first sting was a complete, amazing success. It couldn't get any better. But it did.

The Second Sting

When Don and Jeannie arrived at our table, Maureen was not a happy camper. Knowing the trick I was supposedly playing on

Don, she had assumed she would be the best-looking woman at the table, a situation she usually enjoyed and took full advantage of. But not this night. Oh, no, not this night at all! When the guys stopped at our table, it wasn't to ogle Maureen. She was totally and completely ignored. She damn well wasn't the center of attention at our table, and she hated it.

Barbara, who had observed Maureen's tricks at previous social affairs, was delighted with the turn of events and piled it on. "Ken, don't you think Jeannie looks stunning tonight? But, there's Tom without a date. Don't you think he would like a dance with Jeannie?" And so on.

Meanwhile, poor Ken, poor housebroken Ken couldn't speak, he was so dazzled by Jeannie. Maureen got madder still. "Ken do this. Ken, do that."

Jeannie seeing this going on, looked over at me for the signal. I nodded. Jeannie then made a play toward Ken. Now this wasn't your everyday flirting. No, this was watching a professional at work. She leaned toward him, batting her impossibly lovely eyes and drinking in his every utterance as if she had never heard anything so interesting. Then she asked him to dance.

Maureen choked as if she had bitten into a green persimmon. "No, Ken, I don't think that's a good idea."

"Oh, Maureen, don't be such a stick-in-the-mud. One dance won't hurt Ken," Jeannie gaily cried out as she pulled the willing Ken to the dance floor.

And what a dance that was. A piece of paper couldn't have gotten between them. The roof could have fallen in; they wouldn't have noticed. The orchestra seemed to play only for them. Ken was in pig heaven. Maybe it would never happen to him again, but for this one night his wildest dreams had come true. He was transported, and would have made Fred Astaire jealous with his dance moves. Swirling, dipping, gliding in circles, they were a show-stopper. Jeannie's long black hair floating around them, her arms tight on his, her impossibly long, slim legs flying about Ken. He was a dancing fool.

Meanwhile, a volcano was going active at our table. Smoke was coming out of Maureen's ears. Her eyes were squinting in anger. Her wiles were useless. Her cowardly, useless husband was making a fool out of her. And Maureen knew that a lot of wives in that room thought she had it coming. What a moment! I helped the tenor of the evening along. "Gee, Maureen, don't Ken and Jeannie dance WELL together!" A few comments like that intensified Maureen's black mood. I was having a good time watching them. Not as good as Ken, but then, who was?

After several stormy dances the happy couple returned to the table and were greeted by a definitely unhappy Maureen. "Ken, get your things. We're leaving!"

And then the absolutely impossible happened: the worm turned. Slowly, with emphasis, Ken faced his wife. He pulled the car keys out of his pocket and threw them on the table. "Maureen, you go if you want to. *I'm not leaving!*"

Was I hearing right? Did Ken say what I thought he said? Did he just tell Maureen to get lost? Yeah! He had! And Maureen did, stalking out without a husband, who by now was dancing with Jeannie again. Ken felt good about himself. In a complete turnaround, Maureen had been publicly showed up by him. Couldn't have been more deserved. My second sting had worked to perfection.

The Aftermath

Don was a happy man again, reveling in the kidding his fellow workers threw at him. His glorious date had rebuilt his confidence and redeemed him in their eyes. Ken was never quite the lapdog he had been. Eventually Maureen dumped him for her boss at the next company she worked for, destroying two marriages. Ken was awarded custody of his beloved daughter. Jeannie married and had two daughters who gave early indications of following in their mother's "Miss Alabama" footsteps. Barbara, to the best of my knowledge, never was around Maureen again, which suited her just fine. As for me, my fellow IBM employees were sure I had somehow been involved in the evening's surprises, but weren't sure just what role I had played. I stayed mum, as quiet as a church mouse. And that's just where I intend to remain.

EARTHQUAKE!

It was the Spring of 1953 and I was looking forward to graduating from Notre Dame. Not only because I was tired of school — although I was — but mainly because I wanted to make some money. My starting pay as an Ensign in the Navy wouldn't be that much, $222.20 a month, but as a student I had been broke all the time. For four years, from the time I entered as a freshman, I knew that next month — or year — would be the same. At last my struggle to pay my expenses at Notre Dame was coming to an end; so you would have thought I would be the happiest guy on campus. Well, I wasn't, not by a long shot. And, surprisingly, it wasn't grades which had turned my outlook sour.

Although an indifferent student, easily devoting more time to playing sports and cards than to studies, I had a sufficient average to graduate — barely — and had completed the required number of credit hours prior to my last semester. So, my last semester, in addition to three required courses, I took some fun courses: two English courses, piano and sculpturing. The Navy was fit to be tied. My scholarship required them to pay any extra fees, and piano and sculpturing weren't high on their lists for aspiring junior officers. Luckily for me, they had no choice but to pay up front. But the Navy was responsible for the first unpleasant event of that last semester.

"Midshipman Stuhldreher," The Commanding Officer of the Naval Reserve Officers Training Corps (NROTC) told me, "I have called you in to give you some bad news, I'm afraid. The staff, after consultation with our contract doctor, has decided you're too ugly to be commissioned an officer in the United States Navy." Too ugly? What in hell was this? I had no idea some sort of beauty pageant was going on. Besides, I knew at least half a dozen other midshipmen who weren't any better looking than I was. I gotta tell you, that was a severe blow to my self-image, a jolt that a young fellow just out of his teens didn't need to hear.

"Too ugly? How did you reach that decision?"

"Mr. Stuhldreher, it's as plain as the nose on your face. And that's the problem. Your nose goes all over."

Well, he had me there. It had been broken several times while playing sports, and looked very much like the first letter of my last name. It veered from left to right, then back to the left. It worked OK though, and with no women on campus, and none in sight during the next two years, my obligated service time, who cared? The Navy, I guess. The Korean War was in its third year, with no end in sight. In fact, it was going badly at the moment. The Chinese, in a huge surprise not anticipated by General MacArthur, had spilled over the Yalu river, hundreds of thousands of them, and smashed our outnumbered forces back south. So, I thought, maybe this was a lucky break for me.

"Sir, does that mean I'm free of my obligated service time?"

"Of, course not, Midshipman Stuhldreher," the Captain replied, flushing my short-lived hopes down the drain, "it means you will have to serve three years as an enlisted man."

Oh Wow! This was terrible! An enlisted man? A college graduate? While all my friends would be officers? Jeez, what a mess! And why three years, for God's sake? The Navy and I had signed a contract calling for me to serve two years on active duty and six years in the Reserve. "Sir, aren't you mistaken? I'm signed up for two years, not three."

"Well, Stuhldreher, there is going to be an announcement this week. Before leaving office, President Truman extended you fellows an extra year, due to the war."

I was astonished. Could Truman do this? Yep, it turned out, he damn well could, and did. Three years it was. This nose business was rapidly turning into a horrible mess for me. "Sir, what options do I have?"

"Stuhldreher, you could have your nose fixed through surgery if you choose to go that route."

Why hadn't he told me that right off the bat instead of scaring me into an enlisted man's uniform? "Sir, that sounds like the best bet to me. Where does the Navy want to do it?"

"Are you crazy, man, the Navy isn't going to do anything. You want to get your nose fixed, that's on you. And if you go that route you don't have much time. The semester is almost up."

Walter "Bud" Stuhldreher

So I spent my last spring break, not in Florida with Annette Funicello and Connie Francis on a bikini beach vacation, but in Indianapolis getting a $300 nose job, $300 that was tough for my Dad to come up with. (It served the Navy right when it was broken, again, during my first year on active duty.)

The next ugly surprise the Navy pulled on me, on top of the nose job and the extra year of service, was charging me $300 for my uniforms, $300 I sure didn't have. My NROTC classmates who had also spent four years as midshipmen, but without Navy scholarships, were to be commissioned as *reserve* officers. They would have their uniforms *given* to them since they weren't going to make a career out of the Navy. But the 28 of us who had Navy scholarships were presumed to be career officers. We would be commissioned as *regular* Navy officers, and had to pay for our uniforms. The theory was that we would be using them for much longer. Holy moley! A *regular* commission? Didn't they spell NROTC with a "Reserve" in it? Hadn't I been in the NROTC for four years? We 28 were dumbfounded with this news, and protested strongly.

We, of course, lost the battle and had to come up with the $300. I and many of my classmates didn't have it. So, good ol' Dad was tapped, again. This was a loan, however; one I had to pay back ASAP. Instead of making serious money for the first time in my life, I had to send Dad my paychecks for a month and a half. I didn't go on liberty once during that period — a strange way to start my Navy time. And, just to set the record straight, not a single one of us Notre Dame graduates with Regular commissions stayed in the Navy past our obligated three years. And if you thought the Navy was treating me roughly over a bad nose, they really screwed another classmate of mine. They kicked Al out for being *allergic to grass!* You would think being at sea would be the best thing you could do for a fellow who couldn't tolerate grass, but oh no, out Al went. (You'd also think the Navy would have discovered that little detail during the previous four years, but perhaps that shows you how swift the Navy can be.)

The final topper in that last semester, one I had carefully crafted to be a breeze, was flunking my final exam in sculpturing class. At the end of each semester the schedule for the final exams was posted. Each class was scheduled for a specific time and classroom. Who ever thought you could have a final in sculpturing? I sure didn't, and didn't even check the schedule for that class. When I accidentally learned my mistake I charged off to the teacher's office to see what could be done. Father Lauck, C.S.C., the teacher, and a fine sculptor himself, took pity on me. It turned out I was the first Business School student who had ever signed up for sculpturing! (All previous students had come from the School of Arts and Letters where the more traditional students were enrolled, the philosophy, English, and history majors. As a business student, I was the class project.) So he passed me with a 70, the lowest score you could pass with in those days at Notre Dame. I would have graduated even if I had flunked the course, but I didn't want a flunk on my record, shabby though it was.

1953 Notre Dame sculpturing class. Father Lauck is in the smock.

Instead of flying unscathed through my final semester, I was operated on to improve my "ugly" looks, had my two years of active duty extended to three, almost flunked a "crip" course, and was commissioned as a regular officer, not as a reserve as we had all believed would be the case. And, finally, courtesy of having to pay for my uniforms, I spent my first six weeks on active duty penniless, a condition I thought was behind me.

So 56 newly minted officers, mostly Navy Ensigns but also some Marine 2nd Lieutenants, graduated from Notre Dame, were sworn in the day following graduation, and left for duty posts around the world. No leave granted, of course. Along with several others, I took the train to Bayonne, New Jersey, for a Navy school. The Navy gave us vouchers for the train or I would have had to hitchhike, but while wearing a brand new uniform! It soon became clear that Bayonne was not the garden spot of the world, in spite of being located in the Garden State. The base was a run-down depot. Strangely enough, it was the same base where two of my uncles had served during WW II. Our fancy officer quarters were shabby prefab buildings. Built just well enough to last through WW II, here they were, still in use eight years after that war ended. The food was minimal, and for recreation facilities we had one baseball diamond, a sport I disliked then and now.

But the worst aspect of that base was its location. To get to it, we had to drive through the city of Bayonne's huge garbage dump that was filled with disgusting debris. Cars had no air conditioning back then, and it was June and very hot. But it wasn't just because the dump stunk that we couldn't roll the car windows down when we drove through. We didn't dare, not if we wanted to keep our hands and arms. The town's officials, in a move worthy of a character in the fine novel, *Catch-22*, had decided to solve a large rat problem by introducing wild dogs to the dump. Well, I guess the rats (wharf rats as big as cats) got taken care of by the dogs, but the dogs, big as small deer, maybe weren't the best solution the city fathers could have come up with. The dogs would hurl themselves against our car as we drove through, scratching the hell out of it, while snarling and barking at the top of their considerable lungs. Any stray appendage would have been dinner for the dogs, so we drove through with the windows up, deeming the heat preferable to being eaten alive.

Do you get the picture? The base, an old depot now operating as a school, was bordered by the Atlantic Ocean on one side, and the city dump, filled with savage wild dogs, on the other. The Atlantic Ocean doesn't sound too bad, does it? I guess I forgot to tell you it was a busy dock with freight ships loading and unloading 24 hours a day. No swimming allowed.

My first day at school started strangely. The roster of class officers was posted. In spite of a minimum scholastic record, and with a below-average (way below) midshipman record, I was listed as #2 class officer. I knew that had to be a mistake. After all, as a student midshipman I had set a record for days on Extra Duty Punishment (EDP), plus I had sunk a $50,000 Navy boat. I protested strongly, figuring keeping a low profile was the way to go, but lost, for reasons unknown to me even today. Maybe the officer in charge of us was a sports nut and had recognized the name. Who knows? In typical Navy fashion, the officers in charge of the school never explained their choice, but it ended up as a good deal for me and my friends. Every morning we would line up in formation, and the section guys would report to me if anyone was missing. I then made the official report to LTJG Holcomb, the officer in charge of all of us. I soon learned he was a laid-back fellow and never questioned my report. This allowed my friends to miss muster and gave them extra time to recover from the previous night's

Walter "Bud" Stuhldreher

excesses, of which there were many. You see, past the dump was New York City, separated from us by the Hudson River tunnel.

New York City! What a great place to be as a young officer when I finally had some money in my pockets. The Brooklyn Dodgers, for example, charged only $1 to attend a game if you were in uniform. While I disliked baseball, a lot of my friends were fans, plus the crowds were great. As a matter of principle, we always rooted for the visiting team, just to get a ruckus started. And with beer selling for fifty cents, that was easy to do. But the night life was the real winner.

Five drunk midshipmen in New York City. I'm on the left in the rear seat

Shortly after arriving at Bayonne, Tom Baker, a Notre Dame classmate, and I bought a 1939 Ford station wagon for $150. (I paid Tom my half as soon as I had paid Dad off for my uniforms.) We were warned that only crazy people dared to drive in New York City, but guess what? Since we had the oldest car on the road, and didn't give a damn to boot, the other drivers gave us a wide berth, and we never had a problem. Heading back to the base through the Holland tunnel, drunk as skunks and unable to see very well, we would drive as far on the right as we could, sparks flying as we shot along banging up against the side of the tunnel. That car was indestructible, and after school was over, we sold it for $75 to some new students.

So we lived it up in the city just about every night, school being a big-time joke. And we were not worrying about making muster in the morning. Exercising my lofty prerogative, I had named two other students as my replacements should I fail to show up. Naturally, they followed my example, and we set a record for percentage of students showing up on time each morning, in spite of some rather large spaces in our orderly ranks!

One Friday night we set out with the car loaded with friends. After visiting one watering hole after another, our usual routine, we ended up at Eddie Condon's place. It was on the second story of a building in Greenwich Village. Condon, a nationally known musician at the time, had a swell band featuring one of my heroes on the trumpet, "Wild Bill" Davidson. At the end of the evening, Wild Bill ended up too drunk to play and asked me to fill in. He and I had previously shared some drinks, and he had heard me claim to know how to play. It was big-time fun. I played as little as possible, not wanting to be found out as a fraud. (I still have a cornet out in the garage, but play the French Horn instead today.) After the joint closed at 2 a.m. Eddie invited us out to his home on Long Island to continue the party. Unfortunately, Condon, unsteady on his feet like everyone else, took a header down the flight of steps and his wife called the party off. Just as well. I was pretty much in the bag myself. Tom had disappeared somewhere, and another Notre Dame friend, Rege, drove me to his home in Mineola, Long Island, to spend the rest of the night. Rege was the damnedest guy, and had a hollow leg. While at Notre Dame, we had drunk together several times, and unlike the rest of us, he

Walter "Bud" Stuhldreher

never showed the slightest sign of being in trouble. So I felt comfortable with him doing the driving.

> **EDDIE CONDON**
> presents Nightly
> Peanuts - Hucko - Clarinet
> "Wild" Bill Davison - Trumpet
> Cutty Cutshall - Trombone
> Gene Schroeder - Piano
> Buzzy Drootin - Drums
> Eddie Condon - Guitar
> INTERMISSION — RALPH SUTTON (at the piano)
> **JAM SESSIONS EVERY TUESDAY**
> Closed Sundays

His parents' home was a small two-story, and the stairs to the second floor were in the corner of the living room. I was to sleep on the living room davenport which was at the foot of the stairs. Rege went upstairs to bed, and I passed out, literally. But shortly afterward, the davenport took off on its own. Now I was used to waking up with the room swirling around in circles after a night on the town but this was crazy. The damn couch was leaping in the air, coming down with a big crash, and then repeating this trampoline routine. I was scared out of my befuddled wits. *"Rege! Rege! Come quick, it's an earthquake! The floor is jumping all over the place!"* Rege came half way down the stairs, told me it was OK, that it would soon stop. Sure enough, the jumping soon ceased, and I flopped back down, thinking maybe I had better cut back on my drinking.

The next morning Rege explained the strange behavior of the floor the night before. It seems that many years before, when his dad started to make a little money, his parents had decided to buy their first house. They had gone looking one Sunday afternoon and found this house. The price was right and they bought it. They spent their first night in it, and at six o'clock the next morning, the floor took off. It was the same experience I had the previous night. It turned out that just behind a bunch of trees and bushes on the corner of their lot line there was a set of railroad tracks. The lot was so small that the tracks were no more than twenty or twenty-five feet from the house. It also turned out that the Long Island Railway *didn't run on Sundays* in those days, and it was a Sunday when they had looked at the house. Other days, when the trains went by, the floor shook like the St. Vitus dance! (Today the Realtor's code would prevent this from happening. That fact would have to be disclosed.) Simple explanation. When the first train had gone by, at six in that morning, I had thought my sins had caught up with me. The other times I stayed with Rege's parents I expected this strange behavior of the floor acting like a trampoline and wasn't surprised when the earthquake hit.

Oh, yes, I guess I forgot to tell you Rege's full name: Regis Philbin. He's a regular guy, and what you see on TV is the same man you would see in real life — a cutting sense of humor and a very nice person. He's a performer who has paid his dues, as they like to say in show business. After all, I knew Regis when he was *the sixth weather forecaster* in Buffalo, New York! Now that's starting at the bottom.

TRANSFER THE BASTARDS

During the last half of the 1900's many high-tech companies developed distinctive corporate cultures. Microsoft and Apple, perhaps, are the most notable. But others did, too: Intel, Advanced Micro Devices, Dell and so on. Within this culture, events happen that become company legends. This is the story of one such legend, an IBM one. It won't surprise my friends and readers to find out I was involved.

Corporate legends are events which become embedded in the history of the company. These events are told and retold at company functions, at watering holes after work, at company schools, and at any congregation of employees. But there is one strange thing about any company legend: at the time it happen no one *knows* it is going to live on, to grow legs, to become larger than life. Legends are immensely popular within corporations where employees identify closely with their employer and fellow employees. Sometimes they get published

183

Walter "Bud" Stuhldreher

in company histories. IBM had at least one book of this nature floating around. This legend is one of my favorites.

The Situation

It was during the late 60's and IBM had divisions then, not subsidiaries as today. My division was the Federal Systems Division (FSD), which was responsible for IBM sales and work projects with government agencies. I worked at Huntsville in the Space Systems Center (SSC), a part of FSD.

FSD was not satisfied with our next year's information systems budget and had directed that it be cut 10 percent, or a little over $2 million. A task force had been organized, and the results were now going to be reported to FSD in Bethesda, Maryland.

The Players

Three SSC employees were going up to Bethesda to make a flip-chart presentation. Gordon Doolittle was the senior guy, the #2 executive in SSC, and was responsible for the engineering and programming functions. Bob Drainey, who reported to Doolittle, was the programming manager and was also in charge of internal information systems. I was the low man on the totem pole, a first-line manager with both programming and auditor duties. I was along to lend some sort of authenticity to the presentation, due to my minor auditing responsibilities. In fact, I was the gofer. My main function was to carry the flip charts and keep my mouth shut unless called on, a very unlikely possibility.

At FSD headquarters the President of the division would receive the presentation accompanied by the division Controller and the Director of Information Systems. A very senior group.

SOUR M.A.S.H. AT SEA - SECOND WAVE

The plans were for Gordon, Bob and me to fly up the night before and stay at the Washingtonian Motel in Gaithersburg, Maryland. It was located just north of Bethesda, and Gordon wanted to stay there since it was the training facility of the Washington Redskins. (They have since moved to plusher quarters.) Located in two buildings, and several stories high, it was much more than a motel. The next morning we would drive the ten miles down to FSD headquarters, make the presentation, be out of there by noon, and head back to Huntsville. Since we had hit the assigned budget cut requested, no problems were anticipated.

The three of us met at Huntsville's little airport in a driving rainstorm. We trudged out to the waiting Southern Airways DC-3, a two-propeller plane. (There were no covered access ramps back then.) Thoroughly soaked by the time we climbed the stairs to the plane, we knew the trip was certainly getting off to a bad start.

"Walt, are you sure the charts didn't get wet?" asked Gordon.

"Yes sir, I have them in a waterproof container," I replied, holding the container up for him to see.

"Good. I want you to be damn careful with them. God knows you have nothing else to do on this miserable assignment."

While none of us enjoyed going to headquarters, particularly to make a dumb pitch, Gordon really hated making this useless trip. He was busier than a one-armed paperhanger trying to ensure IBM met its responsibilities in the Apollo program. Successfully getting three astronauts to the moon and safely back seemed just a tad more important to Gordon. And going to

Walter "Bud" Stuhldreher

headquarters was like going to the IRS: nothing good could come of it.

The rain picked up strength as we sat on the runway. It was no longer a rainstorm but a torrential downpour. So we sat there and waited. And waited. Gordon was 6'5" tall, very thin, and very uncomfortable in his coach seat. (All IBM employees traveled coach in those days.) He started bitching to Bob. From time to time the pilot would announce that due to the storm, here and at our destination, National Airport in Washington, D.C., we wouldn't be taking off for a while. (National Airport has since been renamed for President Reagan.) Each announcement was greeted by more bitching from Gordon. By now many of the other screwed travelers were bitching, too. The attendants, meaning well, decided to placate the sullen bunch by passing out free drinks. And that's where my troubles started. They passed down the aisle with trays full of miniatures, and the passengers helped themselves. I saw Gordon's long, skinny fingers grabbing as many as he could swipe, and Bob was doing the same. Uh oh, I thought, if those two keep this up, I'd better stay sober. At least one of us should be in shape to drive to the motel, which was 30 miles from the Washington airport. Each time a flight attendant passed by they would grab more, stuffing them into their pockets. IBM employees were required to wear suits on planes in those days, so they had plenty of pockets. Both jacket and pants pockets were starting to overflow.

Seeing me refusing the free miniatures, Gordon yelled at me in horror, "Stop that! If you don't want them, we do!" Figuring they had enough by now, I pretended I didn't hear him.

Gordon and Bob had liberally tossed down several of the miniatures by now, and were showing signs of it. They laid into me. "You wimp! Is this stuff too strong for a Notre Dame man?" was one of the kinder epitaphs hurled at me.

Damn, I thought, the plane hasn't even left the ground yet. This was shaping up badly. Where were the attendants? Sitting in their jump seats, ignoring the disgruntled passengers around them, swigging down the free booze along with everybody else. God, I prayed, at least the pilots were sober, weren't they, or was I the only one left who knew his own name?

Eventually the plane took off. There were only two women passengers aboard. All the rest were businessmen, and most had to make a connecting flight in Washington. That connection was now hopeless. I was sober, but just as bereft of hope. Gordon and Bob were singing ribald songs by now, accompanied by many passengers. Joining in were the two flight attendants, who were living up to their universal nickname in those days, "stews."

We had trouble landing at National due to the rain, finally arriving at midnight. We climbed down the slick, wet staircase to the tarmac, and headed for the safety of the terminal. What a downpour! I still don't know why they permitted us to land. We were the second to last plane allowed to land that night. We swam up to the Hertz rental counter and Gordon asked for our car. Not saying a word to Bob or me, grabbing the papers and key, he disappeared into a rest room. He soon came out wearing nothing but a pair of swim trunks, black socks and shoes. Throwing his bag at me, he put up his umbrella and yelled, "I'm getting the car. You guys wait here." Now remember, Gordon was 6'5" and didn't weigh 160 pounds dripping wet, which, of course, he was. Ignoring the amazed stares of the crowd at this crazy apparition, he headed out in the rain. In those days there was a roundabout with grass in the middle which separated the terminal from the parking spaces for the rental cars. Gordon, oblivious to the honking cars, disdained the sidewalk around the circle and walked straight across two roads of traffic to the Hertz section.

Pretty soon a Plymouth pulled up next to Bob and me. Gordon got out, told me to drive, and sat in the front passenger seat. Bob got in the rear. I was not sure Gordon had gotten the right car, thinking I had overheard the rental clerk saying something about a Dodge. Sitting down behind the wheel I asked, "Gordon, are you sure you got the right car?"

"Will you just shut up and drive? Of course it's the right car. The key worked didn't it?" He had me there. The key, with a Hertz tag, was hanging from the ignition, so I drove off in the pouring rain. Gordon was vocal in complaining about my stupidity. Bob was glassy-eyed and silent in the rear seat. When the car swayed both of them clanked nosily due to the many miniatures in their pockets.

As we headed north on the Parkway, I grew more uneasy. The car was handling roughly, which was unusual for a rental. I managed to see the odometer, and was flabbergasted to see it read 35,867. A rental car with that much mileage? It didn't make sense; they were usually less than a thousand. I reached over and opened the glove box. Oh, damn! There was a pair of gloves and sunglasses in it. "Shit, Gordon, this isn't a rental car. It belongs to somebody. His personal stuff is in the glove box, and there's over thirty thousand miles on this wreck!"

"Will you shut the hell up and just drive! It's almost 1:00 a.m. now, and we're a long way from the motel. This can't be someone's car. The keys worked!"

But drunk as he was, I was convinced he had made a horrible mistake. I didn't care that the key had worked. I was driving a

SOUR M.A.S.H. AT SEA - SECOND WAVE

stolen car on an IBM business trip, and I wasn't going any farther from the airport.

I made a U-turn, right through the dividing hedgerow, and headed south back to National. Unfortunately, the bushes ripped off the muffler, and we were now making a hell of a racket - almost as much noise as Gordon was making inside the car, yelling curses at me. Bob was still quiet in the back seat, nearly comatose. "Gordon, if you are so sure you got the right car, look at the rental agreement and see if it was for a Plymouth." Bitching loudly, he pulled the sodden mess out of his pocket and tried to read it through rain splattered glasses. I could tell, even in the dim light, that he was going to be no help: he had the agreement upside down. I snatched it away from him and took a peek at it myself. Damn! It said "Dodge" plain enough. "There Gordon. I told you it should have been a Dodge, not a Plymouth!"

Not so sure of himself by now, he mumbled how come the key worked? I didn't know, but I was sure I was driving a stolen car. As I drove nosily back to National Airport, I wondered what would be the least offense the police would charge me with: a stolen car, a naked man next to me, two drunks, or a car with no muffler? And in the middle of the night. Whew! What a night, and with most of it left to go.

Pulling back into the Hertz space at National, Gordon grabbed the key and, once again, disappeared into the night. I almost hoped he wouldn't find us again, but soon a Dodge appeared next to us. Gordon flopped out exclaiming, "Well, that sure beats all. The key worked in this one, too." I was also amazed, but was thankful we had finally gotten the right car for our trip, and the wrong car was back undetected. I left the Plymouth where it sat, wondering what the owner would think when he drove off with no muffler. At least he had his gloves, sun glasses and car. It could have been worse.

I deposited Bob in the back seat of the Dodge; his legs no longer worked, and with a near naked, wet Gordon next to me, we started off once again for the motel. By now it was 2:00 a.m.

Finally arriving at the motel an hour later, we stumbled into the large, ornate lobby and found, just like everything else that had gone wrong on this trip from hell, that our reservations had been lost — or claimed by someone who had arrived on time. Oh, man, I was wiped out and no room? What a mess! There was a large column in the middle of the lobby surrounded by a leather seat, so we sat there while the harried staff tried to find us something. And — I swear I'm not making this up — just then the U.S. Junior Davis Cup Tennis Team came through the front door. Seeing Gordon sitting there in swim trunks, still holding an open umbrella over his head, (never mind that it wasn't raining inside) they stopped and stared.

Bob and I knew, but of course the tennis team didn't, that Gordon had no use for "preppies" or "damn preppies" as he called them. The team members, dressed in J. Crew blue blazers, button-down white shirts, Khaki pants and white buck shoes, each carrying several tennis rackets in wooden presses, were certainly preppies. Gordon, staring back at them, yelled, "Anyone for tennis?" They fled. I would have, too.

We finally got rooms and a very short night's sleep. None of us felt like much the next morning as we left the motel for headquarters, but at least I didn't have a hangover. Bob and Gordon sure did, and I felt good about that. Served them right. I had never been cursed so loudly and long as I had been the previous night. I kept offering to stop for rancid pork chops, etc., as we headed in, but all they could do was groan.

Bob made the pitch, shakily moving through the charts. It went well, as it should have. We had achieved headquarters' objective. Bob arrived at the last chart which showed a grand total of $2.3 million shaved off the Information Systems (IS) budget and stopped. John Jackson, the President, started to say something, but I, the gofer and chart carrying peon, spoke up for the first time. "No, Bob, you're not finished. There's one more chart to go."

"No, Walt. I'm done," replied Bob, knowing he was at the end of his planned pitch.

To my dying day I will remember the controller, Bill Coker, hunching forward and peering at the flip charts. "No, Bob, he's right. I can see that there's another chart back there."

Bob was totally confused. How could there be another chart? He flipped over the one he was holding, and stared in horror. Gordon stared in dismay. You see, angered out of my skull by their terrible treatment the previous night, I had *added* an extra chart while in my motel room. The ol' chart carrying peon had improved upon their cost cutting. The final chart now read:

Savings to date	$2,300,000.00
Transfer Doolittle & Drainey	250,000.00
Total savings	$2,550,000.00

Gordon and Bob were devastated. They both loved living in Huntsville, and both loved their jobs. They desperately wanted to be there when man first went to the moon. They were speechless. In their worst nightmares they had never thought about transferring out of Huntsville, but *their* pitch was suggesting just that. And to the most senior executives in the division, the very guys who could make it happen. They had no idea — yet — where the damn chart had come from.

Coker, the controller, spoke in a low voice to the Director of IS, Carl Harwood, "Carl, I had no idea that they made that much." (Remember this was in the late 60's and salaries were much lower then.)

I spoke up for the second, and last, time, "Don't forget all the mistakes they make. You'll save that money, too."

I got up and left, waiting for them in the car. To this day I don't know what happened after I left, and I don't care. It couldn't have happened to two more deserving guys.

If you think it is impossible for three people to leave a building, share a car to the airport and ride the same plane back home with two of them never speaking to the third person, you are wrong. That is what Gordon and Bob did to me. I didn't give a damn that I had pissed off two senior executives in a big way, and I didn't care what they intended to do to me. Whatever happened was worth it. I had evened the score.

A Corporate Legend is Born

OK, the event had happened. Now it had to pass into company lore, and this is how it happened. At IBM we had many functions which required a Master of Ceremonies. "Win" parties where we celebrated important contract awards, promotion parties, parties for departing employees, etc. We had plenty of the latter as we took Huntsville employment from 2,300 down to 1,100 by the time I left. (It was eventually reduced to zero.) I was often asked to be the MC for several reasons. I could tell a joke, knew almost everyone, and most important, wasn't afraid to poke fun at anyone, no matter how senior they were.

During my planned remarks I was usually interrupted and asked to tell the story about our trip to FSD Headquarters. You wouldn't believe who asked for it: yep, Gordon Doolittle himself. At first I couldn't believe it. After all, it didn't reflect well on him. Drunk, abusive, stealing a car while on company business — not much to go on there. But I got used to him requesting it, and enjoyed seeing how much he like hearing the damn story, particularly the punch line. As I neared the end he would lean forward, listening intently. I would always pause before finishing the story, "Don't forget how many mistakes they make. You'll save that money, too." He then would double over with laughter, totally enthralled. Beats me.

As such things go, the story got out of Huntsville and I was asked to repeat it at the many locations my division was in. And so the legend became part of the company lore.

Aftermath

Gordon eventually took early retirement from IBM and became a successful aerospace consultant.

Bob quit IBM about a year after our trip. NASA, in a particularly atrocious decision, refused to let IBM appoint him to an important position. (Normally IBM fought NASA on deals like this, saying NASA had no right to approve/disapprove appointments. But IBM chose not to fight this one.) What was sickening was that NASA didn't doubt Bob's ability to do the job. Rather, he didn't have the appropriate college degree — as if a degree obtained twenty years earlier in one discipline instead of another made a hill of beans difference. They ignored the

Walter "Bud" Stuhldreher

many years he held responsible positions and delivered the goods for NASA. Such stupidity.

So Bob quit and headed for Hollywood. He had somehow learned that the movie companies were dissatisfied with the procedure they had to undergo when hiring extras. For example, if they needed ten short Mexicans who knew how to fire a rifle, they had to run ads in the movie newspapers, or call agents, or try whatever they could think of. It was time-consuming, expensive and cumbersome. Bob computerized the entire process. All they had to do then, and today, is place one call and the extras were located for them. Bob became a multimillionaire. He later called me about coming out to work for him, at three times the dough I was making at IBM. My wife, Barbara, didn't want to move west, plus she wasn't too fond of Bob, so I never pursued it. Damn! I always thought I would have made a great Hollywood mogul.

THE COAST GUARD, A DOG AND A DRUNK

This story was originally published in the United States Power Squadron's monthly magazine, Scuttlebutt. *For obvious reasons it didn't tell the whole story. This one does.*

The July 1974 newsletter of the Huntsville, Alabama, chapter of the U.S. Power Squadron (USPS) contained what seemed to be an interesting request. The local facility of Wyle Laboratories and the Coast Guard needed some boats in "average" condition, operated by skippers with "average" experience, to undergo some tests. The tests were designed to record the skippers' reaction times, and the boats' operating characteristics, during *stress* conditions. In return for volunteering his services, each skipper would receive an 8 x 10 picture of his boat underway, plus a data sheet attested by the Coast Guard regarding his boat's particular statistics. It didn't specify just what the *stress* conditions would be.

195

Walter "Bud" Stuhldreher

It seemed to me a great way to do some good for boating in general and to have an interesting afternoon by myself. I was an active member of the local unit of the USPS, and we were promoting safety on the water for boat owners. We taught new boat owners the rules when on the water, how to handle a boat, safety requirements, and how to care for their boats — just about everything a boat owner needed to know to be a safe boat operator. So I signed up my four year old, 16-feet long, open-bow rider tri hull with a 120 horsepower inboard/outboard power plant. She was bright red and named *Family Affair* after a popular TV show of the time. The name also reflected my hope that my wife and three small kids would enjoy her, too. We had spent plenty of hours enjoying various family outings on her. You did notice she was only sixteen feet long? Five people was pretty much her limit, and crowded at that. It was tough to set any speed records with her loaded, so having her to myself for a boating afternoon looked plenty good to me.

Wyle Labs and the Coast Guard were eager to record as many different types of boats as possible and quickly accepted my offer. An instructor with USPS (me) looked like a fine candidate for operating a boat under stressful conditions. Later on, as you shall see, Wyle Labs and the Coast Guard somewhat regretted their hasty decision, but that was far in the future.

Early one hot, sunny Saturday morning, August 24, 1974, I reminded my wife of my commitment to the Coast Guard that afternoon. She replied I could do whatever I wanted to as long as I took the children along. After my unwise answer of, "That's not exactly what I had in mind," the issue was quickly resolved. As you might have guessed, my departure for the boat dock at noon was not a lonely one. To give you a feel for it, here are a few representative questions I handled.

"Why can't I bring my jumping rope?"

"Are you sure you have enough Cokes? I only see nine and there's six of us kids, plus Slicer." (Each of my three kids had received permission from their *mother* to bring a friend. Slicer was a neighbor's 67-pound dog of uncertain parentage. According to the kids, he loved the water. Unknown to me, he hated anyone in a uniform.)

"Why do we have to go 25 miles to Limestone Creek — why can't we just go swimming?"

"Who is the Coast Guard? Are they the same ones who yelled at you last week for going too fast?"

"I don't know why you're so mad about my loaning one of the life preservers to Donna — you were able to borrow one from Mr. Campbell."

"We have to go back. I have to go to the bathroom!"

Well, I reflected, if the Coast Guard wanted an average boat they were going to get their money's worth in me — one overweight skipper, six kids ranging in ages from four to ten, and one extremely large dog who wasn't mine. And the wife was going to get an unexpected treat: an afternoon to herself. At least the sun was going to be shining in one part of Huntsville that afternoon, just not on me.

One mile after leaving the dock my crew reported the soft drinks were gone and what did I intend to do about it?

"What do you mean, gone? I had nine for the whole afternoon and we've barely gotten started. If all you wanted to do was eat and drink, you should have gone to McDonald's with your mothers. Now, shut up. We're going to get in some serious boating for a change."

I won't bore you with the rest of the grisly details, but let me put it this way: the next 24 miles didn't get any easier. And I sure didn't wait for the sun to get over the yardarm before I started dipping into my beer supply. Which comic used to say, "Booze is the only answer"? Whoever he was, he must have taken six kids cruising in a small boat, once.

Our arrival at the test course was greeted with polite amazement, open skepticism and complete dismay. The Wyle people and the Coast Guard personnel were running things from a pontoon boat. It was cluttered with electronic gear, walkie talkies, camera equipment, bull horns and other exotic stuff. The kids were enchanted; things were looking up. The Wyle and Coast Guard people didn't look as happy.

As I pulled alongside, they tried to fend me off, stating that the refreshment stand was ashore. I let them know we were there for their tests, gave them my name, and asked when would it be my turn to run the course.

"But sir, this test isn't possible with such a crowded boat."

"No sweat, mate, I'll simply put them on your boat. Kids, get going!"

"But, sir, we don't have room for them — hey, that damn dog lifted his leg — stop him! Listen, kids, please don't unplug anything else — and don't touch that cable!"

Oh, well, I figured they were trained to handle emergencies — let them see if they were up to it. As I pulled away with an apprehensive Wyle official on board I asked him what the drill was.

"Well, Walt, do you see those two buoys? We want you to come through them once at 2700 rpm, once at 3100 rpm, and once at full speed. We'll repeat the runs, giving you different instructions each time. We're interested in observing your reactions, and your boat's handling characteristics in stress situations."

Gee, that didn't sound too tough. I lined up for the first run and away we went — and promptly wiped out two buoys this side of the chute! I hadn't told the Wyle guy I was having trouble seeing. One of the kids had knocked my prescription sunglasses overboard while attempting to catch a butterfly. And the beer wasn't helping, either.

"Hey, you didn't tell me about them!"

"Well Walt, we have — had — two buoys on this side for alignment purposes. I guess we can get along without them. But listen, is your boat all right? What's that clanking noise?"

"No sweat — its just empty beer cans."

"Wow, it's pretty early in the day for that, isn't it?"

"Listen, Jack, did you ever do 25 miles in a 16-footer with six kids and a dog? Ha! I didn't think so or you'd understand all the empties! Now let's get on with it."

And get on with it we did, a total of nine passes. Keeping her on the right rpm's, dropping speed as directed, turning sharply as directed, kept me fully occupied. Then came the big moment I had been waiting for: "Walt, floor her!" Oh, wow!

Walter "Bud" Stuhldreher

Here we go! Pushing the throttle all the way forward, getting the boat on plane quickly, steering sharply into the turns, and heeling her way over was great fun! Except the empty beer cans were bouncing back on the deck and hitting the Wyle guy in the chest. He didn't look too happy.

And speaking of being fully occupied, the Coast Guard guys back on the pontoon boat had their hands full. As we returned from completing the runs they sadly told us we were going to have to repeat them. It seemed one of the children had removed one of the pens from some sort of automatic recording device. (It turned out she had decided to write her fourth grade friend who was at camp.) They were mad as hell but, secretly, I was proud she knew how to write!

After some discussion the Coast Guard reluctantly concluded I had better go round again — they needed the data from my type of boat. But, please, would I please tell the kids to stay away from their gear, not yell through the bull horns at each other, and to keep a close watch on the dog who was continually lifting his leg. I tried — with no noticeable success, however.

"You drunken sod," the Wyle guy exclaimed, "it'll be a cold day in hell before I go through the course with you again!" and started to climb out.

Grabbing his belt, I hauled him back in yelling, "Listen, Mr. Wyle, the run won't be official without you on board, so sit your ass down and shut up!"

"You're calling me an ass? My name isn't Wyle. That's who I work for."

Brushing the empty beer cans off him I said loudly so the Coast Guard could hear, "If you didn't drink on the job, Jack, maybe things would go better." From that time on I called him "Jack"; never did know his real name.

So a truculent "Jack" and I went off again for nine more passes. As I later pieced together from the kids, that's approximately the same number of times Slicer tried to "leave his mark" on a transducer. The Coast Guard eventually detailed one man full time to watch the dog. He was lucky; his uniform only got ripped a little bit. Slicer sure did hate uniforms!

After completing the runs, I throttled back to idle and sat there enjoying the silence, basking in the knowledge I had performed nobly while doing mankind a service. Jack, who again had been slammed with empty beer cans during the final, full speed run, stared at me. "Just what in the hell are you doing sitting here?" he asked, "and what do you have to be looking so smug about? Get me back to the pontoon boat NOW!"

I sat there happily, blearily squinting red-eyed at him, and asked (equably I thought) "Why should I want to go back? There are six kids, a large dog and several Coasties on it, and it's a toss-up who's maddest at me." I had also spotted black smoke drifting from the Coast Guard boat. I was pretty sure they weren't signaling that a new Pope had not been elected. Either Slicer, or a kid, had once again sabotaged an electronic gizmo.

We finally returned to the pontoon boat. Jack hurriedly jumped off, glaring at me as he left; why, I had no idea. The Coast Guard happily transferred the kids and Slicer back to my boat. I grudgingly received them. The 25 miles home were going to be a long trip.

Over Jack's vociferous protests, the other Wyle Lab employees who were working on the pontoon boat offered to pay for the gas I had consumed. I made a counter offer: I'd pay for the gas if Wyle would pay for the soft drinks and snacks. (I figured around $7 would cover the gas — no way I was going to get off that cheaply on the goodies.)

Wisely, Wyle Labs refused, and my Tobacco Road entourage and I proceeded back to Huntsville, stopping off at Decatur for two dozen cokes and snacks. At 5 p.m. we arrived home, sunburned, dirty and — one of us — hung over. Asked by their mother how the boat trip had been, the children were unanimous in their response:

"Terrible, just terrible! Daddy wouldn't let us swim. We only had one coke apiece, (a big lie, but no one, especially their mother, was going to believe me). Baby brother lost his sneakers, and we're going to write the President about how badly the Coast Guard treats dogs!"

Yep, just an average day on the water. An "average" boat owner operating his boat under "average" conditions. About the only thing they had gotten right was the "stressful" part. I was so stressed I promptly passed out in bed. And you might say even that simple act was stressful, what with the wife yelling at me as I did so. Her threat, to never let me take the kids boating again, was the best thing anyone had said to me all day.

A Curious Ending

In November, a few months later, my employer, IBM, transferred us from Alabama to Maryland. I had arranged for the Mayflower Company of Indianapolis (my hometown) to handle moving our possessions. I had instructed them to send an empty van because I wanted all our household furniture, one of our cars and the boat to be shipped in the same van. I was very angry to see a half-full van pull up on the designated day. They assured me they could get all our stuff on it and, stupidly, I agreed to let them try. Well, they came close, but the boat didn't make it. So we, in our other car, and the van, pulled away for Maryland. The boat looked mighty forlorn sitting there on its trailer. The Mayflower people assured me it would arrive shortly after we did, on the next van they had going to Maryland. They lied.

After we were somewhat settled in, I called the local Mayflower office in Gaithersburg: "Where in hell is my boat?" They said they would look into it and get back to me. I called again in two weeks. Same answer. I called again two weeks later. Same answer. "Look, that same excuse is getting kinda old. It's been over a month since we got here, and my boat isn't in sight yet. Just when may I expect to get it?"

A long silence ensued. "Look, to be truthful, we don't know where your boat is."

"MY GOD, YOU'VE LOST MY BOAT!"

"Sir, we didn't say that; what we said is, we don't know where it is; we definitely haven't lost it, we simply don't know where it is."

"CAN YOU PEOPLE HEAR YOURSELVES? YOU HAVEN'T LOST IT, YOU JUST DON'T KNOW WHERE IT IS! WHAT'S THE DIFFERENCE?"

The conversation went downhill from there, as did future conversations. I won't bore you with the details but letters and phone calls over the next two months resulted in the same end result: no boat. I filed a claim which was promptly rejected. It still wasn't considered lost. In retrospect, I believe they couldn't admit to themselves they had managed to lose such a big piece of goods. While they could admit breaking something, a table leg or a mirror, which they did all the time, losing a boat was outside of their experience. It sure was outside mine. They continued to reject my claims. I escalated things to their home office in Indianapolis with no luck. I was very unhappy.

Then, almost four months to the day since we had left Huntsville, I received a strange phone call while at work. On the line was the general manager at the Montgomery County Airport, a small Maryland airport for owners of Piper Cubs and small planes. "Sir, do you own a red boat, about sixteen feet long?"

"I used to, but it's been lost for several months."

"Well, we don't understand what a boat is doing at our airport out here in the country, but there's one here. Do you think it could be yours? It has a registration form in the glove box with your name on it."

"Gee, I don't know. Does it have an Alabama identification decal on it?"

"Yes, sir, it sure does."

Holy smoke, if this doesn't beat all! A boat at an airport? How could my boat, being moved by a huge, reputable moving company, end up at an airport in the middle of nowhere? It didn't make any sense. I promised the airport manager I'd drive out as soon as possible. The next morning I went by the airport on my way into work.

I couldn't believe it. There on a trailer sat a filthy red boat looking fifty years old. But it was mine. As I got out of my car to take a closer look I was staggered to see the bow, or front end, was stove in. A two-foot hole had transformed my sleek racer into a derelict. After locating a repair shop in the yellow pages, I hitched her to my car and trailed her into Silver Spring, Maryland.

Shortly after I arrived back at work the repair shop called me. "Say, are you the guy that just brought this holed 16-footer in?"

"Yeah, I'm the one, what's up?"

"When we took her off the trailer it fell to the ground. Did you know your trailer was broken in two when you pulled your boat this morning? That was a mighty dangerous thing to do."

Of course I hadn't known the trailer was busted in two. Apparently, the weight of the boat had held the damn thing together. "Sir, I sure didn't know it was busted or I never would have trailed her in that condition. I guess I was lucky we made it in one piece."

So, in addition to the boat, my trailer needed repairs. The Mayflower office agreed to the repairs. They had been flabbergasted to learn that my boat had been discovered sitting at an airport, and never did figure out how it happened.

With the boat finally repaired, I picked it up one Saturday morning and trailed her over to Chesapeake Bay for our first boat outing in months. But something was wrong. She handled poorly and didn't come close to her former top speed. I took her back to the repair outfit, but they couldn't find anything wrong. We both concluded the accident had somehow damaged her internally, and that her running characteristics had been impaired. I reported this to the Mayflower people and what did they want to do about it? (I suspect they were extremely tired of me and my boat by this time.) It soon became clear they had no intention of replacing her. Nor, in fact, did they believe my claim that she didn't handle as well as before they got their clumsy hands on her. (My adjective, not theirs.)

"Sir, while we believe you think your boat isn't as fast as she was, and that she handles differently, you can understand our position. We have no way of knowing if that's true, but we do have a proposition for you." I suspiciously asked them what it was. "Mr. Stooduddy" (that's as close as they ever got to correctly pronouncing my name), "it so happens we have an appraiser with boating experience. He's agreeable to going out on your boat with you to see if he sees anything wrong. OK?"

I reluctantly agreed. A week later we went out for a trial spin. The Mayflower guy handled her well, obviously being the first Mayflower employee I had met who knew what he was doing. "Walt, I've tried every maneuver I could think of, and she seems to handle OK. If she isn't the same boat as she used to be, I can understand your disappointment, but there really isn't much I can do about it. If you had *some way to prove her characteristics were changed* then, possibly, I could approve some sort of monetary adjustment for you, but since we both know that isn't possible I'm sorry to say you're just out of luck." With that definitive statement he headed her back to the dock.

"Sport, hold on for just a minute. It so happens you're talking to the only boat owner in America who can supply the evidence you're looking for." Stunned, he looked at me in amazement and asked what I was talking about. I smugly produced the official Coast Guard report titled *COLLISION AVOIDANCE TESTS*, dated 24 August 1974 (see copy of report at the end of this story) — the report I had drunkenly earned that kid-filled day back in Alabama; the tests that the Wyle Lab sucker and I had run, not once but twice; the report that had seemed useless when I finally received it. I didn't really care about the test results, but I sure did want the 8 x 10 picture of my boat underway with her intrepid skipper at the helm — the same picture that my wife had torn up when it had arrived at the house. For some strange reason she didn't want to be reminded of that day every time she saw the picture up on the family room wall. I never have figured women out.

The Mayflower guy couldn't believe his eyes. How in the world could an owner of a private boat, a small boat at that, have managed to get the Coast Guard to run expensive tests on his boat? The S.O.B. had the evidence that was going to cost his company money! I swear his eyes bugged out as he read it. My cup runneth over. He asked me how I had managed this stupendous feat?

Lying through my teeth, figuring I had some satisfaction coming after all the trouble they had put me through, I told him it had seemed a reasonable thing to do knowing the Mayflower Company was going to be moving my boat in the near future.

He gaped at me. What was I talking about?

"Well, it's this way: you know we IBM employees are moved so often we say IBM stands for 'I've Been Moved.' We all have horror stories about bad moves, so I thought it would be prudent, knowing Mayflower would be moving my boat, and having heard bad stories about you, to have a record of my boat's performance characteristics."

Whew, what a whopper! But the poor sap swallowed it, hook, line and sinker. He responded, "Jeez, I never! The home office isn't going to believe this one," and nervously took the report.

Walter "Bud" Stuhldreher

    He and I knew my poor boat could no longer go as fast as stated in the report, and that going fast was a boater's favorite thing. He named a figure; I countered, and we split the difference. Two weeks later I received a $2,500 check from the Mayflower Company for a boat which had cost me $3,500 several years earlier. The boat still carried us around on many happy excursions and accompanied us to Florida when I was transferred from Maryland in 1976. Not too shabby an ending for a drunken boating outing. And to think: going boating while intoxicated was the number one thing the United States Power Squadron, of which I was a proud member, indeed, an instructor, warned new boaters about. But it had sure paid off for me.

SOUR M.A.S.H. AT SEA - SECOND WAVE

COLLISION AVOIDANCE TESTS

HULL: Type <u>DeepVee</u>
DATE: <u>24 August 1974</u>
   Mat'l <u>FRP</u>
WIND: from <u>—</u> at <u>0</u> mph
   Length <u>16 Ft. 7 in.</u>
Sea condition <u>Smooth</u>
   Beam <u>85 In.</u>
   Weight <u>2000 lbs.</u>
LOCATION <u>Limestone</u>

LOADING: <u>100</u> lb gear
BOAT NO. <u>7</u>
    <u>8</u> gal. fuel
POWER
    <u>3</u> people
Inboard _____ hp

Outboard _____ hp

Outdrive <u>120</u> hp
THROTTLE LOCATION:
Jet _____ hp
Starboard side
Single <u>X</u> Twin ___

STEERING, Lock to

Lock:

Midship to Port:

Stg. Wheel Turns <u>1-1/4</u>
Rudder Angle <u>—</u> °

Midship to Stbd:

Stg. Wheel Turns <u>1-3/4</u>

Rudder Angle <u>—</u> °

PROP ROTATION:

Left Hand: _____

Right Hand: _____

Counter: _____

W.O.T.	Cruise or ¾ Throttle		½ Throttle
Speed	35 mph	27 mph	22 mph
Stopping Distance	205 ft	150 ft	105 ft
Speed	36 mph	28 mph	20 mph
Best Turn to Stbd Diameter In 180 ° Turn	210 down to 120 ft	170 down to 60 ft	110 to 175 ft
Speed	33 mph	29 mph	21 mph
Best Turn to Stbd (cutting throttle) Diameter In 180 ° Turn	180 down to 70 ft	160 down to 50 ft	110 to 130 ft

UNCLE TIM'S WAKE

Have you ever been to an Irish wake? I hadn't, and I didn't want to go. This was during the 30's when Irish wakes were more common than they are today. I was six or seven, and the last thing I wanted to do was see some dead guy, even if it was Uncle Tim, one of my favorite uncles. I would not have wanted to go, even if it wasn't anyone I knew. Perhaps I'd better explain.

My grandfather, Daniel Brosnan, came over from Ireland in 1889. Why? Let my mother, Mildred, God rest her soul, tell the story:

"In the latter part of the 1800's, there was a great exodus of the people from Ireland.
The causes are varied — the oppression of the English Rule, the lack of hope for the establishment of Home Rule, the unfair

Walter "Bud" Stuhldreher

Land Tax Enactments, the exorbitant taxes imposed by the English, and other unjust rules.

It was a period of discouragement, and only natural that many young men and women wanted to follow others who had left Ireland. Many had gone to America to start a new life in a new country with the hope of peace, justice, and opportunity." (From an unpublished memoir written about 1975.)

Wow! Mother was still ticked off at the English around 100 years later! And her mother, my grandmother, was far worse. I can still remember her sitting in a chair next to our Magnavox combination record-player and radio, where the entire family gathered each night to listen to the latest WW II news. The sonorous voice of the famous broadcaster, Edward R. Murrow, would be describing the heroic feats of the English people during the terrible nightly bombing of London. Mother Brosnan, sitting in her favorite leather chair, would be knitting, and the long needles would flash ever faster as she got madder. "I know you think a lot of this man (Murrow) but he must be confused. The english (she refused to use caps when referring to the English) have never done anything good!" And faster and faster the needles would fly. To continue.

Grandfather returned to Ireland and married Mother Brosnan on July 29, 1891, in the Pro-Cathedral in Dublin. Its real name, the Provisional Cathedral, was to get around an English law. In Ireland, Catholic cathedrals were not allowed in the same cities where a Church of England was located. In this case, St. Michael's Anglican Church had formerly been a Catholic church until it was seized by Henry VIII. Bettie and I visited Dublin in 1995, and the big Catholic Church there is still called the Provisional Cathedral, or "Pro-Cathedral," some 400 years later.

After his marriage, three brothers, three sisters and Grandfather Brosnan left Ireland. Five came to Indianapolis with him and one brother, Michael, went to Australia. Michael never married, and became immensely rich — how, I don't know. One brother, James, had eight children, six daughters and two sons. Two daughters became nuns. One son and one daughter married. The other four children, Pidge, Nora, Nell and Tim never married. They lived together in a big apartment in downtown Indianapolis for the rest of their lives. This type of arrangement was very common among Irish families in those days. My family would visit them often, usually on Sundays, and everyone had a grand time. Nell, Pidge, and Nora, none of whom weighed a hundred pounds, were little wisps of Irish charm, and doted on us five children. If I'd had any sense, I would have spent more time with them over the years, instead of playing sports and reading comic books. They were fun to be around. Interestingly, while we called Tim "Uncle Tim," the sisters insisted on being called by just their names. In reality they were our cousins, but with a huge disparity in their ages and ours.

Uncle Tim was a big fellow with a red nose. He always dressed in a black suit, stiffly starched white shirt, dark tie, high-topped black shoes and white socks. Like all my Irish relatives, and I had more than I could count, Uncle Tim hated to see an empty glass. A roguish charmer with the ladies, he could tell wonderful stories, and treated us children as grown-ups. Very tall, he was not slim, but not heavy, either. I would sit at his feet and listen intently. What a brogue! What stories! His three sisters thought the world of him, as we all did. And so the drink would flow. Toasts were made, the English were damned, and the good works of the Catholic Church were praised. This was the usual Sunday visit routine.

Walter "Bud" Stuhldreher

I don't know what caused Uncle Tim's death, or how old he was; all adults seemed old to me then. He was probably in his early forties or so. He was a cop, but since uniformed police were not a large presence at his wake, it is doubtful he was killed in the line of duty. But many of the friends in attendance there had to be policemen. (As in most large American cities in those days, in Indianapolis 99 percent of the force were Irishmen.) And, much against my will, I was taken to the wake, for the first day, anyway. Typically, Irish wakes lasted three days, and Uncle Tim's sure did.

Dressed up in our Sunday best, even though it wasn't a Sunday, downtown we went. I was filled with dread. As it turned out, I didn't have anything to worry about. I discovered that if you wanted to have a good time, go to an Irish wake. What a party! The large apartment was filled to overflowing, full of happy Irish families. Half the city was there — all the kids, grannies, spinsters, bachelors, and old people. The most notable bachelor was Hizonnor, Mayor Al Feeney, accompanied by his widowed mother, Marguerite Feeney. Mayor Feeney, a local Irish boy who had made good, was a beloved figure in the Irish community for many years. My favorite memory of him has to do with slot machines.

One of the local country clubs got into financial difficulties during the depression, not an uncommon problem for country clubs in those hard times. To keep the club afloat, the manager installed slot machines, which were illegal, of course. Marguerite Feeney became quite fond of the slots at the club, playing them as often as she could get one of the black-and-whites (police cars) to take her out there. One day she heard that the police were going to raid the club, and called her son, the Mayor, to find out if this was true. He confirmed the rumor. Mrs. Feeney immediately tipped off the club manager who hid the slots until the raid was over. The raid, to no one's surprise, turned up nothing. Mrs. Feeney then extracted a promise from her son, the Mayor, to *always* tip her off in advance of future raids. He agreed, not wanting to displease his mother. He also realized that it was better for her to gamble there in private than maybe to get arrested in a public joint. The raids continued with no results, and the public was satisfied that justice was served. In later years the Ladies Professional Golf Association (LPGA) played a yearly tournament at the Country Club of Indianapolis, the Mayflower Classic. What would they think if they knew their venue had been saved by a combination of illegal slot machines and an Irish Mayor who loved his mother?

Back to the wake. The star, of course, was Uncle Tim. Partially hidden by the baby grand piano, he was standing up in a corner, and looking very lifelike, holding a drink in his hand. (Often at Irish wakes the deceased was posed in a lifelike position. It was his/her party and the deceased wanted to be part of it.) Mike Duffecy, a young family friend who had played piano in Hoagy Carmichael's Dance Band on cruise ships, was pounding away at Uncle Tim's favorite tune, *Easter Parade*. Folks were dancing, singing, knocking the booze down and telling jokes in loud voices. I wondered: if this was the first day, what will the next two be like? Fat chance that I was going to find out! The carefully observed rule was that kids came only on the first day. Darn!

But something was troubling me. I asked Pidge "Why isn't Uncle Tim drinking?"

"What do you mean, Buddy?"

"Well, every time I look at him his glass is always full." (And, young though I was, I knew that definitely was unlike Uncle Tim.)

Pidge looked at me, pitying my lack of education, both in Catholic and Irish traditions. "Buddy, I'm surprised at you!" she said in her lilting brogue, "Tim is in heaven, and everybody knows that in heaven, your glass is always full."

Whoops! Never again made that mistake with Nell, Nora, and Pidge at future wakes. The deceased was always in heaven, and the glass was always full. Even today, over 60 years later, that vision of heaven still sounds good to me. Now there's an Irish tradition I can live with and hope to die with.

THE CATHOLIC CADILLAC

There was going to be a Protestant wedding, and our daughter Beth was going to be in it as a bridesmaid. It didn't turn out as anyone planning it had hoped.

Background

Beth had gone to middle school and high school in Merritt Island, Florida. Her two best girlfriends had gone to school with her throughout this time, and now one of them was getting married. The groom was a fellow she had met at the University of Florida, a penniless student. He lived in a trailer which was so shabby you could see the grass under it by looking through the cracks in the floor. But love triumphs over all, and the marriage was set.

The wedding was going to take place in a small church, indeed, more like a chapel, on Merritt Island just south of the

Kennedy Space Center. Unless you have been there, you might be surprised to learn that there are several orange groves in the area between the unincorporated town of Merritt Island to the south, and Kennedy Space Center several miles to the north. As usual around orange groves, there were small, shabby homes where the workers lived. Work in the orange groves meant minimum wages and a job for only a part of the year, so the yearly income of the workers was low, and the houses reflected that as did the church.

It was very hard to find the church. Not many street addresses were used in that part of the woods. The church was small, rustic, and somewhat rundown, so why had the bride picked it? Simple answer: she hadn't; the groom had, or, to be truthful, his father had. It seems the groom's long-dead grandfather had been an architect, and had designed the church. At the time, the grandfather had owned the land and felt the workers needed a church. So now the pressure was applied to have the ceremony in this church. Since the bride and her family were not regular churchgoers, this venue was agreed to, albeit in a lukewarm manner.

The Rehearsal Dinner

Things started to go badly at the rehearsal dinner the night before the wedding. Between courses, the prospective father-in-law casually gave the bride a form to sign, saying it really didn't mean much. He handed her a pen, and showed her where her signature was needed. The bride, Lucy, didn't give it a thought, and accepted the pen. Lucy's mother, however, four times married and with three successful divorces behind her, knew better.

"Lucy, how many times have I told you *never* to sign anything without reading it first!" she said and grabbed the form.

Well-versed in marriage documents, and a veteran of many acrimonious lawyer meetings, she quickly and competently read the damn thing. "Lucy, you aren't signing this!" she said.

The father-in-law-to-be retorted, "Without her signature, there isn't going to be a wedding!"

Lucy turned to the feckless groom, "Mitch, what's going on?" He replied that he didn't understand what all the fuss was about and that her mother was over-reacting. To please his father, would she please sign the form?

Lucy's mother was not to be swayed from her self-appointed course. "Lucy, come here with me right now. Beth, you come, too." (Beth was studying to be a lawyer at this time.) And off they went to the women's rest-room to talk it over.

Lucy's mother was right to have stopped Lucy from signing unread what turned out to be a prenuptial agreement. The agreement stated that in the event of a divorce, neither Lucy *nor any children born during the marriage* would have any claim on Mitch's assets. Well, it was reasonably ugly behavior to ask a bride to sign a pre-nupt without telling her what it was, but what difference did it make? Why was Mitch's father so hell-bent on protecting the nonexistent assets of a deadbeat? Lucy's mom smelled a rat, a great big wharf rat. (Wharf rats are common to both wharves and orange groves, and they are as big as cats.) Mama stormed out of the rest-room yelling that the wedding was off. She was trailed by a crying bride and an angry bridesmaid, Beth.

Now Mitch was yelling at his father; his mother was cringing down into the table; Beth was shaking the set of papers declaring, "Only an idiot would sign this."

Walter "Bud" Stuhldreher

The bride was in tears. The rest of the wedding party didn't have a clue about what was happening. All they knew was that this rehearsal dinner was going down the drain. They never made it to dessert. The wedding was off.

Beth engineered a meeting immediately after the truncated rehearsal dinner had imploded. Lucy, her mother, and Scotty (Lucy's current stepfather), the groom's parents and a shaken groom gathered together in the restaurant manager's small office. Beth was trying to save the wedding. The meeting didn't start well, not with Mitch's father demanding his lawyer be present. "Mr. Yancy, there's no need for a lawyer here. After all, no one's related yet. Let's just try to understand why this pre-nupt agreement is so important to you. Since Mitch doesn't have any money, it's a mystery to us."

The battle lines had been firmly drawn in the Florida sand: on one side were Lucy, her parents and Beth, the would-be lawyer; on the other side were Mitch and his parents. Mitch's mother never opened her mouth, obviously wishing this disharmony would just disappear, but his father, red-faced and irate, was just getting started. He was a short, dapper man, pudgy and florid, with prominent red veins in his nose. Because I grew up in a large family which was half Irish, I knew what those red veins meant: he was a drinker.

"Beth, I don't know why you're involved in this. It's something which should be between Lucy and Mitch."

"Well, I am involved so you might as well as get used to it! Why did you try to play such a dirty trick on Lucy? Not telling her what she was signing was unforgivable!"

The father reacted poorly to this attack on his manners. Patrician in bearing, attire and diction, if you closed your eyes you would have sworn it was the ghost of Franklin Roosevelt speaking. He obviously thought his blue-blood lineage reached back to the Mayflower. He also thought, like so many Ivy League graduates, that he had been sent here to Earth for one purpose: to help the rest of us unwashed, ignorant masses, by providing guidance in our struggle to survive.

"First, Beth, you will never use that tone of voice to me again. Second, it's clear that as merely a law school student, and at a second-rate law school too, you don't know what you're talking about. Who ever heard of Alabama Law School, anyway?"

Whew! He might as well have waved a red flag in a bull's face. He certainly didn't know what — or whom — he was taking on. What followed wasn't pretty. The groom's father continued to insist that the pre-nupt be signed, or there would be no wedding. It also became clear to the bride, her family and Beth, that the groom wasn't going to stand up to his father. Beth asked, once again, why it was so important since Mitch was broke.

The father answered, surprising Lucy, her parents and Beth, "He won't always be." He went on to explain that many decades ago, Mitch's grandfather, for reasons known only to him, had bought 87,000 acres from the Indians for five cents an acre. While the Indians' legal claim to the property was vague, that didn't matter since no one else wanted the parcel, which was mostly marshland and water. Mitch's grandfather's friends thought his spending $4,350 for it was a waste of good money.

Years later, the government wanted it and bought most of it to be part of the Kennedy Space Center, which occupies 140,000 acres. The area was perfect for NASA's planned spaceport. It wasn't much good for anything else. And it was on the edge of this property that the orange groves were located and the church had been built.

You could have knocked Lucy's family over with a feather. But her mother was a fast recoverer, especially when money was the topic. "How much did NASA pay Mitch's grandfather?" she purred, sheathing her claws.

"None of your business, lady," replied Mr. Yancy, recognizing a gold-digger when he saw one. "But enough so that a sizable trust fund has been established for Mitch. The proceeds will become partially available to him at age 30 and every two years thereafter."

The tenor of the meeting immediately changed. Avarice was in the air, at least for Lucy's mother. But not for Beth.

"Lucy, it's insane for you to consider signing this document, which takes away rights which are yours. Don't you care what happens to your children?" *What children? I asked myself, was there something about the wedding I didn't know? The smell of a shotgun, for instance?* (Since I hadn't been invited to the rehearsal dinner I was hearing the whole story from Beth after she returned home.)

Things still had not been cleared up when we left for the wedding the next morning. We didn't know if there was going to be one or not. But Beth and I were traveling in style to the rustic chapel that was buried in the remains of an orange grove and was surrounded by migrant workers' tin-roofed shacks. We were going in style in a new Cadillac.

I had recently bought the Cadillac in a misguided attempt to prepare for my early retirement which was three years off. I had been brought up in a very conservative household, one where, if money wasn't loved, it was damn well respected. My parents had lived through the depression, and like so many other depression survivors, they had a healthy respect for money and an unhealthy fear of not having it. Thus I was taught to have two things in place before retiring: a paid-for home and a new car, also paid-for. So I had done this. I had paid cash for a retirement home in an Orlando retirement community (daily commuting the 44 miles to the Cape), and had paid cash for the car, a new Cadillac, my lifelong dream. But as I said earlier, this was misguided advice. I would be retiring at 55, and probably would have 30 or 40 years in front of me. How could any car last until I died? I should have stuck to the used, less expensive cars my reduced income would provide. But, oh no, I had to have a gas guzzler with expensive repair habits and a propensity to burn oil at an alarming rate. The car was subsequently nicknamed "Valdiz" after the tanker which went aground in Alaska.

The Wedding

We soon discovered the wedding was on, after all. Mitch had found his backbone. He had told his father he intended to marry Lucy, and didn't care if she signed the prenupt or not. And to shut up about it. My impression of Mitch went up a notch or two, and that was the zenith of my good feelings about him.

It was *not* a shotgun wedding, and while they are still married 15 years later, Lucy remains the breadwinner of the family. Mitch, a professional student when she met him, has proved remarkably good at it — still studying without a smidgen of a degree to show for it.

Well, you might reasonably ask, what about the trust fund? There was one, all right. It was not as large as Mr. Yancy had led everyone to believe, but it could have been a very nice thing for them. The first installment, for instance, would have been enough for a down payment on a home. Mitch had other ideas. It, and the other payments, have disappeared in poorly thought out business ventures. The first installment bought a travel business, a business Mitch knew absolutely nothing about. It went under in six months. The next venture, a pizza business, lasted about the same length of time. I think you have to have a real talent for losing money to mess up a pizza business in a college town, in this case, Gainesville, Florida. Gainesville is a mid-sized town with 50,000 students attending the University of Florida, its only industry. Mitch managed to lose in the pizza business, too.

But all this was in the future. For now, we had a wedding to attend. It soon became obvious things were strained between the people at the alter and in the front pews. No one was talking to anyone else, not even the bride and groom. Lucy, understandably, was ticked off at Mitch's father and at Mitch for not immediately standing up for her. Mitch was definitely pissed off at his best man, his father. Mr. Ivy League himself was mad at the world, a world which had not done his bidding. Mitch's mother was sitting by herself, a condition she had become used to, what with being married to a man so far her superior.

The bridesmaids, who didn't know even half the story, were nervous throughout the short, and strange, ceremony. The minister, who didn't know a soul in the whole deal, since none of them attended his church, wasn't sure what was coming next. The bride and groom had written their own vows, a decision the minister had argued against during his only meeting with them, and with good reason; for they stumbled through their vows badly.

SOUR M.A.S.H. AT SEA - SECOND WAVE

Lucy's parents were dazed by the events: a disastrous rehearsal dinner the night before, and now an original church ceremony, albeit a blessedly short one. In spite of her parents' lengthy marriage credentials, this was their first wedding in a church. There were many guests attending for Lucy who had gone to school in Merritt Island, and few for Mitch, making the attendance decidedly lopsided in her favor. While a recorded music selection had been discussed, it had been discarded and the usual organist played. It wasn't her day either, for it turned out the organ hadn't been played for some time and was badly out of tune. (The church was used by the migrant orange pickers when work was available; then sat vacant until the next crop came in. Thus, the minister was part-time.) For me, a practicing Catholic, the wedding seemed mighty strange. I was used to the formal old rituals, with altar boys in white cassocks flitting about. An elderly priest handling the centuries-old ceremony with practiced ease. Everybody standing, sitting and kneeling in unison. And those with hangovers from the liquid rehearsal dinner the night before would be sweating mightily. Yeah, this one was different, all right. And about to get even more so.

The guests emptied out into the hot Florida sun. The grassy lot was partially shaded by the many pine trees. Only one thing was amiss: where was my car, my splendid Cadillac? Not where I had left it, that's for sure. I hurriedly covered the grounds, looking everywhere a car might be. There were not many places a car could hide. It was a small church with small grounds. No paved parking lot, just grass and a dirt road. And no Cadillac. I panicked. I ran over to the minister, who had probably been congratulating himself for having gotten through the morning unscathed, and I yelled at him: *"Where's my car?"* As if he could know.

"Sir, what are you talking about?"

Walter "Bud" Stuhldreher

"My car, where is it? I left it here on the grass before the wedding and it isn't here now!"

"Calm down," he told me. "It has to be here somewhere. It couldn't have just driven off by itself."

He and I walked around the church. No four-door, gray Cadillac with leather upholstery appeared, and I completely lost it.

"I knew it, I knew it! My first Protestant wedding and my car gets stolen. A million Catholic weddings and funerals and no problems! But one Protestant wedding, even out here in the sticks with no one around for miles and my new car gets stolen! How do you explain that?" I guess if I counted them up, I could find out how many ways I had just insulted that poor minister. I'm not sure, but there were many.

He got mad at me, not that I blame him, at least not now, many years later. He told me off, and took his sweet time doing it. How could I possibly blame the religion involved? Cars get stolen everywhere, every day, and probably at Catholic churches, too. If my car was lost, and he still wasn't sure I hadn't just misplaced it, how dare I accuse his religion of being the cause? I was a religious zealot. He was glad he would never have to see me again in this life, and he was pretty sure he wouldn't be seeing me again in the afterlife since the odds were that I was going to hell, and he definitely was not. I can't remember all of his tirade, but you get the general idea. To heighten the moment, at least one good thing came out of my car's being stolen: the rest of the wedding party and guests were listening avidly to this loud argument, and had forgotten their troubles.

Just about now, to my everlasting shame, Beth came driving up in *my Caddy!* It seems that in the wreckage of the previous night, the stuff to decorate the married couple's car had been forgotten, and she had left to buy it! Without telling me! Oh, Lord, I was in for it now. That minister had a good time telling me off again, with emphasis and glee! My "Catholic" daughter had stolen my "Catholic" car. Damn! The Holy Rollers couldn't have done any better. I was just lucky this wasn't a church where snakes were handled, or I would have been wearing a rattlesnake as a going-away present. I truly slunk out of there, tail between my legs. I apologized profusely as I crawled over to my precious Catholic Cadillac, and sped off, leaving Beth to fend for herself. The wedding might have been dry but the rest of that terrible day wasn't.

A curious ending

I won't blame you if you don't believe what I'm now going to tell you, but I swear it's the truth. Two weeks after the wedding, that sanctimonious minister left his wife and ran off with the organist! True! And did I howl when I heard about it. I didn't have much to brag about in my performance out there, but he sure topped me. Saved by lust.

THE PATRIOTIC SWIMMING POOL

In 1945, at the end of World War II, Wernher von Braun's German rocket team surrendered to the U.S. Army. They were sent to White Sands, New Mexico, to show the Americans how the V-2 rocket worked. Then in 1950, the Army decided that an inland site was too confining, a decision prompted in part by an unfortunate occasion when the transplanted German team put a V-2 into a cemetery south of Juarez. From then on the larger rockets were launched out over the ocean from Cape Canaveral. The von Braun team itself was moved to Huntsville, Alabama. The Germans were delighted to be out of the arid Southwest and into a wooded, hilly area that reminded them of their German countryside.

The local residents were not pleased with their arrival. A delegation from the town was returning to Huntsville from Washington, DC, when they learned the news. They had successfully, so they thought, persuaded Congress to give a large

Walter "Bud" Stuhldreher

tract of land west of Huntsville to the town. They intended to develop it into an industrial park. It had been used during WW II as an ammunition storage area. Instead, they had inherited some foreigners, and eccentric ones at that. It was a severe blow, one they deeply resented.

Thanks to von Braun's intelligent leadership the Germans were assimilated into the local community in an extraordinarily short time. By 1952, only two years later, former Luftwaffe Sergeant Walter Wiesman was President of the Huntsville Junior Chamber of Commerce, elected by a membership that was 70 percent World War II veterans. "So am I!" Wiesman pointed out.

Von Braun had insisted his fellow Germans do three things to help them gain acceptance by the town. First, they would not live next to each other in enclaves, but rather, in different sections of Huntsville. Second, they would attend all community events. We would see them putting up chairs at outdoor high school band concerts, for example. Third, their children would attend public schools, not private schools as first planned.

The local school system was not satisfactory to the Germans when they arrived. They requested ten changes they wanted the School Board to make. If not, the Germans would start their own school. By now, with a staggering influx of educated aerospace workers flooding into Huntsville, and naturally, also wanting a first class school system themselves, the Board quickly acquiesced.

But one weakness the Germans couldn't fix was a shortage of skilled home builders. Since builders could sell everything they put up, quality didn't matter much. Amenities, such as neighborhood swimming pools, were ignored. In fact, the only

SOUR M.A.S.H. AT SEA - SECOND WAVE

pool in town available to the space workers was owned by the American Legion. And it was a round pool, not the rectangle one most engineers would expect. Why a round pool instead of the normal rectangle? Well, totally different from the houses surrounding it, the Legionnaires had built a round clubhouse with a round bar and dance floor within. They decided the pool should match their clubhouse. It made for difficult swimming competitions for the members' children in that the length of the lanes was different. None of the space engineers ever accepted the shape of the clubhouse and pool as a desirable engineering accomplishment.

But if you wanted to swim, or have a place for your kids to swim, you joined the American Legion. And that's what I did.

The IBM facility manager, Steve Ramminger, did too. In the normal process for membership, Steve was interviewed by the Legion membership committee, a collection of white, middle-aged rural Southerners. Steve was asked if he had served in the Armed Services.

"Yah, of course," he replied.

"Which branch?"

"The Air Force."

"Where?"

"Mostly in North Carolina."

Satisfied, the committee passed Steve with flying colors.

You see, even with Steve's German accent, the American Legion membership had been somewhat misled. Yes, Steve *had*

Walter "Bud" Stuhldreher

served in the military during WW II, the *German* military. And in the German Air Force. Had he really served in North Carolina? Yep, Steve sure had served there, but in a POW camp, after he had been shot down and taken prisoner by American forces.

As near as I can tell, Steve answered all their questions truthfully. He just didn't elaborate on his answers. And Steve's kids and my kids enjoyed the swimming pool tremendously.

MY FIRST COLLEGE FOOTBALL GAME

This story was rejected by Sports Illustrated *in 1988. I thought it deserved a better fate.*

During 1988, *Sports Illustrated* ran a series of Junior Achievement ads titled: "Do We Ever Outgrow Our Need For Heroes?" The March 21, 1988, issue featured a picture of four old time football players sitting on horses — the legendary Four Horsemen of Notre Dame. The one on the right, Quarterback Harry Stuhldreher, was my uncle. This picture, arguably the most published sports picture of all time, was featured on a United States postage stamp — back when they cost thirty-two cents. Interestingly, the picture almost wasn't made.

In 1924, sportswriter Grantland Rice wrote his famous column on the Notre Dame vs. Army game, titled "The Four Horsemen Ride Again." When the victorious team returned to South Bend, a young Notre Dame student showed up at the school's practice field with four horses from the South Bend Coal & Ice Company. He wanted ND's backfield to pose on the horses. They refused. Coach Rockne, angry that the practice had been interrupted for so long, asked what the holdup was. The players told Rockne it was a dumb picture: 1. Football wasn't played on horses, polo was; 2. Only one player would hold a ball, not all four as the photographer wanted; and 3. Their practice uniforms were dirty and torn. Rockne didn't believe these excuses, and wanted to know the real reason. It was that all four of them, including the two who had been brought up on a farm, were scared of horses. Rockne, patience exhausted, ordered them to get on the horses, pose, and get back to practice. That's why, in the picture that made them famous for life, not one is smiling and all look unhappy. They were lucky Rockne had the last word, but then, he always did. They were also lucky the picture turned out OK. Photography was an inexact science in those days and multiple pictures, to ensure getting one good one, were the rule. But the only photo snapped was a hit.

And it was this uncle, Harry Stuhldreher, who was responsible for my first college football game being the most exciting one of the hundreds I have attended over the years. Only, of course, I didn't know it at the time.

Uncle Harry coached at the University of Wisconsin from 1936 to 1949. Before playing an away game against Purdue, which is located 60 miles northwest of Indianapolis, he would bring his team into Indianapolis to work out at the Butler College field on Friday afternoons. (Butler College is now Butler University.) Where the team stayed afterwards I don't know, but I do know where Harry and his staff went: our home. His many Indianapolis friends, sportswriters, famous and not-so-famous strangers would then congregate for really noisy parties. In self defense, my parents invited all the neighbors so they wouldn't complain about the noise, and they ended up being

Harry's good "Naptown" friends, too. It helped that we lived in a big house and only three doors from a Catholic church. This meant that most homes in the neighborhood were Catholic families, so noisy parties were not unusual. It's possible that some of the neighbors didn't drink, but I don't remember any who didn't.

Saturday mornings, after these parties, my two brothers, two sisters and I would creep downstairs wondering what exotic sights would be in store for us. The record was one gentleman sound asleep in the fireplace, another under the grand piano, and one lady *in* the piano. We kids would then drink the remains in all the glasses we found which weren't empty. Eventually my parents would depart for West Lafayette for the Wisconsin - Purdue game, arriving in time for the Bloody Mary tailgate parties in the parking lot which started around 10 a.m.

One such Saturday morning — either 1938 or 1939 — the local head sportswriter, William (Bill) F. Fox, Jr., of the *Indianapolis News*, called inquiring about a friend he had misplaced the night before. Then a thought struck him: "How would you and Bill (my twin brother) like to see the game today?"

"Would we — you bet we would!" We were only seven or eight years old and going to a college football game!

Mr. Fox picked up Bill and me and drove speedily north to Purdue. He parked right next to the stadium, and we went up to the press box where we watched the game in style. And what a game! Wisconsin was down 13 - 0 with six minutes to go, and Purdue had the ball. The few Wisconsin fans started straggling out of the stadium, figuring the famous Wisconsin song "On Wisconsin, on Wisconsin…" wasn't going to be heard again. In those days the coaches didn't call the plays, the quarterback did.

Walter "Bud" Stuhldreher

To the surprise and dismay of the Purdue coaches and fans, the Purdue quarterback threw a pass — right into the hands of a Wisconsin player who returned it 63 yards for a touchdown. Now the score was 13 - 7 with a little over five minutes to go. The boisterous Purdue fans quieted down. A few of the Wisconsin fans paused at the top of the steps leading out of the stadium. The Purdue team was clumped together on the sidelines listening to the coaches berate them. The Purdue squad took the field, lining up to receive the probable on-side kick. The Wisconsin kicker tried one, but it went too far, bounced a couple of times and was caught by a Purdue player on the 25 yard line, where he was quickly tackled.

Bill and I looked over at Mr. Fox in the press box. We were excited and thought that now Wisconsin still had a chance. Mr. Fox just shrugged and said, "Well, it's a close game now, and at least Harry's team won't be shut out. But, boys, don't get your hopes up. That interception was the Badgers' only spark this whole afternoon, and Purdue does have the ball."

Bill and I shrank back in our seats, understanding Mr. Fox was probably right. After all, he was a veteran sportscaster; we were just kids.

Purdue, obviously intent on running out the clock tried one running play after another. Apparently the coaches had gotten the quarterback's attention, and Purdue passes were not in the program now. We were bitterly disappointed when Purdue managed a first down with less than three minutes to go. Darn! But Wisconsin held them during the next series and Purdue was forced to punt from their 34 yard line with a little over a minute to go.

It was a great kick under the circumstances, high and long, and fielded by a Wisconsin receiver on his 15 yard line. In fact the kick was too good, because the kick sailed way past the Purdue defenders as they rushed toward the Wisconsin receivers. The Wisconsin punt receiver charged up the field, picked up a wall of blockers, and cut towards the sideline at the 50 yard line. His blockers knocked down Boilermakers one by one. With great protection the Badger player ran over the goal line untouched. Touchdown! And the score was now tied at 13 - 13.

Bill and I excitedly jumped up and down, disturbing the reporters who were typing furiously. "Hey, calm down, you two," yelled one of them.

Mr. Fox told them to let us be, "Their uncle is the Badger Coach."

The point after split the uprights. The happy Wisconsin team kicked off and the dispirited Boilermakers could only manage two ineffective passes.

Wow! What a game! Down 13 - 0 with the other team in possession of the ball, we had pulled out the win against heavy odds and with almost no time left on the clock!

In those days sportswriters typed their columns during the game, then got them to their paper as speedily as possible. Since Purdue's stadium at West Lafayette was only 60 miles from Indianapolis, Mr. Fox had arranged for some Indiana State Troopers to escort him back immediately after the game. To tell the truth, that 60 mile high-speed run, with the sirens going the whole way, was even more exciting than the game.

When our jubilant parents arrived home several hours later they said, "It was a great game. Too bad you kids didn't get to see it." They were astonished to learn that Bill and I had seen it — and from better seats than they had, too!

Well. I've seen some great games since then, but never again from a press box, never again from the 50-yard line, and I have never had a police escort again. At least, not from a football game.

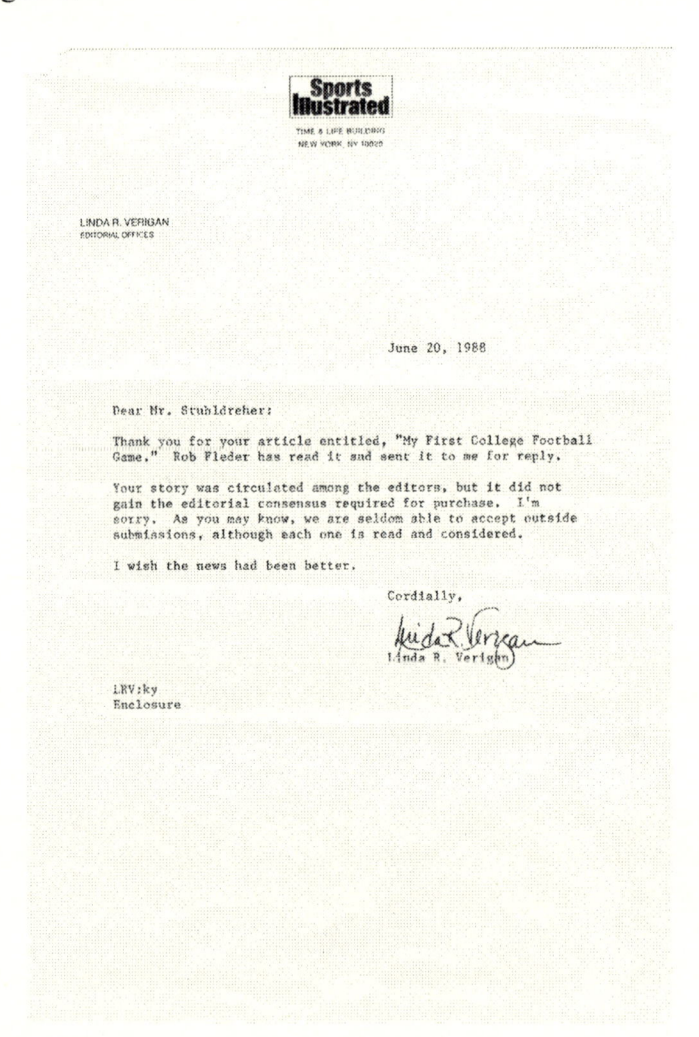

Sports Illustrated
TIME & LIFE BUILDING
NEW YORK, NY 10020

LINDA R. VERIGAN
EDITORIAL OFFICES

June 20, 1988

Dear Mr. Stuhldreher:

Thank you for your article entitled, "My First College Football Game." Rob Fleder has read it and sent it to me for reply.

Your story was circulated among the editors, but it did not gain the editorial consensus required for purchase. I'm sorry. As you may know, we are seldom able to accept outside submissions, although each one is read and considered.

I wish the news had been better.

Cordially,

Linda R. Verigan

LRV:ky
Enclosure

THE BADGER GAME

This is a tale of six turbulent months of my life, a period of Damon Runyonesque proportions, peopled with FBI agents, IRS agents, local police and corporate chicanery. Of sex entrapment and sex scams. Of trying to sell, improbably, machines to grow grass to farmers surrounded by hundreds of acres of grass.

Of airplane accidents and former jail inmates. And, just to keep the caldron bubbling, a firing squad or two. As in all my stories, all the incidents are true.

But since I'm not sure how libel laws work, and I damn well don't want to find out, some names are not real. I have been fired twice in my life. Once by US Steel over a golf game. This describes the second firing, caused by "The Badger Game." Don't know what that game is? Neither did I, at first. But I learned.

Walter "Bud" Stuhldreher

Background

It was early in the 60's and I was working in the farm industry in Indiana. Specifically, for a company that had one product, a prefabricated building in which to grow grass. Rapidly. With no dirt involved. Thanks to Slyvania "Grow Lux" lamps, General Electric heat pumps, and a new technology called "hydroponics," our system produced grass six inches to eight inches high in a week. This "grass" was not marijuana, but feed for cattle. Since the farm industry is notorious for not accepting new ideas, and we were trying to sell grass when the farmers could grow all the grass they wanted, free, we had our work cut out for us.

Of course, there was more here than met the eye. Our system worked year round. Weather was not a problem. Winter or summer, drought or flood, hot or cold, our system didn't care. Grass — fresh green grass every day, seven days a week, twelve months a year. Thus the system promised, and delivered, amazing results for those farmers willing to try it. The grass was used as an additive, a natural supplement to their regular feed. Our system was not cost-effective for the small farmer or for ones with cheap livestock, but if they had diary cows for example, we could prove their milk output was higher with our grass in their diet. At breeding operations with expensive horses, the mares we fed got pregnant at a higher rate than those who didn't eat the stuff. We had great success in Kentucky with almost all the famous racing stables using our system.

But, in addition to introducing a new element into the farming industry, a tough proposition, the system was expensive. Our cheapest unit sold for $5,280, and bigger units sold for as much as $20,000. A lot of money in 1960.

One of the "Four Horsemen" Comes to Town

Working for a company trying to sell grass to farmers presented me with another problem. My Uncle Harry was coming to town and Mother was in a dither. Uncle Harry had been the quarterback of Notre Dame's famed Four Horsemen. He was a former head football coach at both Villanova and the University of Wisconsin, a nationally known sports figure, and had been featured on a zillion boxes of Wheaties, the pinnacle of sports recognition at that time and still a very important symbol. He was employed by US Steel to make speeches — 250 speeches a year. A sought-after speaker, he had four basic speeches and modified them to suit the audience. The speeches usually stressed teamwork, which then permitted him to swing into talking about how important teamwork was at US Steel, his employer. (US Steel paid all the expenses required to get Harry to the town for the speech. The sponsoring organization was pleased to let this subtle reference to US Steel into the speech in return for getting a nationally known figure for free.)

So when Harry hit town a lot of publicity came with him. The closest comparison I can think of in today's sports-mad populace would be Michael Jordan coming to town. Harry generated about the same level of interest. During his visit Harry would be busy with interviews and attending cocktail parties hosted by the organization that had brought him to Indianapolis, but he always made time for a visit with the family. Mother wanted everything to go smoothly during his visit, but was at a loss as to what she should tell Harry about my occupation.

"Why not tell the truth?" I asked, reasonably.

Mother was horrified. "I have no intention of telling him you work for a company that grows grass in the air! He would be mortified! His only brother's son doing that!"

"Well," I responded, "it wasn't like I was breaking the law. Besides, I'm sure Uncle Harry would be interested in such an operation."

Mother was adamant that Harry was not going to know the truth about my current employment. I agreed not to bring it up, but what was I to tell him if he asked what I was up to? Mother didn't have an answer to that, but said she'd think of something.

To tell the truth, I kinda agreed with Mother. When at a social affair, I would be asked what I did for a living. I would respond, "I sell farmers a machine which grows grass," and conversation would quickly come to a halt.

Sure enough, after the drinks were poured, Harry talked to all of his nieces and nephews who were there, then asked me what I was up to. Mother jumped in, and answered for me, telling Harry that I worked as an accountant for a company in the farm industry. Then she quickly changed the subject before he could ask anything further. It worked. Harry left town the next morning not knowing that I worked for a company which grew grass. Mother was happy.

The Players

Our new corporation was a strange conglomeration of entrepreneurs. The President was Jack Lane, a very nice guy, and not just because he had hired me as Controller. The Executive Vice-president was Bob Kayne. Did you see the movie *The Flim-Flam Man?* George C. Scott played a crusty old man who was always just two steps ahead of the law. He

SOUR M.A.S.H. AT SEA - SECOND WAVE

specialized in cheating strangers out of their money in various scams. I swear the writers must have known Kayne because he not only looked like Scott's character, he acted liked him. Kayne had somehow gotten hold of the patent for our system; rumor said it was from a card game in which he cheated, and that was his ticket into the business. He didn't have an engineering background, nor any other background we could uncover. He did have a terrible dye job on his hair and eyebrows. The other top guy, although not on the payroll, was our corporate Secretary, Charlie Parrow. These three guys were ex-Air Force pilots from WW II, and that was the source of my first problem with them.

Like most former war pilots, they loved to fly, and the business was giving them a chance to relive their days of glory. The business owned a four seater, single-engine, propeller plane. I believe it was some model of Cessna. They used it to transport prospects to observe operations where one of our units was installed. They used it for sales conferences. They used it for every conceivable trip they could dream up, and they were furious that I was adamant about not going up in it.

Wild horses couldn't have gotten me to fly with any of them, for reasons I couldn't tell them. First, the plane wasn't maintained properly. There was no regular maintenance schedule I ever heard about. Second, they were not full-time pilots with all their attention focused on flying. Occasional pilots, with rusty skills, they simply didn't inspire confidence in me. Let me share a few stories with you so you'll see I'm not exaggerating.

On one trip Jack, our CEO, overshot a landing at a rural airport and ended up in a neighboring farmer's pea patch. The propeller flung the peas over the front of the plane, covering the windshield with green goo. Jack promptly gunned the plane into

Walter "Bud" Stuhldreher

a 180-degree turn and, without being able to see through the windshield, got her back into the air. Karl, our sales manager, was furious with this dumb stunt. He wanted to know why Jack hadn't shut her down; they could have pushed her back to the airport. Jack said he would have been embarrassed to have been caught overshooting the runway! Karl didn't think much of that explanation.

A couple of weeks later, Charlie was piloting the plane over the Okefenokee Swamp in Florida when the engine quit. The only passenger, a prospective buyer, was scared to death. Charlie told him, not to worry, they had simply run out of gas in the main tank. He would just switch over to the auxiliary tank and they would be fine. Charlie then leaned over, and pushed a metal rod which was in between the pilot and the front passenger's seat. It broke off. Charlie exclaimed, "Whoops! I meant to get that fixed!" The lever to switch from the main gas tank to the auxiliary tank was busted. But Charlie managed to jury rig the damn thing and got them down safely. To no one's surprise, we lost that prospective sale.

The last story I'll share with you, out of several more I could relate, happened when Jack and Karl were 10,000 feet high over Iowa one day in the fall. An early winter storm had caught Jack by surprise and he was in trouble. "Karl, wake up, I've got something I must tell you." Karl came to and asked what's up? Jack replied that there was a cloud system below them, and he couldn't fly the plane through it without ice quickly building up on the wings — so much ice that the plane would become unstable and crash. Furthermore, they were running out of gas, and things looked bad.

"Jack," Karl asked, "why did you feel you had to wake me up to tell me such terrible news?"

Jack didn't answer, just asked Karl to help him look for a hole in the clouds which would permit them to get down to earth without losing the wings. Jack finally found a hole, down they went, ran out of gas, and landed on a dirt road. The landing was so hard that Karl suffered a back injury that causes him pain to this day. That plane was a flying hearse.

We were a small, publicly owned corporation with seven directors, mostly brought on to help with our sales effort. You can't succeed in the farm business unless you have a professor from a well-known agricultural university on your board. Ours was Professor Yardley from Purdue University in Indiana.

Another was "Cash" Bradley, who ran an enormous dairy operation outside of Indianapolis. He had earned his nickname, of which he was very proud, by being as tight fisted with a buck as anyone I ever knew. Electric milking machines had been successfully introduced to the dairy business, but he thought manual milking was best. He also thought dairy workers from Holland had the softest hands in the milking business, and had brought several over to handle his prize stock Indentured, they were paid pitiful wages and worked seven days a week. The few times I was out there, it was always strange to see them in their wooden shoes. Cash had also experimented with using music to soothe the cows so they would produce more milk. Certain music, such as loud sounds, actually curtailed production, while other types increased production.

Cash was well known in local circles, if infamously, by the manner in which he had gotten control of his operation. It had originally been owned by his parents, but he had convinced them to sign over the homestead and business to him. Then he promptly threw them off the land and into the poorhouse. Nice fellow.

Walter "Bud" Stuhldreher

The Badger Game

Another director was Larry Brown. Larry, a CPA, ran a large diary operation for two Indianapolis brothers who had inherited a fortune from their grandparents. Not liking to work very much, in fact, not at all, the brothers had turned this particular business totally over to Larry to run. Larry, it turned out, was an unsavory character, one in whom the FBI was interested. The Feds came to see me one morning. It seems Larry and his wife, a gorgeous 12-car pileup beauty, were operating a scam, called the "badger game" on unsuspecting businessmen. The scam consisted of his wife picking up out-of-town businessmen in bars who were looking for a good time. She would take them up to a hotel room where they started undressing. Then Larry would bust into the room, screaming bloody murder, and threaten to tell the businessmen's wives and families about their terrible behavior if they didn't pay off. They had no choice but to do so. In those days such marital misbehavior was not tolerated. But one guy had complained, and since they had sometimes crossed state lines while pulling off this extortion, the Feds had been brought in.

This news came as a complete shock to me. Larry, a CPA, had seemed an OK guy. And besides, his wife was damn easy on the eyes. The agents were interested in learning if I knew anything about Larry's scam. I, horrified, said certainly not. They then wanted to see all checks involving Larry, either ones we had received or payments to Larry.

"Why," I asked?

"Just looking around, nothing specific in mind," they said.

I wasn't sure what do to. I knew diddley squat about such things as search warrants and figured perhaps I better cooperate with them. I dug out the checks. The agents studied the fronts and backs, then they returned the checks to me without comment and left. I promptly called Larry and told him what I knew. After all, he was a director of the company. He didn't blame me for "working with the FBI" as he called it. I wouldn't have said I was working with them, not yet, that was to come, but was relieved that Larry wasn't upset.

Going Public

The other top guy in the corporation, but not on our payroll was John Hofler, our lawyer. When we had decided to go public in an intrastate offering, we couldn't get permission from the Secretary of State's Office to do so. It wasn't as if we were turned down, it was more like nothing ever happened. After several weeks with no action, someone tipped off Bob Kayne that "we had the wrong lawyer." What did that mean? He was told nothing would ever happen unless we switched lawyers. After asking who we should get, several names were suggested, one of them being John Hofler. So we hired him to get the Secretary of State's office off the dime. He said no problem, and that it would cost $21,000. Although not yet on the board at this time, I protested the size of his fee. He cheerfully told me only $1,000 of it was his fee. The other $20,000 was to be paid "under the table." And this, he firmly told us, was the only way the Secretary's office did business. (It was a Democratic administration. I suppose it might have worked the same way in a Republican administration, but then, we'll never know, will we?)

We paid the $21,000 and got permission to sell stock, which we did for three dollars a share. Jack, Bob and Charlie got 20,000 options at one cent per share, Karl, Don, our plant manager, and I got 5,000 options at one dollar a share. Things were looking up. All we needed was for the company to start making money, a goal yet to be achieved.

The next surprise was when our CEO, Jack, got booted out of the corporation in a coup engineered by Bob Kayne. Seems Bob wasn't happy being #2 and spread enough lies about Jack to do him in. Jack, essentially a nice guy, didn't have a clue what was going on. Since Jack had hired me, I figured my days were numbered, so I was equally shocked when Bob asked me to replace Jack on the board and become Treasurer. I felt sorry for Jack, but was overjoyed to be a director of a publicly owned corporation, small though we were, before the age of thirty.

A Profitable Sideline Shot to Hell

In order to grow grass six to eight inches high in seven days, our system required very good seed — certified oat seed. (Today, it is common practice to use certified seed for most crops, but it wasn't back then.) It was not possible to sell an expensive system unless we could assure the buyer a supply of good seed. We did this by contracting with farmers to buy their output if they would use certified seed. This worked OK in the United States but what about Venezuela? We had sold a number of units to wealthy land owners there, and they, too, needed a continuing source of seed. Our sales manager, Karl Nutting, and I stepped in to fill the need. (Bob and Jack wanted no part of this operation, insisting our base business was selling the system, and they had enough on their plates as it was.)

KARL E. NUTTING

Nutting Named Distributor for Hydroponics, Inc.

Well known to farmers, dairymen, cattle and horse breeders in this area, Karl E. Nutting of Muncie has recently been appointed distributor for Hydroponics, Inc. throughout Eastern Indiana and Western Ohio.

As head of the distributorship (known as Green Feeds of Indiana, Inc.), Mr. Nutting will appoint dealers throughout the area to handle the sales and installations of Hydroponics equipment.

Hydroponics, Inc. is the producer of new farm equipment that grows green grass from seed —for feeding cattle, dairy cows, horses, hogs and poultry—365 days a year. The new Hydroponics equipment actually produces as much as 1,500 pounds of grass per day—rain or shine, flood or drought! It is the modern, scientific grass growing equipment that is credited with keeping farm animals healthier, more productive and contented ... by providing their natural food all through the year. One of the first Hydroponics units in this area is now in use on the farm of Homer Jackson, near Gaston, Indiana.

A native of Muncie, Mr. Nutting resides at 51 Warwich Rd. with his wife and two children: Karl Jr., 11, and Kyle Nan, 5. He is a member of the board of directors of the Delaware County 4-H Horse-and-Saddle Program, of the Muncie Lighthorse Club and the M-Bar-D Westerners, and of the Indiana Quarter Horse Association.

Karl and I formed the S & N Grain Company. Karl contracted with the farmers. I handled packing the seed in bags and shipping it to New Orleans where American Express took over. They arranged with a maritime carrier to transport the seed to Venezuela, plus they handled the banking requirements. One day I surprised the hell out of an Indianapolis bank when I told them I needed to arrange for an "irrevocable, confirmed letter of credit." Foreign business transactions weren't common in those days. This instrument protected both the shipper, us, and the buyer, Communications de Venezuela, S.A., our customer. I wouldn't ship the grain until the letter had been established. American Express would verify that the grain had been shipped, and the bank would then release the funds to us. Our customer, by the way, was a subsidiary of ITT, a giant American company. It was operated solely by Germans who had escaped from Germany either during, or after, WW II. (This was also true of the oil business in Venezuela.)

My contact was Wolfgang Jastram, hardly an Hispanic name. He owned up to having been in the Luftwaffe; however, he claimed never to have gone against English or American fighters — only Russians. In those days, I never met a former German soldier or aviator who didn't make the exact same claim.

This sideline really didn't take up much of our time. Once started, it went along quite nicely. Karl and I made profits equal to around 50 percent of our regular salaries from it, so it was a very nice sideline. But it came to a halt one Saturday morning.

Economic difficulties plagued Venezuela then, the same as they do today, forty years later. So the government, in a desperate bid for votes, decided to nationalize the large farms and give the land to the peasants. Of course, the large farms were owned by our customers. The nationalization process was simple in its execution. The government just lined the owners up against their walls one Saturday morning and shot them. Too bad. That was the end of the S & N Grain Company.

In common with most young businesses, the grass-growing business was cash poor. Friday paydays were a close encounter, and sometimes Jack and Bob had not taken their salaries. I grew quite tired of this and, using my new found status on the Board, convinced Charlie and Bob that a long-term loan from a Chicago firm I had located made sense. The lending firm insisted on representation on the board, and Bob agreed, if reluctantly.

The IRS

I was next visited by the police and the IRS. Larry was in the spotlight again. It seems a disgruntled employee at the large dairy operation he was running had alerted the IRS to a problem. They, in turn, had brought in the local cops. Here's the deal. Dairy cows, in order to give milk, have to be pregnant or calving. Thus, they give milk about 300 days a year. What does the operation do with the offspring? If they need additional milk cows they keep the heifers and sell off the steers. Farmers who raise cattle for beef are the usual buyers. Both sexes are sold if the milking barns are full. But Larry's operation wasn't reporting any receipts from such sales. Where had the money gone? If Larry had skimmed it off, he had not reported it on his tax returns and the IRS was very interested. If the operation had received the dough, but not reported the income to the IRS, that was another problem. Either way Larry was up to his neck in trouble. Like the Feds before them, the IRS and the police wanted to review all checking transactions involving Larry and the operation.

Geez, I thought, this routine was getting old in a hurry. They did their stuff and I did mine, once again notifying Larry that he had new scouts on his tail. He didn't say much.

The Lusty Inmate

My next problem was with Bob, our new CEO. He insisted we hire his son, a person we hadn't known existed, to work in our small manufacturing plant in the rear of our property. First, we didn't need another employee; second, the kid had no experience in metal working, the only skill we used; third, and worst, he had just been released from the State of Indiana's prison in Michigan City, Indiana, after doing a stretch for armed robbery. I, along with Don, our plant manager, protested, but

Bob overruled us. We had to let a good employee go and hire an unskilled jailbird. Damn!

Depending on your viewpoint, hiring the kid wasn't the best thing Bob ever did. Bob had a wife much, much younger than he was. She had a lot of rough edges, no social skills whatever, and when we had to be around the happy couple our wives were very uncomfortable. So I didn't mind it much when the kid soon started bragging that he was "screwing my old man's chippie." What a mess.

Corporate Chicanery

What happened next made the above incidents look like small potatoes, very small potatoes. It was my habit to closely review every check we cut, front and back. Reviewing the backs of all the canceled checks is a swell way to catch a gambling problem in a plant. Reviewing the front is the way to catch someone altering the payee, thus enabling them to cash the check. So I became very nervous about some Canadian checks Bob had authorized payment on. Further inspection revealed Bob was in the process of obtaining Canadian patents on our system, not in the corporation's name, as his contract required, but in his own name. The patents, all those currently in existence and any future ones, were to be the property of the corporation. That was Bob's contribution to the business, rather than cash which the other founders had thrown in.

I was in a tough spot, and had to accuse my boss of fraud. Predictably, Bob got mad and claimed it wasn't true. I showed him my evidence which convinced him lies weren't going to work. What did I want him to do? I said he had to immediately turn the Canadian patents over to the company and I would forget his mistake. He next launched into a long harangue about how he had sold the American patents to the company for less than they were worth, that the company wasn't growing fast enough to suit him, and that he deserved ownership of the international patents. If I knew what was good for me, I'd shut up and forget about the whole deal.

I responded I couldn't do that. What he was up to was illegal, and I had no intention of keeping quiet. He glared at me, then took his gloves off. "Stuhldreher, if you'll go quietly I'll arrange a payment of $10,000 to you. That's more than you make in a year. But if you sound off, I'll fire your ass and you'll get nothing!"

I thought the offer over for a couple of minutes while reflecting on my minuscule bank account, then told him to shove it — I intended to tell the other officers and board members how he was cheating their corporation. And then I left his office in hurry.

The next several weeks passed in a strange, Alice in Wonderland, existence. Bob and I conducted the corporation's business as if nothing was amiss between us. An unspoken agreement evolved to keep the business going in spite of our growing enmity. Unreal. I was busy traveling the state lining up support for my side while Bob was doing the same for his side. Jack, the deposed CEO, happily supported my efforts and advised me on how to try to gain the necessary votes at the upcoming special Board of Directors meeting to discuss my revelations.

I started with Cash Bradley. I pointed out to him, that not only were Bob's actions illegal, which he didn't seem much interested in, but would unavoidably hit Cash in his wallet. (He had bought several hundred shares.) It got his attention when I discussed how their precarious market value was sure to be depressed when this news got out, but he remained noncommittal. However, I had hope because, if nothing else, Cash was intensely interested in anything involving his wallet.

I next visited Professor Yardley at Purdue University, and had no trouble getting his agreement to support me at the Board meeting.

Since Bob and I had been told we would not be allowed to attend the meeting, this left three directors: Charlie Parrow, our Secretary; the banker from Chicago; and Larry Brown, CPA and well-known crook in FBI, IRS and local police circles. I wrote Charlie off, knowing he was a big-time crony of Bob's. The banker immediately agreed Bob's actions stank to high heaven and would be at the meeting to support me. OK, I now had two members for sure in my corner, the professor and the banker. Cash was a maybe. Charlie was definitely out. What about Larry who was not exactly a choir boy? In spite of my rocky relationship with Larry, I had one thing going for me with him. *Larry hated Bob more than he hated me.* You see, in spite of being warned off several times, Bob had continued to hit on Larry's wife.

I had a long meeting with Larry, and emphasized how I had always shared my knowledge of what the various authorities were up to, that I really had no choice but to cooperate with them. Bob, on the other hand, was a snake who had ignored Larry's reasonable request to quit trying to get Larry's wife in the sack. Oh, but I laid it on good! I left, not sure what Larry would do, but feeling pretty good about my chances to survive. Two votes for sure, and only needing one of Cash's or Larry's. Yep, I was doing much better that I had anticipated. Jack was eagerly plotting his return to the business.

Sex at a Bad Time

Then, one week before the meeting, Chicken Little decided to pay me a visit. Actually it was Professor Yardley. He informed me, with tears in his eyes, that he could no longer support me. It turned out he had done a really stupid, indefensible thing the previous weekend. He had agreed to go drinking with Charlie and Bob while they tried to obtain his vote. Failing to sway him, they had gotten him drunk and photographed him in several comprising positions with a whore. They had showed him the pictures the previous day, pictures he had no memory of being taken. Hell, he didn't even remember the whore. They coldly informed him that the University and his family would be shown the pictures if he didn't vote for Bob. I understood his position, told him no hard feelings, and wished him well. (He would need all the good wishes he could get. Bob and Charley were sure to hold the damn pictures over his head every time they wanted something from him in the future.)

Whew! My high-flying outlook had just crashed in flames. I now had just one sure vote, the banker's. Bob had two, Charlie's and the professor's. I now needed both Cash's and Larry's, a long shot if I had ever seen one. Just to let you know Mrs. Stuhldreher hadn't raised an idiot, I had, surreptitiously, arranged interviews and had three job offers on the table. Still, if I had my "druthers," I'd "druther" stay with the grass business.

The Special Board of Directors Meeting

The day of the special evening meeting was strained and tense. My wife was definitely unhappy with the mess, Karl and Don weren't sure where the company was heading, no matter who won. Jack was waiting on the sidelines, hopeful his ouster

Walter "Bud" Stuhldreher

was going to be reversed. Bob was nervous and his Texas accent had never been stronger. I was pretty nervous myself.

As dusk approached I became even more nervous. Larry had called me and said he might not make the meeting, that he had been informed there was a warrant out for his arrest. (About time, I thought.) I tried to persuade him the cops would have no reason to be at our office that night, that he would be perfectly safe. Larry wasn't buying it.

I then came up with a plan, desperate as I was to get him to the meeting. "Call me at 6:30 and ask if any cops are here. If there are, I'll tell you and then help you get in through the window in the men's rest room." From there he could go up the stairs to the meeting and they would not be able to see him. He surprised me by agreeing with this shabby plan, and I left for the airport to pick up the two bankers coming in from Chicago.

Well, damn it all to hell, the cops did arrive at our building around 6 p.m. Someone, I later suspected Bob, had tipped them off Larry would be there that evening. And so they sat downstairs, like two large lumps of police gristle, and complained that we didn't have a spittoon for their chewing tobacco. Surprising me once again, Larry called to see if the coast was clear. I told him it wasn't. He came anyway, climbed through the small window in the men's rest room, with me pulling him through, and went upstairs without being spotted. Whew! I still had a chance!

The meeting lasted for hours. Finally the banker came down and gave me the bad news: I was out by a vote of three to two. (Cash had voted for me after all. Larry had not, and after I had helped him through the rest room window so he could attend!) Then, the banker went on, even though the outcome was certain, since the notice of the meeting had specified two votes would be

SOUR M.A.S.H. AT SEA - SECOND WAVE

taken, one for me and one for Bob, another vote was taken. Surprise! By a vote of three to two, Bob was also voted out. *Larry had switched his vote!* He had gotten even with both of us! I've always thought he did better than Solomon with his decision about the baby. What a master stroke! Of, course, this left the business in a leadership vacuum, what with both the CEO and CFO dumped on their asses. Hell, Larry didn't care, he had done all right. Gotten even with a pair of enemies.

Aftermath

Amazingly, Bob ignored the director's vote throwing him out of the business, and stayed as CEO, dashing Jack's hope of a comeback. He paid off the Chicago loan, which the bankers called in when I was voted out. He then filled the two vacancies on the board with cronies and got himself reelected as CEO.

Don, the plant manager, and Karl, the sales manager stayed on until Bob ran the business into the ground. They surfaced owning the American rights to a South African patent, a system which produced enough electricity from chicken manure to supply the chicken farm's total power needs. (The chicken droppings produced methane gas. The gas powered the generators, and the droppings, by now having no smell and no longer attracting flies, were sold as premium fertilizer to city dwellers with small gardens.) They wanted me in the business and took me over to a large chicken operation in Illinois where the system had been installed. I had joined the Federal Government after the grass growing debacle and decided against another job in the farm industry.

After all, if I was embarrassed to say I made my living by growing grass, how would I handle admitting I collected chicken manure? It staggered the imagination to think how Mother would handle it. "Mother, you never liked to say I was in the grass business. Well, I've got good news and bad news. The good news is that I'm out of the grass business. The bad news is that I now handle chicken crap!"

The Feds nailed Larry under the Mann Act, which prohibited taking females over state lines for immoral purposes. I'm not sure if the law was intended to include wives, but it was good enough to send Larry up for a while. The last I heard of Larry he was still in, and the IRS was waiting for him to get out so they could have their pound of flesh.

Bob's son ended up back in jail, again for armed robbery, so I guess Bob had his wife back to himself. For a while, anyway. I lost track of them after that.

Jack stayed in Indianapolis and, a true entrepreneur, kept enough small businesses going so he made a nice living. I don't know what happened to Charlie. Professor Yardley finished a successful career at Purdue University, having resigned from the board soon after the special board meeting. We exchanged Christmas cards for a few years and then stopped.

A Curious Ending

In 1965 I interviewed for a job in the space business with IBM in Huntsville, Alabama,. The interview was going well until I told them I had been fired two jobs ago. To IBM's credit, they didn't quit looking at me immediately, but decided to investigate the details involved in the firing. They talked with the lawyer, John Hofler, who had taken us public. He told the truth, said I "was a stand up guy," and had done the right thing even though it cost me my job. So I was a very rare hire for IBM, in fact, the only one I ever heard of — someone who had been hired in spite of an earlier firing. I stayed for the rest of my career until IBM transferred me to Houston three months prior to my fifty-fifth birthday. How could anyone live there, the humidity capital of the United States? Not Bettie and me, that's for sure. I took early retirement and returned to Tallahassee, where I play bad golf, a decent French horn and write stories such as these.

IT'S STRADIVARIUS TIME!

It was the summer of 1951 and I was in the middle of my second-class midshipman cruise — the one between my sophomore and junior years. The one where we split the eight weeks between the Marines and Navy Preflight Training. We had left Little Creek, Virginia — and the Marines, thank God — and had just arrived in Pensacola, Florida.

To say I was glad to see the end of Marine training that summer would be the understatement of all time. It was a miserable experience of marching, living in tents, undergoing extreme physical tests, and having to fire rifles every day. For a city boy like me it was hell on earth. To top it off, when I sank a Landing Craft Vehicle Personnel (LCVP) boat, I was given permanent Extra Duty Punishment (EDP) as a result. The captain of the *USS Sanborn* had done his damnedest to court-martial me for that mishap, but couldn't because I was a midshipman. So every day, when the base and the rest of the

Walter "Bud" Stuhldreher

midshipmen knocked off for the day at 1600 (4 p.m. for you landlubbers), I marched on the tennis courts until 1800 (six p.m.). With my despised 16-pound rifle over my shoulder, I marched to one end of the tennis court, made a 180-degree Marine turn, and marched back. For two numbing hours in afternoon heat, every day, except on Saturdays and Sundays when I got to march four numbing hours, from two o'clock to six o'clock. I actually prayed for rain; it was cooler then.

Posed Marine publicity photo of Notre Dame midshipmen for newspapers back home. I'm on the left studying the end of the rope — why, God only knows.

Now we were in Pensacola. The Navy trained aviators there, at least for the first part of their training. Three fields were actually in use in those long-ago days: Pensacola, Saufley and Corry. I'm not sure what type of training took place where, but I do remember the Navy's stupidity in selecting Corry for one of its training sites. A paper mill was located just west of the runways. Since the prevailing wind was from the southwest, this meant the heavy, dark gray smoke from their smokestacks drifted across the runways. The embryo pilots, who found

262

SOUR M.A.S.H. AT SEA - SECOND WAVE

piloting the trainers difficult enough, were baffled by the six foot layer of gray smoke which hovered just above the runways. They would descend to what they believed was the runway, and when they thought they were a foot above Mother Earth, they would shut their engines off or lower engine speed dramatically. Then they would drop, sickeningly, the final six feet instead of the expected one foot. It was said that more landing carriages and wheels were damaged at Corry than at any other military base in the U.S. And this had been going on for years when we arrived. We were there to learn what Navy flying was all about so that we could make an intelligent decision when, at the end of our senior year, we could select normal ship duty, Naval Flight Training, or the Marines.

Yep, Pensacola looked great, especially when I found out that my EDP orders had been lost in the transfer. You can bet that I didn't turn myself in as I probably should have. After all, I wasn't an "officer and gentleman" as decreed by Congress; I hadn't been commissioned yet. I was just a dirty, tired, college-age kid playing at being in the military. Not even a "wet behind the ears" Ensign, the lowest of the low. As a thin, tall midshipman trying to keep a low profile, sinking 36-foot boats worth $50,000 wasn't the way to do it. I resolved to walk a straight line at all times to avoid more problems. I almost made it.

After regular hours were over, one recreational activity which appealed to me was swimming in the ocean. I'll tell you, cold beers and tepid water beat the hell out of marching with a heavy rifle! One day I got to talking with an attractive young lady in a skimpy swim suit who invited me to a party that night in her home. Gee, that sounded great, could I bring a friend? Sure, we have room for one more. What time, and can I bring anything? Nope, just your appetite and your friend. Seven o'clock, and she gave me the address. It was on the base, and on

Officer's Row. Damn, things were looking up! Been here a week and already had a date! Not exactly, as it turned out.

George Griffen, a Notre Dame classmate, and I showed up promptly at seven. So did four other midshipmen. Rats! The testosterone level was pretty high on that front doorstep. The girl's mother greeted us graciously and invited us in. Jousting in an unmannerly manner to sit as close to the beautiful daughter as possible, we pretty much made fools out of ourselves. The young lady loved it, of course. Two other girls were there. They were not as good-looking as the daughter, but were a hell of a lot easier on the eyes than the midshipmen I'd been surrounded with that summer. Still, the numbers were not good; the girls had crafted odds of two to one in their favor. Oh well, it beat EDP.

After beer and chips had been passed around, and the jousting had subsided, the evening's entertainment commenced. The girl's father sat down in a corner of the living room and got out his violin. A violin! I thought, I'm going to have to sit here and pretend I'm enjoying myself? EDP was looking better. He started sawing away. It turned out he was a four-striper who had been selected for Rear Admiral, so the candy-ass Academy midshipmen were hanging on his every saw with great interest and rapt expressions. They teach brown nosing as a class at the Academy, I thought. This evening was going rapidly downhill. First, too many guys, and second, having to listen to a violin. But then things got worse.

George passed out. Toppled right out of his chair. I was mortified. Unknown to me, George was a full-fledged alcoholic, and hid his condition well. He had looked perfectly straight-faced when we walked over to the den of music. I sat down next to George, pretended it was a planned move, and continued to listen to the hen scratching. Then George stared snoring. Low

SOUR M.A.S.H. AT SEA - SECOND WAVE

wheezes at first, then rising gloriously to full-sounding fog horns. The violinist would falter. I would elbow George into silence. The violinist would pick up his cadence, and George would repeat his performance. It was awful. Finally the four-striper stopped playing and asked who knew this fellow? I ashamedly answered that I did, and after looking at my nameplate, the Captain, soon-to-be Rear Admiral, ordered me to remove myself and my friend from his home. We returned to our barracks. I was red-faced and angry over having missed an opportunity to spend time with someone other than a midshipman or Marine. George was oblivious to it all, stumbling happily along and singing a dirty song. I could have killed him.

The next morning I was summoned from class to meet with an angry officer, the one in charge of the midshipmen detachment. "Midshipman Stoodlemeir," he roared, (I thought it wise not to correct his pronunciation), "just what in hell did you do last night? I just got the chewing out of my life from Captain Wilson. Something about you ruining his daughter's party last night! What the hell went down, anyway?"

I told him what had happened, and that I was very sorry about my friend's bad manners. I also said, mistakenly, that we hadn't ruined the party, maybe interfered with it a little.

Wrong thing to say! "Listen you, I'll be the judge as to what damage you drunks did last night. Captain Wilson is mad as hell; that means I'm mad as hell also!" He summoned the Master-At-Arms who, apparently, had been waiting outside the door. A Master-At-Arms is an enlisted sailor, normally a Chief Petty Officer, which this one was, who serves as a cop. "Charlie, what do you think would be the appropriate punishment for someone stupid enough to spoil a captain's party?"

Walter "Bud" Stuhldreher

"Well, Sir, EDP seems to fill the bill."

"Charlie, normally I'd agree with you, but that poses a problem. Midshipman Stoodlemeir here, according to a set of orders that was delayed, but I just received, is supposed to be on permanent EDP already. An order he didn't feel it was necessary to share with us as he should have."

Damn, my past had caught up with me!

"Sir, since the midshipman is already on EDP that doesn't fit the situation, does it?"

"My sentiments exactly, Charlie. As of now, Midshipman Stoodlemeir is back on EDP until his sorry ass leaves our command to return to whatever sorry school he came from. And since normal EDP won't fill the bill I'll count on you to come up with something that will."

"Aye, aye Sir, I'll take care of it." And the Chief Petty Officer surely did.

When I reported to the chief at 1600 hours (4:00) he was waiting for me. He first had me sign for a rifle, another 16-pound monster. "Sonny, you get to march in this nice Florida sun every day carrying this," he smugly announced. "But since that would simply be normal EDP, I've decided your case deserves special gear. Here's a Fourth of July present for you." And he handed me a rucksack which was so heavy I almost dropped it. "Careful, sonny, we don't want to damage government property, do we?"

As a matter of fact, I didn't give a damn if I did, but thought it wise not to share my traitorous thoughts with this avid defender of freedom. He continued, "It probably didn't weigh as much before I filled it up with rocks. Say, sonny, do you know how hard it is to find rocks in Florida? I had to scare these up, just for you!" Oh boy, I wouldn't have minded one bit if he hadn't found any.

Next he led me out to a nearby track area, affixed the damnably heavy pack on my back, handed me my new rifle and pointed. "See that track, sonny? You're going to run around it until I say you can march. Then you march until I tell you to start running again. We're going to keep doing that for the next two hours. I don't think you're going to like it much, but that's your problem isn't it?" And off I trotted.

At first it wasn't too bad, I was young, thin, and in reasonably good shape. What I didn't understand was that the Navy knew a lot more about various punishments than I did. That pack got damn heavy after a couple of laps. My legs started to cramp; sweat was running down my face so heavily that I had trouble seeing. I waited anxiously for Captain Bligh to yell I could start marching, but of course he didn't.

After a couple more laps I stopped to upchuck my lunch. "You son of a bitch keep moving. Throw up while you run!" So I did. Then my legs gave out and down I went. "Gee, sonny, you've only been out here fifteen minutes and you're on your ass already. This is going to be fun. Now you just sit there until you're ready to go again, I'm in no hurry." And he returned to his chair under a tree, the only shade for miles around.

"How about some water?" I squeaked out.

"No, sonny, I'm afraid I didn't bring any." After I got my breath I started the drill once again.

Walter "Bud" Stuhldreher

And so it went, me running, upchucking, falling, and repeating the miserable drill. Finally it was 1800 hours (6:00). My two hours were up! I sat down, hard, not sure if I was ever going to get up again. "Sonny, what do you think you're doing?"

"Chief, it's 1800 hours, my time is up for today."

"Gee, sonny, did I forget to tell you that time not marching or running didn't count towards the two hours you owe me? I'm sorry but you owe me another thirty minutes so get your sorry ass in gear and move it!"

Well it was 1845 (6:45) before the sadistic sombitch was satisfied. He strolled back to the arms locker, me staggering along side of him. Collecting the pack and rifle he genially said he'd see me at 1600 hours tomorrow for some more fun. The bastard was thoroughly enjoying killing me.

The next three days were more of the same. I, of course, was getting in too late for dinner, even if I had felt like eating, which I didn't. I would go to bed, pass out, and haul myself painfully out of bed the next morning. I was a mess. Some junior officer learned what my EDP had turned into, and reported to the officer in charge that, in his opinion, it had gone too far. The top gun came to the track area that afternoon and promptly changed things. He approved the rifle and pack but made Captain Bligh reduce the pack's weight. And only marching was to be required. It was still one of the toughest drills I'd ever been through, but at least it was bearable now. Finishing at 1800 hours meant I could, once again, eat dinner. And, wouldn't you know it, that was the source of my next affront to the military establishment of the United States.

They had a curious rule at Pensacola that summer. We midshipman weren't allowed to walk to meals. We had to march with at least four middies at a time, and with a fifth middie in charge. It was just more bullshit the military is so fond of, and meant we had to wait until other middies were ready to go. One evening I was the fifth to show up which meant I had to march the four of them, and myself, to dinner. On the way, one of the middies scratched his crotch. A passing female sailor immediately put *me on report for making an obscene gesture towards her!* Another stupid regulation, one I hadn't known about. The person in charge of a unit was placed on report for anything untoward a member under his command did. Maybe this would have been fair if the guy in charge had a chance to discipline his troops, but we weren't in charge of anyone. I didn't even know their names! Nevertheless, rules are rules, and I was on report.

The top gun looked at me incredulously the next morning. "I swear, Stoodlemeir, you just can't seem to stay out of trouble, can you?" I assured him I was innocent and explained what happened.

"I'll tell you what, Stoodlemeir," he said in a conspiratorial whisper as he leaned towards me, "the next time you see that ass hole, why don't you get even with him and beat the shit out of him!" And chuckled uproariously at his shallow wit. "Meantime, of course, you're guilty of the crime as accused. A formal report of this incident will be made to your school. By the way, where do you go, anyway?"

"Notre Dame, Sir."

"Ah, well, they probably won't look too favorably on this report, will they?" he said, and commenced laughing uproariously again.

Walter "Bud" Stuhldreher

He was damn right about the last spear he threw at me. Shortly after reporting back to school that fall I was summoned to the NROTC Captain's office. An unsmiling Captain held several pieces of paper in front of him. "Been a busy lad this summer, have you? Sunk an expensive boat belonging to the Navy, did you? Caused a scene at a Captain's party in his own home, did you? Made an obscene gesture toward a female Navy person, did you? *God in Heaven what were you thinking? You are a disgrace to this command, this university, your parents and yourself!*"

On and on he ranted, never giving me a chance to get a word in. I mean, he went on for at least twenty minutes before, thankfully, he ran out of breath. "Sir, I can explain, mostly, what happened. It really wasn't as bad as it sounds." Whoops! Not what the Captain wanted to hear. It turned out he didn't give a rat's ass (his words) what I thought about anything. I was there to listen, and listen I did. He finally booted me out of his office, telling me he was going to keep his eyes on me, that I was dead meat as far as he was concerned; that if he could heave me out of the program he would. Unfortunately for him, it didn't appear I could get thrown out for summer midshipmen training transgressions. Too damn bad about that, he concluded.

Then, surprisingly, he switched the conversation. "I am pleased by your showing during the exercise in the flight trainer." For the first time I noticed his Navy wings above his salad bar. (The rows of ribbons on his left chest.) "Yes, sir, you did just fine. The report says you were the only midshipman, out of sixteen in your flight, who didn't throw up during the acrobatic exercises. Good show, that!" I didn't have the heart to tell him it had been a close encounter, that I had the barf bag in front of my face the last half of the exercise. And probably didn't upchuck because I was the only middie aloft that day without a trace of alcohol in his system. In addition to EDP I was restricted to the base. We later learned the pilots had tried to get us sick on purpose. It was their way to try to sort out the natural flyers from the pretenders. The Captain had one more thing to say, "Oh, by the way, you are due in the President's office after your last class tomorrow. Now get out of here."

The next afternoon I trudged up the side stairs of the Administration building (only graduates were allowed to use the main stairs). This is the building under the famous Golden Dome. I looked forward to this meeting with the president, Father John J. Cavanaugh, C.S.C., as much as a root canal without Novocain. I found his office and went in, to be greeted by a smoldering priest with a smoldering pipe. Father Cavanaugh didn't ask me to sit down, just peered at me without enthusiasm. "Stuhldreher, I can't believe how much trouble you have been in during the summer. It's obvious you don't know how to conduct yourself off the campus. What's more troubling, you've trashed a famous name, one which is closely identified with this university. I'm terribly disappointed with you."

The Four Horsemen of Notre Dame. Uncle Harry Stuhldreher, Quarterback, is the fellow on the right.

I just stood there, trying to appear 2'6" instead of my normal 6'2". Father Cavanaugh continued, "It goes without saying, either your deportment improves or your presence on this campus will no longer be permitted. Think it over, your nine lives are up, as far as I'm concerned. You may leave now." Then he called to me as I slunk out of his office. "And, Walter, much as it pains me, I'm going to have to inform your parents about our conversation. It's a shame that you have disgraced a fine family." Pained him, huh? I was pretty sure it was going to pain me a lot more than him and I was right. The next phone call from my father was short, nasty and explicit. Shape up or ship out.

I'm going to let you in on a secret: that was one summer I'd just as soon forget, but here I am, fifty years later, telling you about it. Sure haven't forgotten it, have I? And, except for sinking a $50,000 boat earlier that summer, really none of it was my fault, was it? At least I don't think so, but I can understand there might be those who disagree. The Navy, of course.

MOOSE MISCHIEF

Traveling Around New England

In May of 2003 my wife, Bettie, daughter Beth, and her friend Kevin and I spent a week in New England, specifically Maine, Vermont and New Hampshire. We had wanted to see that part of America for some time, realizing it would be very different from the Georgia-Florida area where we live. Boy! were we right, as different as night and day.

We landed at the Portland, Maine, International airport, and after picking up our very nice rental car, we headed to a floating restaurant for lobster. That lobster pie was the perfect way to start a trip in New England! Expensive, but delicious.

Notice I said "a very nice rental car." When I called Avis to reserve the car, the agent said the quoted price got us a midsize car. Realizing the four of us, all tall people, with an outlandish amount of luggage, would probably be more than the car could comfortably handle, I asked how much extra the next bigger size car would cost.

"Three dollars."

"You mean per day?"

"No sir, per week."

I could hardly believe it, why hadn't she tried to sell more car if the price differential was so small? I pressed on, escalating in three dollars increments. I topped out at a Buick LeSabre with all the bells and whistles. I actually asked what the next bigger car would be when I quit. The agent replied it would be a Cadillac, and I really didn't want to know how much extra it would cost; it was much more expensive. Looking back, I realize I should have specifically asked how much more. Maybe it would have only been $20 more a week. Avis's definition and my idea of the price differences was very different.

Heading west to our resort in North Conway, New Hampshire, we soon realized the road system was vastly different from what we were used to. I believe I-93 is the only road up there which carries much traffic. On the east-west two-lane roads, which we traveled on 95 percent of the time, we literally could go for miles without encountering another car. During that week we were *never* passed by a car, nor did we pass one. Try that in Georgia or Florida! There was no road kill on the pavement. No dead possums, snakes or armadillos as in

Florida. No birds either. During our week there, I saw less than a dozen birds, excluding gulls in coastal towns,. Perhaps the migratory birds hadn't yet arrived for the summer season.

There were no large open spaces visible, just a succession of small towns interspersed with very small farms, and trees everywhere in between. There were two interesting road signs which we saw all over New England. One was "Pavement stops in 500 yards." That's it. Just a sign telling you the pavement was going to end shortly. Not why, not for how long, just that it was ending. It was pretty scary the first time we encountered such a sign, but we got used to them. They turned out to be road improvement projects, but unlike most such repairs which left one lane open for use, they wiped out both lanes. We bumped along on what was left, usually a dirt roadbed. Strange. Another ubiquitous sign was "Moose crossing — next 5 miles (or 10 or 20)." Now I'm not exactly sure what a driver is supposed to do after seeing one. Slow down to 20 miles an hour? Ten miles an hour? Even at ten miles an hour, I suspect that a moose, quickly darting out into the road, would cause an accident. Never did learn what to do. With a normal top speed of 50 mph, we were going slow enough. A further reduction in speed would have tied us with snails, if there are any up there. And New Hampshire doesn't kid around with their speed signs. We found out the roads permitted safe passage only at the recommended speeds. Exceed them at your peril.

The houses were typically what you would expect to find in New England. Wooden, with contrasting shutters. The paint was uniformly new, the style Victorian. The people, though, were entirely unexpected. We were expecting taciturn, reticent New Englanders, as described in the many novels where the locale is set in that area. Not true. Without exception, they were friendly, open, loquacious and eager to help. Some of the nicest people I've ever been around. And the food! Those people serve huge helpings of delicious food. Would you believe you can buy lobster rolls at McDonald's? Yep, sure enough. Good, too. We never had an average meal there. Eating in a variety of places, we found every meal outstanding. The restaurants serve the largest helpings and the most diversified menu offerings I have ever run across. Another interesting aspect of New England, at least to us southerners, was the cold water. Right out of the tap, it was wonderfully cold. Not like down in Florida.

A McDonalds's ad sign

The Old Man of the Mountain

A pall was hanging over the communities of New Hampshire, however. The "Old Man of the Mountain" had slipped to his demise on May 4, 2003, shortly before we got there. A huge granite outcropping in the White Mountains looked like the facial profile of an old man and had probably been in existence for thousands of years. He is featured on their new state quarter, on the state flag, and all state highway signs show his outlined face. Mugs, tee shirts, and souvenirs of all kinds carry his image. As one of the locals told us, "The folks here are devastated." We ate at one restaurant where the marquee simply read: "R.I.P. OLD MAN." We were flabbergasted that they felt so strongly about it. A state committee has been formed to figure out a proper replacement. What can they do? A fiberglass replica won't be the same.

I loved the quaint names of the towns we passed: Sugar Hill, Waterville Valley, Sandwich, Center Harbor, Rumney, Twin Mountain - to name just a few. Restaurants, too, had great names: Clark's Trading Post, Hobo R.R., Loon Mountain Pub, Flying Moose Restaurant, The Clamshell Restaurant, and my favorite, The Hungry Rhino, complete with a picture of a brown rhinoceros. Do you suppose there are many rhinoceroses up in the New England mountains? I wanted to stop and ask the restaurant where the name came from, but was outvoted three to one on that idea.

We took a trip up The Mount Washington Cog Railway. The first cog railway in the world, it was built in 1869. ("For tourists, like you," the railroad engineer responded when I asked him why it was built. Think of that: a cog railway built up a

Walter "Bud" Stuhldreher

mountain 6,280 feet high that long ago. What tourists, I wondered.) One reason we took this trip was, unlike the climbers of Mount Everest who do it "Because it's there," it was at the top of this mountain, in the terrible storm of April 1934 that the highest winds ever recorded on earth were experienced. Two hundred and thirty-four mph! The morning we were there, snow still lingered in the sheltered areas and a stiff wind was blowing. At the top is a rustic snack shop. There were Appalachian Trail hikers, plenty of them, who used the rest rooms to take sponge baths.

Moose Mischief

One noon, after eating lunch in Franconia, NH, (passing up where I wanted to eat, "Polly's Pancake Parlor") we went next door to a bakery shop with the wonderful name "The Grateful Bread," only to find it was closed. A sign on the door said "Closed today from 12 to 3." Strange sign for a place of business. Bettie guessed it might be closed because of a funeral.

Driving along a few more miles, we entered the town of Sugar Hill and encountered a traffic jam. Cars were parked along both sides of the narrow two-lane road, making driving difficult. (Road shoulders in New Hampshire were typically only a foot or so wide; thus the cars were parked halfway on the road.) A crowd of people, mostly dressed up, were gathered in front of a church. Passing slowly by, we noticed many were walking towards another church, some carrying food. Bettie guessed the funeral was in one church, the reception in the second one.

Next door to the second church, just before Sugar Hill's Meeting House, was our next shopping destination, Harmon's Cheese & Country Store. In a very old building, the Harmons had started a store in 1954. It had been purchased by the Aldrich family (Bert, Maxine and Brenda) in 1981, who continue to operate it in the same tradition. In addition to cheddar and other cheeses, the store offers "Unusual one-of-a kind delicacies" such as pure maple products, smoked salmon, smoked baby clams, Pacific oysters, berry preserves, and New England common crackers. Also blue crab meat, she-crab soup, kipper fillets, Zelda's homemade jams, NH lollipop tree preserves, mountain brook marmalades, soldier beans, Kenyon's Indian Pudding, and Gormly's Maple Apple Drizzle. My favorite item was Grampa Gilman's Skin Care, olive oil and honey wax discs, offering "pure and natural relief from chapping." Down South, we don't have many problems with chapping but I thought you Yankees might be interested.

Brenda Aldrich, the proprietor, greeted us with a cheery hello and told us to look around. Meanwhile we had to excuse her for running out front every few minutes. She was in sympathy with the mourners, and wanted to handle the situation delicately, but cars for the funeral attendees were taking up her customers' parking places. Bettie said someone important must have died since there were so many mourners. (We all hoped that she wouldn't say the funeral was for The Old Man of the Mountain, and it wasn't.) Mrs. Aldrich replied that yes, it was someone important. In fact it was a "five town" funeral. Very sad. I asked her what she meant by a "five town" funeral. Well, a prominent businessman who lived in Sugar Hill and owned a motorcycle shop in Littletown had been killed by a moose. His wife was a Vice-Principal at a school in Franconia. Since he coached high school golf in Bethleham and played trumpet in a jazz band in Berlin, it was a "five town" funeral.

I was fascinated by her answer. "Killed by a moose? How?" I asked Mrs. Aldrich, and learned that he had run into a moose while on his motorcycle. "Gee, does that happen often?" Mrs. Aldrich didn't know, but thought it was rare.

The topper was Mrs. Aldrich's kindly refusal to sell Kevin a used book. (There was a small bookcase in the store with used paperbacks for sale for 25 cents and used hardbacks for 50 cents, with the proceeds going to a local charity.) Kevin was nonplused by her refusal and asked why. "I haven't read it yet," Mrs. Aldrich replied, "and I never sell a book until I've read it. I'm a real book lover!" What a great answer! I loved her for it.

But all those moose signs had left me wondering. How many cars hit a moose a year in New Hampshire? I decided to find out and called the New Hampshire Division of Motor Vehicles. After first swearing I wasn't an ambulance chaser trying to drum up a source of business, I finally got an unequivocal answer: didn't know.

I pressed on, "Just what do you know?"

Ah, the right question. "In 2002 there were 1,490 nonfatal road accidents with an animal."

"How many involved moose?"

"Don't know. We don't break down the non-fatalities by type of animal."

Damn, this was like pulling teeth. But surely some involved moose?"

"Yeah, some for sure."

OK, now for the $64,000 question: "Were there any fatalities caused by a collision with a moose?"

"Yeah, one fatality."

So, as near as I could find out, in 2002 there were at least several moose collisions with one fatality. There seem to be an inordinate number of "Moose Crossing" signs, given only one fatality, but I suppose there's an added benefit to the signs in that they probably keep the tourists alert and that's good. As you can tell, they certainly got me thinking. And there was at least one fatal road accident in 2003, the fellow on his motorcycle.

The moose in the road reminded me of other animal-in-the-road incidents. It reminded me of riding in a twelve-passenger, commercial van while coming home to Merritt Island, Florida,

Walter "Bud" Stuhldreher

from the airport in Orlando. It was April, and the normally lethargic male alligators were on the move since it was mating season. We smashed into a big fellow, and it tore up the van's transmission. A driver of a Camero, hot on our tail, scrunched the alligator, and tore up his transmission also. The big alligator slowed up some, but kept on moving. That female must have been one good looking gator! Incidentally a big gator goes five hundred pounds while a mature moose weighs three times as much, so hitting a moose with a car is bad business. I've since wondered who got the moose meat.

When I went to pay for our purchases, Mrs. Aldrich surprised me once again. "Oh, I don't take credit cards, a check or cash will do fine." An out-of-state check from a stranger was preferable to a credit card? We later decided I must have an extremely honest-looking face.

Due to bad weather we missed going on a planned whale watching excursion but otherwise packed in a lot of sightseeing into a short week. It's a great part of our wonderful country to see and I recommend it highly. And if any of you go, will you please let me know what they did about replacing the Old Man on the Mountain. I'd like to hear the end of that story ... and watch out for moose.

THE PSA PGA

Golf is a lifetime sport, so they tell us, and with certain modifications, it is. I cannot play the same game I played 20 years ago, or even 10 years ago. But ONE GOOD SHOT a game is enough to bring a golfer out for another round. Golf has been a source of friendship, self competition and outdoor activity from my teen years through to the geezer years. Here are a few golfing stories.

Azalea Festival - 1955

The Navy had requested one unmarried officer from the *Kleinsmith* to represent the Navy at the 1955 Azalea Festival. Although I had no idea what my duties might be, it sounded good, so I pulled rank and volunteered. Arriving in Wilmington, N.C., I was greeted my one of the many officials. (You could tell them by their blazers, badges and perpetual smiles.) "Look here, son," he said, "here's the keys to a brand new convertible, it's yours for the week." Since the Festival ran Thursday through Sunday, this was the first of many exaggerations I was to run into that week. "And you have been assigned as escort to Queen Barbara White, from Salem College. You also are going to have as much Wild Turkey as you want." (Wild turkey? Was it any good? As a city boy from Indiana I had only a passing acquaintance with turkeys. I had eaten it at Thanksgivings and maybe a couple of other times a year, but had never had wild turkey, that's for sure. This was supposed to be a plus?) The enthusiastic greeter continued. "Now that's what I call a real good deal for you, son." At least that's what I think he said. His Southern accent was stronger than White Lightning. "Yes, sir, a beautiful gal to squire around, a great car, and all the finest whiskey in the world to drink! Now all we ask of you are two things: Show up sober at required appearances and don't smash up the car. You think you can handle that?"

You betcha! This deal was sounding better and better, especially now that I understood Wild Turkey was a fine Kentucky bourbon.

He next introduced me to Miss Barbara White from Salem College. And Miss White introduced me to a picture of her fiancé, a huge fellow whose tee shirt had to have been bought from a tent and awning store. "Just so we understand each other this weekend, you need to know that Bubba is a football player and is very possessive about me. So don't be getting any ideas."

SOUR M.A.S.H. AT SEA - SECOND WAVE

Barbara White, Salem College

Since Miss White was a hellava looker, she must have been reading my lustful mind. But seeing King Kong there, with a shave and a shirt on, drove the impure thoughts out of my mind, all the way to Vatican City, if you want to know the truth. And my old teachers from grade school, the nuns who used to hold twelve-inch rulers between us at dances, would have been proud of me that weekend. They could have held a yardstick and not touched either Miss White or me!

One of the feature events that week was the $12,500 National PGA Azalea Open Golf Tournament at the Cape Fear Country Club. Think of that! The whole purse was $12,500! Chicken feed today, but it was and is a reasonably important tournament. Previous winners included many of the big names in golf, and I saw almost all of them at the tournament that year. One evening, while waiting in a hotel lobby for my queen to get ready, something she was always doing that weekend, I saw Dow Finsterwald crossing the lobby. He had shot a wonderful round that day, in the low sixties, and I went over and congratulated him on his fine play. He thanked me, but then said, "Did you see that six-footer I missed on #13? I should have made that!" A typical golfer's answer. Shot a round that duffers like me could only dream about, yet he was critical that it should have been better! What a great game.

Golf in Cleveland, 1957-1959

Have you ever heard the term "rat-golf?" Well, that's the kind of golf I played in Cleveland when I lived there in 1957-1959. Here's what it was like.

Cleveland, in spite of a population of over a million, only had two public golf courses. One was a 9-hole course called "Little Muni." The other had 18 holes and was called "Big Muni." That's where I played. In order to speed up play, the authorities had removed all rough, traps, trees, and anything that would slow down the golfers. It was like being in a WW I "No man's land," since golf balls were forever whizzing by your head. Sometimes they didn't make it by! We hit out of divots the size of craters. (Maintenance was a low priority at Big Muni.) Good golfers were rarely seen there. They wanted a truer test of their skills, and wangled invitations to the private clubs.

The worst feature, of many bad ones, was the starters' insistence that a new group tee off every eight minutes. It didn't make any difference if a foursome was in the fairway waiting for the group ahead to finish putting and clear the green, down came the tee shots, accompanied by a useless chorus of "Fore!" It probably did speed up play; however, it didn't do much for the quality of play.

In order to get to play on Saturdays and Sundays, the only days available to the working stiffs, of whom I was one, we faced a daunting procedure. Since reservations were not allowed, every guy in our foursome took his turn getting to the course around 4 a.m. Parking in the dark, he scurried to the hill behind the starter's shack. A four-foot long tube, straightened out at the bottom, was the objective. Selecting a well-marked ball so it could easily be identified later, he dropped the ball into the tube. Then he immediately bent over to hear how far down it dropped until it was stopped by the balls in front of it. The distance it dropped told him, roughly, how many foursomes were in front of him and when we might expect to tee off. He then returned to his car, either to sleep (if possible), drink coffee, or eat anything he had brought with him. The small pro shop, complete with rest rooms and a snack shop, didn't open until 7 a.m.

The other three members of the foursome slept in and arrived around 9 a.m. After listening to a sleepy guess as to our probable tee time, we putted on the small putting green and drank coffee out of plastic cups from the snack shop. There was, of course, no practice range where we could warm up our swing. The Big Muni wasn't much into amenities.

About half an hour before we expected to tee off, we stationed one of our group next to the bottom of the tube where it flattened out. He could see the next four balls in line. When our ball was in sight, he called the other three guys over so we would be ready to tee off when our ball was first in line. If we missed our turn it was, "Next week, Baby" (which reminds me of Dick Vitale, the basketball announcer).

At one time the tube was simply an open track, and all the balls were visible. This system was changed when too many fights erupted. One group would accuse another of putting their ball farther down the track, in the middle of the lined-up balls, rather than at the top where they should have taken the last position. While fights remained common on the course, courtesy of angry golfers chasing someone who had hit them

Walter "Bud" Stuhldreher

with a ball, at least the enclosed tube ended fights before the course opened.

All of my regular foursome worked at the same place, US Steel. After finishing the round, we met at a bar for drinks and sandwiches, replaying the round, lamenting the bad bounces and either congratulating, or commiserating, as the case might be, on living through one more round without getting hit. Yep, you had to be tough to play Big Muni. We also had to be tough when we dragged our half-baked asses home to face the wrath of our wives who, once again, had believed us when we had said, "I'll be home in time for lunch, honey."

PGA Golf in Indianapolis - Early 1960's

They used to hold a PGA tournament at the Indianapolis 500 Speedway golf course in the early 60's. The course was a shaggy one, with several of the opening holes (#1 through #4) outside the track, then nine holes (#5 through #13) inside the famous two and a half mile oval, then the final holes (#14 through #18) once again outside of the track. This meant you finished the first nine holes miles from the club house. But the worst feature was the terrible layout of holes #5 through #13 which were inside the track. Since tens of thousands of cars parked in the infield on qualifying days, and on the day of the race, it was absolutely level. Not a raised green, tee or bunker in sight. A really boring nine holes. Jack Nicklaus played it once and never returned. I understand it has been rebuilt since then, and, supposedly, is a much finer layout, but I haven't seen the new course.

One tournament, I followed Bob Goalby around all day. I can't tell you what he shot, I don't remember. What I do remember is Goalby's coming off each green but not proceeding to the next tee until the guys behind us had hit into the green.

One of them was tearing up the course, making one magnificent shot after another. Goalby waited to see these remarkable shots, exclaiming out loud, "Damn, did you see that! What a shot!" His admiration for his fellow competitor's shot making skills was evident. I was struck by his conduct, openly admiring his competitor's skill. So different from other big-time sports, I thought. It could happen only in golf. I still feel the same way.

The Capital City Golf Gang - 1989

Every golf club has a bunch of old duffers who tee up every week day. Retired, they leave the weekends open for the younger members who are still working. We call those young dudes "flat bellies" — you know, the guys who can still see their belts and shoes without bending over, the ones whose waist measurements haven't expanded past their chest measurements. We pretty much despise them and their 250 yard drives. Our expectations are much lower. In fact, our favorite sayings are "The grass looks a lot better looking down on it than up at it," and another: "You know you're old when you have more doctors than friends." Another is how we pick out a shirt to wear prior to eating out. We always choose a color which matches what we're going to eat that night so it won't show when we spill food on our chest. You get the idea. Just surviving to play another day is triumph enough. Accordingly, we have an unspoken rule to never talk about our ailments; it's too depressing, and no one wants to hear about another guy's troubles.

One exception is our PSA numbers. I swear that, collectively, we know more about prostate cancer, and the various treatments available, than any urologist in Tallahassee. I'll never forget the time when the young lady driving the beverage cart overheard us discussing our numbers and asked, "Is that some sort of SAT score?"

We solemnly answered her, while hiding our snickers, that indeed it was. It, too, determined our chances for a good life!

The first such gang I joined in Tallahassee was at the Capital City Country Club, the oldest country club in Tallahassee. When it started in 1908, initiation fees were one dollar, as were the annual dues. Quite a bargain. The oldsters tee off at 12:30 every weekday and have been playing for years. I once asked old Doc Morris, who ran the deal, how long they had been playing. "Don't know, Walt," he replied, "I've only been in it 35 years."

Before my first round, one of the players, Dick Ervin, a retired Chief Justice of the Florida Supreme Court, warned me about displaying bad manners on the course. "Walter," he informed me, "never, never throw your clubs. I used to be guilty of that, but I haven't thrown one in 15 years." Later I learned the Judge was around 85 at the time he said this to me. I also learned he had played golf there all his life, and figured he had played over 7,000 rounds at Capital City, starting when it was a 9-hole course with sand greens. So, I reflected, when mad, he had thrown his clubs until he was seventy years old! Since I wasn't even 60 yet when I got his etiquette lesson, and had never thrown a club in anger, I figured my manners would hold up all right.

One of the Judge's favorite stories, and he had many, was the first time he played golf with the Duke of Windsor in 1949. The Duke and the Duchess were regular freeloaders at the huge plantations in Thomasville, Georgia, a small town about 25 miles north of Tallahassee. Their private course, Glen Arvin, was the oldest in the area, having been formed in 1892. Thomasville was very active in those days for one reason: the southbound railroad lines ended there (South Florida was still a swamp). Congressmen in Washington, D.C. had encouraged the railroad to extend the lines down to Thomasville, even though it didn't carry enough traffic to justify the expense. But the congressmen needed a place to install their mistresses away from official Washington society. They owned plantations there, and used the railway to visit their mistresses and play golf in the winter. Quail hunting was also a big winter activity. This was a strange source of the money needed to establish these beautiful plantations, and the town, but I guess no one cared. Especially the local merchants.

The Judge knew, more than he probably wanted to, about the Duke's unsavory manners on the golf course. A smallish man, the Duke thought his "you know what" didn't stink. Since he thought he was still royalty, he never carried any money. This didn't stop him from betting, but it did stop him from paying off when he lost. Of course, when he won he expected to be paid immediately. And since he carried no money, he left it up to the other members of the foursome to pay his caddie, a privilege they would have gladly passed up. So the Judge was prepared for his introduction to the Duke.

The Duke announced himself to the Judge with all the gravity the small man could muster: "*I* am the Duke of Windsor."

This was prior to the Judge's election to the Florida Supreme Court, and he was the Attorney General for the State of Florida that year. So the Judge fired back, "And *I* am the General!" Then, smiling ever so slightly, he turned away.

One other story about the Judge. Several years ago the small Florida coastal town of Panacea, his birthplace, decided to erect a statue of the Judge, their most famous native son. The Judge tried to talk them out of this, telling them they should never erect a statue of a living person; the person might yet get into trouble of some kind, and it would embarrass the town. The Mayor replied, "Dick, you're too old to get into trouble!" And Panacea went ahead.

I've often wondered if the good citizens of the Irish town of Ballybunion regret their statue of Bill Clinton holding a driver. They built it after Clinton, while President, played the famed Ballybunion Golf Club with 20,000 people watching. Clinton cheated his way to a score of 95. Incidentally, it is the only statue of Clinton anywhere in the world.

One last story about Capital City Country Club. The oldest club in town, it not only had the "movers and shakers" in its membership, it was also somewhat inbred. (Still sells chewing tobacco in the pro shop.) I can best illustrate this by relating what happened one afternoon on the course. A small club, we pretty well knew everyone else, especially the other golfers. But in the foursome in front of us was a guy we didn't know. I asked Tom, a retired orange grove farmer, if he knew who he was. "No, Walter, I don't know his name, but I know what he is: **a damn Yankee from Atlanta!**" Along those lines, early on they had told me the difference between a "Yankee" and a "Damn Yankee." "Yankees" move back north. "Damn Yankees" stay.

The S.L.U.G.S. - 1994

I next joined Killearn Country Club where I joined an old duffers' gang which tees off every Monday, Wednesday and Friday mornings and is called the S.L.U.G.S. This stands for **S**pencer's **L**ighthearted **U**nskilled **G**olfer's **S**ociety. It was named after its founder, Tom Spencer, who is too old to play much now. We're extremely fond of Tom. Not only is he a very nice guy to play golf with, we also admire him greatly. Tom has a son who's mentally challenged. Every morning Tom takes him to his job and picks him up every afternoon, never complaining. And Tom always has a positive attitude. There's a guy to admire.

Our present leader is Burt, a genius at getting free things for the group. A few weeks ago, for example, we played at the Florida State University Golf Course for the low price of $12.75, which included cart fees. I don't know how he does it. We have an annual best ball tournament, a "S.L.U.G.S. Fest," where we play in sixsomes with our non-golfing wives (husbands and wives do not play in the same group). Burt produces enough prizes for everyone to win at least one prize, and usually more than one. Drinks abound, and special food, contributed by local merchants, is plentiful.

The members are a disparate bunch. Warren is called "The Linguini Kid." Once — that's all it took — he wore a gruesome pork pie hat that was much too small for him. Furnished at some sort of Italian event he had played in, it had "The Linguini Open" emblazoned across the front.

Fred, 84 years young, still carries his bag and doesn't carry a driver, saying he doesn't need one, the course is too short. You could write him off as an eccentric except that, until this year, he shot his age several times a month. Shooting your age is our Holy Grail, and most of us have as much chance of achieving that goal as Ponce de Leon had in finding the water which would bring eternal youth. (Much of his search was in this area.) One of my favorite stories about Fred happened on the day his wife met mine. Bettie commented that she believed their husbands played golf together. Fred's wife answered: "That's right, but Fred is a *good* golfer!"

Dan has, like most of us, a swing like no-one else's. Winding up like a baseball player, Dan violates everything you are taught about a good swing. He takes a mighty cut, ending up with all his weight on his right foot, his left foot waving in the air, the reverse of a good golfer. Who cares? Dan plays a very good game and shot a 78 the last time I played with him.

"Stan the Man," so named because he doesn't weigh 120 pounds dripping wet, simply raises his clubs over his head, then drops the club on the ball. No strength involved whatever. But if his little white pellet is one inch off his desired path he gets mad. I mean the sucker hits them straight! Inside 80 yards Stan is a killer. I swear he gets up and down over 60 percent of the time. You could be two strokes better when you arrive near a green, but then when Stan whips you, it takes the wind out of your sails.

Dick is a retired professor, thinner than an exclamation mark, and wears two gloves. He doesn't care what he shoots, or what you shoot. He is out there to enjoy himself, and he does.

Del, everyone claims, could play Santa Claus without needing any kind of artificial help. Tall, with a widening waistline, he has a thick shock of long white hair, dense white eyebrows, a thick white mustache and a long white beard, so he truly could. The pony tail would have to be hidden, but that's it. He is an ideal Santa Claus except when it comes to betting on golf. Then Del plays an excellent game and doesn't give away gifts or money.

Rich, a big heavy guy, has a swing no-one else wants. Come to think of it, neither does Rich. He spends more time in the woods than Paul Bunyon ever did. We have suggested he wear a big cow bell so we can find him more easily, but he hasn't taken us up on that kind suggestion.

Forrest, a tall former actuary, is from the planet Moron. Nothing else explains his eccentric habits. More than once he has shown up at the first tee without his clubs. He is one of the worst cart drivers we have, and that's saying something. Forrest once managed to throw me out of the cart and we weren't even on a hill. At least once on each hole he forgets there is another guy riding in the cart with him. While you stand there by your ball, without a club, you helplessly watch Forrest driving off down the fairway. Just this morning I saw Forrest in the pro shop. "Hey, Forrest, haven't seen you for a while. Where you been?"

"Oh, I've been out of town — don't remember where." And he nonchalantly went on signing in, leaving us to wonder about him, once again.

Charlie is a redneck. A swell guy, very funny, but I'm sorry, that's what he is. His southern accent is so thick I often have trouble understanding him. Once, on a golfing trip we passed through Monticello, a small town near here. Charlie started telling us about his second marriage which took place in the town hall there. He had all of us in the car in hysterics. Seems the town gives newlyweds a brown paper sack of goodies which includes Tampax, two toothbrushes, a paperback Bible and a box of condoms. In addition to telling us about that remarkable gift, Charlie went on to tell about his first wife attending his second wedding and yelling, "**Go, Girl, Go!**" in a loud voice. She was cheering the new bride on, he told us.

Bill is a Naval Academy graduate and a proper, retired four-striper. He has read some of my stories and is fond of telling the guys how thankful he is that I was never in his command. I'm pretty sure I am too.

Walter "Bud" Stuhldreher

Glenn is never called that, "Zip" being our name for him. Why? Simple. He was Assistant Operations Manager, Information Systems, for the University of Akron for 25 years and that's the school's nickname. They got that singular nickname because the zipper was invented in Akron. See the important and useful stuff you can learn if you just read my stories?

Ben is a retired professor of philosophy and more wordy than Plato. You have to wait for Ben to shut up before each swing. But he is surprisingly knowledgeable about a variety of current subjects, thus is an interesting, if annoying, golfing companion.

Les wears a cloth fedora adorned with the metal insignia of every country and city he's visited, and he has traveled all over. The hat makes a nice, tinkley sound as he swings. And what a swing! Les takes two abrupt practice swings and, while still in motion, steps up to his ball without stopping and hits in earnest. Looks like he's afflicted with St. Vitus's Dance. As Les says "If I can synchronize my lunges and lurches I've got a chance to hit the ball!"

Another fellow who's traveled all over is Geoff. Born in England, he worked his entire life in South Africa. I'm not sure how he got to the United States. Most of the guys don't say much about their working careers, which is a shame, since some, like Geof, could tell some interesting tales.

Geoff, like many of us, has an incontinence problem. (If you ever have prostrate cancer surgery you'll know what I mean.) Since our course has 27 holes, with only three rest rooms on the course, this leads to problems. With lots of trees available, this worked out OK until the neighbors started complaining. Apparently golfers taking a whiz in their backyards wasn't high on their social agenda. Accordingly, the club passed a rule:

Either use the rest rooms or hold it. We feel this rule is discriminatory towards us older golfers, but so far we haven't gone to court over it. That's been discussed, however.

Gary is a large, very friendly fellow with more friends than anyone else. Gary has never met a stranger. When I was diagnosed with diabetes he was extremely helpful to me while I was learning to cope with it. This was sorta strange since Gary, who is also a diabetic, has never taken proper care of himself. A side problem of diabetes is poor circulation in the lower legs and feet. When Gary had to have his toes removed I sent him a card which my wife, Bettie, thought was in terrible taste. The front of the card showed a framed jock strap hanging up on a wall. The inside showed ten framed toes up on a wall. The caption read: "I've heard of guys nailing their jock strap up when they retired, but their toes?" Gary loved it. I knew he would. I guess it's a guy thing.

Dick, from Napierville, Illinois, is an urbane fellow, easily the classiest dresser among us. He is on the Club's Advisory Board, so he often identifies himself with the Club's management. Since the S.L.U.G.S. enjoy bitching about the way the club is being run, we watch our comments around Dick. Sometimes, anyway.

Finally, Harry, a retired orthopedic surgeon. When I first met Harry I was surprised to learn he was retired since he was so young, so I asked him why. He told me his eyes had gone bad, and he could no longer see well enough to operate. I then promptly stuck my size thirteen shoes in my mouth by exclaiming, "Oh, God, I hope you quit in time!" He looked at me strangely, but assured me he thought he had. Hell, what's one more blooper? My life has been full of them.

Walter "Bud" Stuhldreher

Not in our group, but a fellow golfer we admire tremendously, is Bob Andrews. Bob is totally blind, and Tina, his wife, is his coach. (Bob lost his sight to a grenade in Vietnam in 1967.) Together they make up one of the best teams in the United States Blind Golf Association. Sometimes, if Tina isn't available, we see Bob playing with Peter Richardson, a part-time club employee, as his coach. Peter is a dashing immigrant from England and has carefully maintained his English appearance, accent and colloquialisms. His white mustache is carefully cut in a Guards manner, and one and all, you are "mate." Very energetic, he is a delight to be around, and tells great stories. Strangely enough, he is a sought-after square dance "caller" all over the Southeast. Imagine. A caller with a strong English accent. Killearn Country Club uses him in all their TV ads. I suppose he projects the "upper crust" image the club wishes prospective members to imagine they will rub elbows with.

Bob Andrews on left, with Peter Richardson

In the summer of 2003 Peter and Bob went to England to play in the British Blind Open at the West Essex Golf Club on Bury Road, Chingford, London. In their instructions to the players they warned them that "A limited number of buggies will be available at West Essex. The golf course undulates with a few sloping fairways and a few gradients. It cannot be described as either easy or hard walking." Doesn't that sound English? Bob did well over there, finishing second in the Open and third in the celebrity pro-am. Since returning, Bob did something we duffers only dream about: he played 18 holes without a three putt! Amazing! Blind and no three putts.

What an adventure! And what a gracious thing for Peter to do. Peter has been Bob's coach for 12 years, so going to other courses with him is not a new experience for Peter. They went to the Ken Venturi Seeing Eye Tournament in Westchester County, New York, four years ago. Bob finished sixth. Bob does have one advantage over us golfers who can see. When playing a new course, neither Tina nor Peter tell him when he's facing a shot over water. No use putting him under undue pressure, they say!

Another club employee we're all fond of is Jack Brookshaw, the Supervisor of the cart guys. Jack is over 40, but looks younger than 30, damn him. An extremely hard worker, Jack has a photographic memory and not only knows every member's name (and there's 800 of us), he knows our wives' names and who plays with whom. More important, he knows who won't ride with whom. That trick saves embarrassing moments. Jack is extremely good looking, charms all the ladies and is the best joke teller I know. He also works two nights a week as a bartender, plus does odd jobs that members want done at their houses. Once, he even considered laying tile for our daughter, and she lives in Atlanta!

Since there are about 40 guys in each of the groups, you can see I have barely scratched the surface in describing them, but these vignettes are enough for you to get the idea. We're not

Walter "Bud" Stuhldreher

much into dressy clothes, only wearing collars on our shirts because the club won't let us play unless we do. The group is big on strong elastic socks which are worn up to their knees. We have one 13-year heart transplant survivor, Harry. There are many joint replacement guys, and just as many, like myself, who need one. Knee braces are big sellers, too.

They are a fun bunch to play golf with, and you never have to worry about getting up a game. Yep, cronies all. I am lucky to be included. Of course, I think I'm the most normal of them all, but there are those who would dispute this.

One of the SLUGS had a problem with his wife who told him she felt he played too much golf and wasn't spending enough time with her. This tickled my funny bone and I immediately developed the following Matrimonial Happiness Matrix.

SOUR M.A.S.H. AT SEA - SECOND WAVE

THE SLUGS MATRIMONIAL HAPPINESS MATRIX

Your objective is to earn five points each week by doing the following activities.

Activity	**Points earned**
Eating out at nice restaurant	1
Eating out at McDonalds, Taco Bell or Golden Corral	1/2
Eating out with mother-in-law along	3
Doing yard work with spouse	1
Doing yard work with spouse knowing there's no cold beer in house	2
Going shopping at store	1
Going shopping at mall	2
Playing cards	1
Going to movies	1
Going to Chick Flick movie	3
Kissing spouse before golf	1
Kissing spouse after golf, before shower	1/2
Taking spouse & dog for walk	1
Taking spouse & dog for walk with pooper scooper	2
Going to church supper	1
Eating meal served at church supper	2
Cleaning dishes after dinner	1
Cleaning dishes after dinner by having dog lick them	1/2

Walter "Bud" Stuhldreher

Telling spouse white lie when asked opinion re dress, shoes or hat	1
Telling spouse truth when asked opinion re dress, shoes or hat	-1
Doing any of the above and NOT turning hearing aid off	Double points
Doing any of the above while spouse has PMS	Triple points

THE SECRET SOCIETY

I'll bet that many of you have sat through boring sessions in grade school while waiting for the slower learners to catch up with the rest of the class. Having spent hours like that during school, I resolved to do something about it so my kids wouldn't have to experience the same stultifying boredom. And the opportunity, or challenge, came when they entered grade school after we moved to Huntsville, Alabama in the fall of 1965.

The first thing I learned about the Huntsville primary school system was that it did not have a program for students with faster learning skills. These programs go by a variety of disingenuous names these days, thanks to the PC police, but you know what I mean. I figured that fixing this shortfall was a good place to start, but how? As one individual, particularly a newcomer, I would have as much leverage with the School Board as a boll weevil.

That year, 1965, was the first year the school sessions were not interrupted so the kids could pick cotton. It was the first year women were allowed to serve on juries.

Not all of the authorities had heard of women attaining equality, however. My wife and I went to the state licensing office to get our driver's licenses switched from Indiana to Alabama. My transfer was speedily accomplished, but Barbara's was not.

"You're going to have to take a road test first," she was told. Astonished, she asked why. "You're a woman," was the short but revealing answer.

Angry, Barbara told them this was unfair, that she was a much better driver than I was. Nope, no dice. Take the driving test or else no license.

Fuming, she did, and passed with flying colors. Still angry, she pointed at me and said, "Now it's his turn."

The examiner was perplexed by this remark. "He's already got his license. Why should he?"

"Because he's a rotten driver, that's why!"

I got out of there as fast as I could before they changed their minds.

Another interesting aspect of living in Alabama in 1965 was the availability of booze. Or perhaps the non-availability would better describe our predicament. The Governor, George Wallace, insisted on an "under-the-table" rake-off on all booze made outside Alabama. The well-known distillers, Seagrams for example, refused to pay this illegal tariff, and they were banned from doing business in the state. That left us with some mighty strange choices. One that I remember was "Alabama Whiskey." Not too informative was that label, nor were the contents very appealing. So we developed a strategy to get decent booze. It involved crossing the state line into Tennessee where regular booze was available. But we had to be extremely careful.

Governor Wallace, aware this ruse was being actively pursued by us lawbreakers, initiated two procedures to stop it. First, he changed the law so that cars caught carrying more than one day's supply of booze would be confiscated, not simply impounded, as was previously the case. If caught, the family buggy now belonged to the sovereign state of Alabama, not merely detained until a fine was paid. Whew! A toughie. Next, he instructed the State Troopers to patrol the Tennessee-Alabama borders. They did this by not only patrolling the borders, but also by having troopers in unmarked cars stationed at liquor stores just over the state line. These troopers would radio the license plate numbers of cars with Alabama tags to their waiting brethren, who then knew which cars to pull over and examine.

We got around this mess by sending two cars to Tennessee on buying trips. One car would buy the booze, then drive around the block or to the other side of the town, where it would be transferred to the second car. The first car would then be inspected when it crossed over into Alabama. The one bottle found would pass the "one day's supply" sniff test, while the second car came happily home. (It was necessary to have some booze in the first car to explain why it had visited the Tennessee liquor store.) Such was life in Alabama in 1965. But back to the school board.

Walter "Bud" Stuhldreher

Mensa

I decided that, as an individual, I wouldn't get far with the school board. I needed to get other concerned people involved. But who? Ah, some Mensa members would do nicely. Their reputation as high-IQ persons should influence the board. But who were they? With no way to find out, I decided to join the almost secret society so I could meet the local members and maybe get a posse up.

My first Mensa meeting confirmed my suspicions of how secretive they were. They had two symbols of membership, an owl and a pin with a yellow head. I could understand the owl, the age-old symbol of wisdom, but wearing a yellow headed pin on the *underneath side of your lapel* was reasonably strange. Who could possibly see it? Was there a secret ritual where two members flipped their lapels over instead of shaking hands? It was never explained to me.

I was working around 60 hours a week, and was out of town 20 percent of the time, so I went directly to the point. I explained to the small group of around 15 what I was up to, and did anyone want to join me? Luckily two did. Both had school-age children.

Bobby G. Willis was a principal mathematician at NASA's Marshall Space Flight Center (MSFC). Even though this was 1966, Bobby G. felt TV was potentially harmful to kids, and was the first person I knew who wouldn't allow one in his home. (His overworked wife, Agnes, with several energetic young children, felt differently.) Bobby G. had a fascinating assignment. He was leading the NASA team to ascertain the correct moment for Trans Lunar Insertion (TLI). The Apollo spaceship would be put in orbit around the earth. At a predetermined *exact second* the engines would be re-ignited and accelerate the space craft from 17,500 mph to 25,000 mph. This was the speed required to break earth's tenuous hold on the spacecraft and send it on the way to the moon which was between 225,000 and 229,000 miles away, depending upon the time of the year. The mathematics involved were immense. Essentially the mathematicians developed the calculations based on where the moon would be in orbit and worked backward — I think!

The other willing member was Asher Fisher, the local TV anchorman. (I did my best to keep Asher from finding out Bobby G.'s views on TV.)

I explained the gifted program and what documents I felt were necessary if we were to have a chance to sway the school board. Bobby G. volunteered to get copies of other states' programs. Asher volunteered to develop background data on the school board members. The more we knew about them the better our chance of success. I agreed to develop the desired fundamentals of a good Gifted Program, and set deadlines for all three of us. We did OK, and after three weeks, felt confident we were ready to take on the board. Accordingly, I notified the board of our objectives, and requested time be allocated at their next meeting for us. They agreed.

The School Board Meeting

At 7:00 p.m. the next Tuesday, the meeting commenced. Amazingly, the seven board members looked like they could be brothers. All were white, middle-aged men, round around the middle, clean shaven and — this is true — all seven had a stogie protruding from their mouths. (Bobby G. was against smoking, too, and I had to whisper to him to keep his mouth shut.) The meeting started strangely. "You people are Germans aren't you?"

Walter "Bud" Stuhldreher

What was he talking about? I am half German; Bobby G. was Scotch/English with a strong Puritan streak, and I didn't have the slightest idea of Asner's heritage. But more to the point, what difference did it make?

Asner spoke up. "Sir, what do you mean?"

He wasn't answered. Instead, the seven started whispering among themselves. Finally, another strange question. "Are you three Americans and have you always been Americans?"

Time for us to huddle. We asked each other what was going on? Bobby G. figured it out. "I heard the Germans visited the board a couple of months ago and demanded ten changes be made to the Huntsville school system or they would start their own school. It ticked them off, but they acquiesced. I bet they think we're Germans back for another bite of the apple."

Asner and I agreed this was probably the case and decided on an approach. "Sir," Asner politely replied, "yes, indeed, we're Americans and proud of it!"

Bobby G. was next: "Americans to a man!"

Finally, I chimed in, "You couldn't find any three people in Huntsville more American than we are! Apple pie, motherhood and Alabama football are number one in our lives!"

What we said wasn't nearly as important as *how* we said it. All the Germans, and there were around three hundred of them living in Huntsville, had thick accents. With all three of us speaking without German accents, the board would know we weren't Krauts.

One of my readers, Richard Blair of Kingsport, Tennessee, wrote about living in Huntsville in 1957. "Oh, I was a GS-5 Math 'expert.' They would run static tests on the Redstone missile, come back with these long rolls of computer printouts. I would take a ruler and measure the distance between points, and do some kind of calculation. I assume these numbers meant something to someone, but not to me. I think how today, this would all be instantly printed out and 1000 adjustments made in a few seconds after the test was run — never touched by human hands. Oh, and my boss was one of the Germans you mentioned in your story The Patriotic Swimming Pool. *I never could understand a thing he said, so I just nodded a lot."*

Our strategy worked, and satisfied that we belonged to the right side of the Atlantic, the chairman continued his inquisition. "What's this group you represent, Mensa, and how big is it?"

Whoops! Didn't want to admit how small we were, that was for sure. I took over. "Sir, Mensa is an organization that's interested in children with faster learning skills having a more challenging school curriculum than what's presently being offered. You can see we're not suggesting a major change, nothing like that, simply one class a day, maybe three days a week, for this type of child to be stretched intellectually. We've supplied several programs of this nature from other states so you can see what's being done there."

Another huddle by the gang of seven. "Well, we're going to have to take this off the table for the appropriate school personnel to examine it and give us their recommendation. But we have one final question: are you sure any of our children will qualify; will there be enough students to justify this change?"

I thought it politic to answer in a general fashion. "Gentlemen, we're sure there will be enough. After all, two out of every one hundred students will qualify, and that's with an average student population. The situation here, with thousands of well educated people pouring in every year to work on the space program, will undoubtedly be skewed towards a more intelligent student body than average."

And this forecast turned out to be true. The *Saturday Evening Post*, a national weekly publication, later ran an article on this subject. It claimed that the students in the Huntsville school system, because of the influx of Ph. D's, and many other well-trained engineers and programmers, were the brightest in the nation. I'm not sure just what hard data they had to justify this position, but it might have been true. In any event the school board did agree to install a "gifted student" program, which benefited many children.

I remained a member of Mensa until shortly after being transferred to Maryland in 1974. There I discovered a gifted student program was already installed, and I quit Mensa. I never did learn why they wore that yellow-headed pin on the underneath side of their lapels.

POPCORN ANYONE?

In the fall of 1985, shortly after our marriage, Bettie and I took a trip. I don't remember where we went, but I do remember staying in a motel and wanting some popcorn. A short trip to the vending machine area showed me what I was after: a sack of microwave popcorn. Great! But before telling you about that sack of popcorn here's some popcorn history.

Prior to 1981, if you wanted popcorn in your home, you had a couple of choices. You could buy popping corn, usually in a glass jar, and the oil in which to pop it. (Of the five types of certified corn seeds the one with an unusually high water content is used for popcorn.) Sometimes you bought the corn and oil together in a jar, but my favorite choice was "Pops-Rite," which was sold in a disposable aluminum skillet. It was covered with a very thin aluminum cover and you heated it over the stove, continually moving it back and forth. When the corn started popping, the thin cover bulged upwards in a very satisfactory

Walter "Bud" Stuhldreher

manner. This may sound childish, but it was exciting to watch! It also smelled good. Unfortunately, no matter how hard you tried, some usually burned on the bottom, but, overall, it was great popcorn.

Then in 1981 the world of making popcorn at home changed forever. Golden Valley Microwave Foods (GVMF) introduced ACT I, a refrigerated microwave popcorn. Imagine! Throw it into the microwave, turn it on, wait until it quit popping, and viola! Great popcorn! Yes, having to keep it refrigerated until you were ready to eat it was inconvenient for the grocery stores and the customer, plus it couldn't be sold in vending machines, but overall, it was a gigantic step forward for popcorn lovers like myself.

In 1984 GVMF really put popcorn into homes with the introduction of ACT II, a microwave popcorn which could be stored at room temperature. And that's the stuff I found in the motel's vending machine in 1985. Bringing it back to the room Bettie and I agreed it was the best popcorn we had ever tasted. I resolved to get some for our use in Tallahassee, but that proved to be a challenge that would have made Don Quixote quail in his stirrups. It simply wasn't available yet in our grocery chains. Finally, by calling the home office (then located in Minnesota, now in Ohio) I got the phone number of their local wholesaler and bought a case of the stuff. Man, was it good!

The legendary stock market guru, Warren Buffett, has always advised investors never to buy stock in a company if they didn't understand the product and industry. Well, I understood popcorn, thought GVMF had a hell of a product, and, quite by accident, found out GVMF was going public. It seems to me that Wall Street never knows, or cares, what middle America is up to. I couldn't find anything out about the IPO, except it was going public at $20 a share.

SOUR M.A.S.H. AT SEA - SECOND WAVE

Although I lived in Tallahassee, I used a stockbroker in Cocoa Beach, Florida. I had used him while working at the Kennedy Space Center and hadn't bothered to find another one in Tallahassee. I called Charlie, and although he was affiliated with a major brokerage house, he had never heard of GVMF. I assured him they existed, were going public at $20 a share, and I wanted some. Charlie next asked me why I wanted to buy their stock.

"Charlie, I like the popcorn they sell."

There was an incredulous silence. "You like the popcorn they sell? Are you crazy? That's no reason to buy stock in their company!" Charlie vented along like this for several minutes. The truth was, he was pissed off that he had never heard of them, and if he or his firm hadn't, it just couldn't be any good. I stuck to my guns.

"Charlie, just buy 200 shares for me. If it goes south I won't blame you. OK?" Charlie argued some more, gave up, told me it was a stupid move, but if I persisted in being dumb he would execute the order. And he did.

That stock came out and never looked back. It just went up and up. It split 2 for 1 less than a year later, in March 1987. Charlie then called me and mentioned the stock for the first time.

"Walt, that popcorn stock - didn't *we* do good on that one!" Now it was my turn to be silent.

"What's this 'we' stuff, Tonto? As I remember you were dead set against it." Charlie's stockbroker-type memory didn't see it that way. He always took credit for getting me into a nice

313

Walter "Bud" Stuhldreher

winner. (He never liked to talk about the losers he got me into, though.) I didn't really care, GVMF was a golden goose. It split again, 3 for 2, in 1990, and sold out to ConAgra Inc. in 1991, for a cash price of $41.67 per share. With the splits, this was $125 for each original share I bought. Yahoo!

The only time I got nervous while owning that stock was when GVMF decided to try to develop a microwave french-fry product. The only reason I didn't sell out at that time was their statement that if their product wasn't superior to McDonald's french fries it wouldn't be brought to market. I thought that was a wonderful benchmark to use, and figured I couldn't lose, no matter what happened. As it turned out they couldn't match McDonalds quality (who can?) and curtailed the effort.

I'm pretty sure the moral in this story is you can't go far wrong listening to Warren Buffett. I may not have his money, but I sure can listen like hell!

LETTERS FROM IRAQ

The following letters were written in 2003 by 1st Lieutenant Jeremy Trentham, U.S. Army, a young soldier in Iraq during Operation Iraqi Freedom. They were sent to his family and given to me by his sister, Christy, who plays trumpet in our church orchestra in which I play the French horn. I thought they were very informative and well-written. They reminded me of the stories of Ernie Pyle, the great news corespondent in WW II, known as "the G.I.'s reporter."

They say a soldier's world in a war is a ten-foot circle surrounding him. He doesn't know the overall picture of the battle he's in, or the generals' objectives. He only knows what's going on around him — and sometimes not even that. I think Jeremy describes his world very well and has given permission to include the letters in this book.

Walter "Bud" Stuhldreher

Jeremy, a native of Tallahassee, Florida, was born on August 14, 1977. He attended Florida State University, graduating in 2000 with a major in history. A member of the Army ROTC while in college, he was commissioned as a 2nd Lieutenant upon graduating. He married Kristen Swartz on March 6, 1999.

His duty posts have included Fort Benning, Georgia, Fort Knox in Kentucky, and Fort Sill in Kentucky. He left there on March 3, 2003, for Camp New York in Kuwait. He was there two or three weeks before entering Iraq. His division is the 101st Airborne supporting the 2nd Brigade, Air Assault.

1st Lieutenant Jeremy Trentham, U.S. Army, Kuwait, just before entering Iraq on March 3, 2003

SOUR M.A.S.H. AT SEA - SECOND WAVE

Sent: Sunday, April 6, 2003

Dear Mom and Dad,

Hello. How is everyone back home? Everyone here is fine. As you may have heard on CNN, I am in Iraq. I crossed the border into Iraq traveling up Highway 80 on 27 Mar 03 at 1:00 p.m. local time. I guess that was like 5:00 a.m. your time. So far everything has been fine.

We spent the first 2 days just driving and trying to get to our first position. Believe me when I tell you that 350 miles in a HMMWV, on what can be described as like an interstate half the time and worse than a country road the second half, was no fun. Highway 80 and Highway 8, which is what we were on the first half, really do remind me of a 6-lane interstate back home. They are paved and have overpasses every couple of miles and really are like I-10 except for the thousands of U.S. military vehicles on them which made it like driving in 5:00 traffic down Thomasville Road in the old days.

The second half of the trip we drove down a road called a pipeline road. It has that name because it has underground oil pipelines on both sides of the 'road.' I put that in quotes because I'm not really sure that it was more than a path through the sand. Some of it packed down and some of it not. This made for a dusty trip. Even the paved part sucked because it was only one lane wide, so if someone came the other way it was in the sand we go. The pavement was full of holes also, which was fun. In other words, the second half was like driving down a partially paved country road in August in an old Ford Pinto with no air conditioning. Lots of fun.:-) But I guess war is supposed to be hell.

Right now I am sitting in our third position since we got in this area. I don't want to tell you the names of the towns in this area. Not because I can't [but] because we will have left here by

Walter "Bud" Stuhldreher

the time you get this. I just don't want the news telling you any crap about there's a major battle here and worrying you because there really isn't much going on. I will tell you I am very close to the Euphrates. I don't see paradise anywhere around here.

I'm trying to describe war to you, but I'm not sure how. It really is 90% boredom. Most of my time has been spent just sitting and writing. We have fired some artillery rounds. About 120 of them so far. Mostly we've been shooting at artillery and mortars that we picked up on radar. I don't know if we did any damage to those targets. I do know that the ones we shot at for an observer had some effect. So far my battery has destroyed 2 vehicles and killed 9 people that I know of. An observer always tells us if we caused any damage. I don't know how I feel about that. Especially since we are currently pretty close to where we were shooting about a week ago. I think I saw one of the vehicles we destroyed and saw the holes in the road we caused. At least the people had been picked up. That really would have bothered me.

To get to the spot where we are now we had to drive down a road where we had fired and where the armor had fought a battle. From here I can see about 8 destroyed vehicles. We passed by dead bodies for the first time also. I think the local population finally picked all of those up, but I can still smell them. It is no picnic. I don't know why I am telling you that. It doesn't really bother me or anything, but I guess I just want to share it with someone. It's not like I didn't expect that to happen, it's just kind of weird when it does happen. It's like watching it in a movie. I can't tell you just how weird this all has been.

There are so many things I didn't expect. I didn't expect to see the number of power lines knocked down that I have seen. On this road we are constantly driving over power lines, driving around artillery holes and around vehicles. It's weird. I have probably seen a thousand dogs since I have been in this country.

SOUR M.A.S.H. AT SEA - SECOND WAVE

I didn't even realize they had dogs and yet I hear them barking all night long. It's kind of like being back home.

I do want to tell you about the weirdest thing that has happened so far. On April 1 (April Fool's Day) I was waked up by someone telling me we had a hot meal for breakfast which was a joke of course:-(. But about 10:00 a.m. my boss started putting together some people and several of our HMMWV's and our large 5-ton truck to leave the position. I thought he was kidding about the reason for this, but he wasn't.

It turned out that some Iraqis had tried to stay holed up in a factory. The kind of factory it was surprised everyone. It was a soda factory. It makes a kind of soda called Kufa. The Kufa Cola tastes just like Sam's Cola, so we liberated a ton of it for our own use. We now have cases of Kufa Cola (Coke), Orange Kufa (Orange Soda), Lemon Lime Kufa (7 Up), and a little Apple Kufa (apple soda? Don't ask me, but it tastes good). Me and my soldiers alone have (or had) 22 cases of the stuff. We are now down to about 12 - 15 (it's hot and we are thirsty). Once we and all the other sections finish what's on our HMMWV's we will start getting some off the 5 ton truck. In other words, my battery will be drinking Kufa until the end of the war. I plan on bringing some of it home just because it has a pop top, Arabic and English on it, and it even says made in Iraq in English. It's weird things like the Kufa that made this a totally surreal experience.

It's also weird that we really aren't that scared anymore. Obviously we are very aware of our surroundings and always on guard, but my soldiers aren't physically shaking with fear anymore. We aren't wearing our chemical suits anymore, just our desert camouflage uniforms. We are not paranoid about wearing our Flak vests and helmets, either. I am actually sitting here with just a T-shirt on, drinking orange Kufa, listening to Third Day on my CD player, and writing a letter. It's not what I expected in combat.

Walter "Bud" Stuhldreher

By the way, it's already getting **HOT** here!! When we crossed the border it was in the 70s and 80s during the day and in the 50s and 60s at night. In the last few days it has been getting in the upper 90s during the day and in the 70s and 80s at night. It's only April for crying out loud. This place will be miserable in a month. I really can't wait for that.

Two days ago I got a letter from Christy [his sister] and four letters from you all including my Hall's [cough drops] and hand sanitizer. Thank you very much. I needed that. I could use some Kool-Aid mix. We have a little but I could use some more. I really wish you could send me some ice. These Kufas only get so cold at night now. Oh well. I also need some large envelopes. I have some pictures but no envelopes to send them in. That would be great.

All of my thoughts now are about home. I have been gone almost a month now and I want to go home. When I left home I had big plans for when I got home. I was going to use all of this money to buy a big screen TV and an X-Box, etc. Now I just want to hold my wife and family, play with my dogs, and sleep in my own bed. Nothing makes you miss home like something like this.

When my time is up, I may try to get a Master's degree. If I moved back to Tallahassee, I would definitely get FSU football season tickets. I like that a lot better than sitting here in this place. Well, I just found out that we may move again soon, so I have to get ready for that. I will write again as soon as possible. I love you all very much and I hope to be home soon.

Love, Jeremy

SOUR M.A.S.H. AT SEA - SECOND WAVE

Sent: Tuesday, April 15, 2003

Hey guys,

Well, do you recognize the envelope and paper? Thank you for this and all the other stuff you have sent me. It is awesome. It's funny though because some of the food you sent me is in the MREs [meals ready to eat] now. The cheese crackers with peanut butter and the Combos are all in there. The Combos you gave me are a different flavor though, because the MRE only has cheddar cheese Combos. Believe it or not, I am sitting here now eating a Tootsie Roll from an MRE. Not bad, huh?

I am currently in the lead as far as the amount of mail coming to me. All my soldiers keep asking me how much I am going to get. It's awesome that the mail has started catching up to us. I have gotten letters from you, Christy, Kristen [his wife], Grandma White, Aunt Jane, Grandma Johnson, and a couple of ladies I don't even know who live in Texas. It is really cool.

As far as the war, I think it is basically over. We are just outside of Baghdad right now, and in about a week we will be moving north near the Turkish border. Judging by your letters I am sure the news will tell you where. I was near, and in, the battle of An Najaf. I shot in support of 2nd Brigade (502nd Infantry Regiment). I know for sure my shooting artillery there made a difference. A captain in my battalion who was with the infantry said as they moved to the city they ran into a wire obstacle. Three Iraqis started shooting at them from on top of a building so they called for artillery. My battery shot 12 rounds of airburst artillery at them and I am told that those people just ceased to exist when we stopped shooting. It's not something I am proud of, but it's my job and it probably saved some American lives. I guess that's war.

I just hope it ends soon and we can start peace keeping; when that happens we will move to a permanent camp with running

Walter "Bud" Stuhldreher

water, porta potties, buildings, real food, and maybe even e mail or phones. That would be so nice.

Right now is kind of a weird time. The war isn't officially over, but we are already trying to keep from hurting people or the infrastructure here. We can't shoot what they call 'killer' munitions like high explosives or white phosphorus (incendiary munitions). The only thing we can shoot is smoke during the day and illumination at night which provides light for the soldiers on the ground. Would you believe that 2 nights ago I shot 15 rounds of illumination into Baghdad to stop some civilians from robbing a bank? That wasn't something I thought I would do. That's why this is so weird. Hopefully things will improve soon.

Well, I need to go. Keep the letters and packages coming because they keep me going. I will write again soon.

Love,

Jeremy

SOUR M.A.S.H. AT SEA - SECOND WAVE

Sent: Saturday, April 19, 2003

Hello From Jeremy In Iraq

Hello everyone. I finally got a chance to send you an email. Don't reply to this because they are sending us somewhere just to send out email. This is just a one-time thing and not a regular thing.

Hello from Iraq. First of all, don't worry. Everyone is fine. So far only one person in our battery has gotten hurt and that was from wrestling another soldier in the battery. The last week or so have been really boring, so to kill time and let out some energy, most of the battery met by one of the howitzers, got in a circle, and started having wrestling matches. Not WWF wrestling, but college style wrestling. Well, this one soldier named Chevalier was wrestling and his foot got caught on an uneven part of the ground. Well, the other guy was pushing against him at the time and it caused him to dislocate his ankle. He was in a lot of pain, but we splinted it, gave him some morphine and called for an ambulance. So far they said that they have to reset his ankle, but there was some damage so he will probably have to fly to Germany to have surgery. He probably won't come back. He was just upset that he wouldn't get a Purple Heart. I guess that's the breaks.

So far I can tell you that war is no big deal. We have not been shot at, but we did shoot about 330 artillery rounds. I have been told that those rounds have made a big difference and kept the infantry from having to deal with quite a few people. Obviously I have seen some things I would rather not have seen, but it has not been too bad. Iraq is a really weird place. There are a few things that have really surprised me. Probably the biggest thing is the number of dogs. They are everywhere. I feel really sorry for them because I think most of them are either wild or abandoned. Some people in my battery even kind of adopted one of them. It is a cute little white and brown puppy.

They gave it a bath and feed it regularly, so it continues to hang around. I think the soldiers did that just because they miss home and wish they could have their dogs with them. I know I do.

There are a lot more green plants here than I thought there would be. It's probably because we have mostly stayed near the Euphrates River. Every time we drive through a town it's like there is a parade or something. Everyone comes outside and watches us drive by. Some people wave, others just stare, but most of the kids beg for food so we throw parts of our MREs to them. It is really sad. I just hope we are making things better for them. We got our first hot meal last night. Until then all we had to eat was MREs. I am getting tired of them. I am just glad that they have gotten better than they used to be. One of the meals is the Hamburger Patty. I really like that one. It comes with two pieces of Wheat Snack Bread, Cheese Spread, and Heinz Bar B Que Sauce. It really is good. Most of the rest of them are just O.K.

I finally started getting packages from you Tuesday. The mail system over here is broke. They told us that since we crossed the border on 27 March none of the letters we have written have even left the country. If you are not getting any letters from me, that is why, because I assure you that I am writing them. For example, I got my first letter from Kristen just today. I'm sure she is writing more than that. Thank you very much for all the junk food and Max Payne. It is exactly what I need. If you get the chance to send any more packages there are some things I have seen sent to other people that would be great. They are Ramen Noodle Soup, Instant Oatmeal Packages, soups in a cup, finger nail clippers, foot powder and anything else you can find like that. That stuff would help me break up the MRE monotony with other meals, and keep me from being bored because we really don't have anything to do right now.

I can tell by your letters that you are able to track where I am going from the news. So far, I was involved in the battles for

An Najaf, Al Hillah, and I am currently about 2 miles outside Baghdad. I can see the city from where I am. A few days ago we were near the Saddam International Airport and I could see one of Saddam's Palaces. It was huge. Some of the soldiers made the long walk over to the palace and brought back some souvenirs. They gave me a piece of marble from the floor. Speaking of souvenirs, there is a lot of hunting and trading going on. Everyone wants to have the best souvenir. The hottest items are Iraqi flags, uniforms, doorknobs and fixtures from Saddam's Palace, parts off of an Iraqi Howitzer, and Iraqi gas masks. The trading here is wild. You would be surprised what you can 'buy' for a pack of cigarettes. Some are selling cigarettes right now for $5 per pack and no one minds paying that much. I guess they are desperate for tobacco. Must suck to have that addiction here and run out.

Right now there is not much going on. We can't shoot into the city because they don't want us creating a lot of damage, so we just sit here all day and play games or whatever we can find to do. I really miss home. When I left I was thinking about the extra money I would be making and what I wanted to buy with it, but I don't care about that anymore. I want to give everyone a hug, play with my dogs, sleep on something besides the hood of a HMMWV, not have to cut a hold in an MRE box to go to the bathroom, take a shower more than once in two weeks, have some ice in my water and never see sand again.:-) I really miss you all and I can't wait to see you. Please keep the letters and packages coming because it is the most important thing I can get right now. Hopefully I will see you all soon.

Love,

Jeremy

Walter "Bud" Stuhldreher

Sent: Thursday, May 15, 2003

    Hey everyone. Well as you can see I will be able to email regularly. I am sorry if my letters have been sparse and sporadic. Part of that is the bad mail system and part of that is my being so busy. If there is someone who I have not been able to respond to, please tell them I am sorry. I will try to thank them during a more peaceful time in my life.

    Yesterday was a great day for me. I finally got to talk to my wife after almost 2 months of not hearing her voice. I also got to email her and the rest of my family. Then I received about 8 of mom's daily packages, another one of dad's cards (which are great by the way), a letter from Thomasville Road Baptist Church telling me I was on their prayer list, a box from someone I don't know, and 2 boxes from my wife. Because of that mail I was able to eat the best dinner I have had since I deployed which was macaroni and cheese, Ramen soup, cookies for desert, and a Coke (even though it had squigglys and dots, I mean Arabic on it, the Coke still tasted pretty good).

    All in all it was a good day. As you can see, good and bad days are dependent on very simple pleasures. For example, the day I can use a real toilet instead of a piece of wood with a burn barrel under it will be a good day. Speaking of mail, I love the daily packages but I am becoming overwhelmed with more than I can hold. Is there anyway we can slow them down a little. I have to give some away. I appreciate all of the hygiene stuff too, but that is getting very excessive. For instance, one of my NCOs not too long ago received 1200 baby wipes in one day. That is great and I appreciate the support, but now that we are stable we are taking showers about every 2 or 3 days, so our baby (soldier) wipe usage has greatly decreased. We are now creating a stockpile big enough to supply the entire army with baby wipes for the next war. I also have about a dozen toothbrushes, tubes of toothpaste, and bars of soap. We are nasty people out here but not that nasty. Thank you for all of the

SOUR M.A.S.H. AT SEA - SECOND WAVE

support but I am worried that I won't be able to hold much more.

As far as food, all I really need right now is stuff to make a meal with so that I can avoid MREs. I have plenty of candy and chewing gum (but I want dad to still include his 2 pieces with each card because it reminds me of him because he is always chewing gum (and it almost makes me cry). I am also good on AA batteries for a while and even if I run out it is possible to get some from the army. I am not saying that I want you to stop because I will eventually run out, it just won't be anytime soon. But please continue to send me letters and cards because they are my world right now (another one of those simple pleasures which make or break my day).

In case you are curious, your food is arriving in one piece. The only things I have had trouble with are Cheese Nips (Crum Nips) and chocolate (unless you meant to send me a blob of it). That's OK though. In my current situation it is better to have too much or have it broken than to have none at all. I would like for someone to send me some Pepto Bismol though. I am fine right now, but almost everyone around me has 'Saddam's Revenge' which was either caused by a virus that is going around or more than likely from the local food everyone has been eating (again in an attempt to avoid MREs). Please send some just in case, and if I don't need it I can sure hand it out because there is a shortage of good stomach medicine because our supply system (like our mail system) is all screwed up. I, and everyone around me, would greatly appreciate it.

I miss everyone at home and hope to come home soon. I still have no date but am told it will be before I die which is good news I guess. Until I see everyone again I hope all is well and I love you all.

Love, Jeremy

Walter "Bud" Stuhldreher

P.S. If anyone is interested, it is getting hotter than hell here and I don't like it anymore. I don't know exactly how hot because I don't have a thermometer, but it has to be over 100 degrees. It's lots of fun, especially at night. Enjoy your air conditioning.

SOUR M.A.S.H. AT SEA - SECOND WAVE

Sent: Thursday, May 16, 2003

Hey everyone. Today was a little bit interesting. It was the first time in about a month I was a little concerned because of all the loud booms going off near me. At about 1200 [noon] today the whole place started rocking and it went on for several hours. At first I wasn't concerned because our Explosive Ordinance Disposal (EOD) guys are always making a lot of racket during the day when they blow up weapons and ammunition we confiscate from the local Iraqis. The only thing was that today's volume and intensity of explosions was a little extreme. After a short time I found out why.

Apparently, a few miles up the road a unit was doing a controlled burn of the brush around their area. Well it got out of control and hit 2 of our main Ammunition Supply Points (ASP's). The explosions went on for a very long time and unfortunately, a young Specialist was injured. That poor kid lost a leg when a piece of shrapnel came down and hit them. I feel bad for them, but I am really glad that was the only casualty. Needless to say, we spent half the day in our helmets and flak vests whenever we went anywhere just in case a piece made it to where I am. The city is still filled with smoke and I don't know how this will affect the training we had planned for the next month or so.

Anyway, I need a favor. In my thinking about what I want to do when I get out of the army I was wondering if anyone could tell me if it is better to buy a house or have my own built. I have always wanted a house that is totally mine, but I was wondering what would be best financially. Ask around and see if anyone can tell me the plus and minus of the two options. I would appreciate it.

By the way, yes, I still see my soldiers pretty regularly and I miss them greatly. They are the best group I have ever worked with and I will always miss them. Well I need to go. There is a

Walter "Bud" Stuhldreher

conference call about to happen and I can get more details about what happened today.
 I will write again soon.

Love,

Jeremy

SOUR M.A.S.H. AT SEA - SECOND WAVE

Sent: Sunday, May 18, 2003

Hello Everyone. I'm sorry I haven't written in a couple days. The email has been down.

I'll start by answering some questions from the emails I just read. I do get haircuts. Several people brought their own clippers so I get my head completely shaved about every 2 weeks. My wife sent me the chocolate which worked out pretty well but it still melted some. I did get the packages from the McFaddens. Their Kool-Aid is really good. It's sort of like Krystal Lite. I drink about 2 of those per day. I also got packages from Uncle Joe/Aunt Judy and from Mrs. Dean yesterday. Tell them thank you very much when you see/talk to them. They got me a lot of things I needed.

Life here continues to get better. The Battalion Supply Officer (S-4) has been taking trips to a little town called Duhok. I am told it is similar to the U.S. and by far the most modern place we have seen so far. They have stores similar to a Wal-Mart and the women wear tight Blue Jeans (a big hit with the soldiers). I haven't been there yet but I hope to soon. When he goes there he buys things we need. Recently he bought a refrigerator so we can finally have cold drinks.

He also bought fans, but those can't run yet because they haven't fixed the electricity here yet. We have generators that supply power for us, but we have a problem with those. They put out 110 volts of electricity just like the U.S. but everything here runs on 220 volts which is what their electrical system runs on. Hopefully they will fix that soon and I can get my fan running. I am told the other day it was supposed to have gotten up to 110 degrees. I believe it. It is hard just to sit and do nothing.

Well I need to go. Thanks for the pictures and I will hopefully be able to write tomorrow. I love you all.

Love, Jeremy

Walter "Bud" Stuhldreher

Sent: Wednesday, May 21, 2003

    Hey guys. Sorry I didn't write to you yesterday. I started checking my e-mail and was pulled away because I suddenly had to drive [to] the Tactical Operations Center. The funny thing was it wasn't that vital that I go because there were about 6 other people with nothing to do who could have gone. That is really annoying when you consider that I had waited over an hour to use the computer and was pulled away after about 5 minutes of reading e-mail. Oh well, that's the army.

    I read mom's questions about my new job, and well the truth is, I really don't have a new job yet. Eventually I will be the Battalion Intelligence Officer (S-2), but I won't start that job until the guy I am replacing leaves on June 15. Trust me, it won't be as cool as it sounds. I will mostly inspect arms rooms and things like that when we get back to Fort Campbell. While I am here I will mostly send up information that we collect to the Brigade that we support. It is just a staff job (kind of boring). Until then I am stuck here in the Ammo and Logistics Operations Center (ALOC) doing basically nothing. I pretty much sit here and play my Playstation all day long (literally). But I am 2/3 of the way through Max Payne and I led Florida State to an undefeated National Championship in NCAA Football 2003!!! I like a lot of people I work with, with a few exceptions of course.

    Anyway, with all of this time on my hands all I can think about is what I want to do outside the army. The only things I can come up with is move back to Tallahassee, own my own home, have kids, and get season football tickets every year. I don't know yet how to pay for all of this, but hopefully it will come to me soon. There is a PX opening here on Monday which I am told is Memorial Day. That will be good because at least I can buy something American (not that I need much with the packages and all). It will just be nice not to have to worry about language barriers, the value of the Dinar, or the sanitary conditions of what you are buying. I am also told that they are going to have fun things to do here on Memorial Day like sports tournaments, a bar-b-que, and a ceremony. Hopefully, I can go with that and it will help kill one more day. By the way, I have been able to start doing P.T. again which I sort of enjoy although it hurts after not doing any for 2 months, and I play volleyball most evenings because we have a pretty nice court. I really enjoy that, actually, even though I am not very good at it.

We still have no power here (besides our own generators) or running water, but we have plumbers and electricians working on that every day. It takes a lot of time because we are staying in buildings that previously held a Republican Guard Air Defense unit. When they left this place was looted and every light fixture, light switch, power outlet, toilet, sink, and water heater was taken so those guys are basically starting from scratch. They should be done by Friday though which will be great.

Oh well, I have written a small book and I need to go. I will write again soon.

Love, Jeremy

Walter "Bud" Stuhldreher

Sent: Wednesday, May 28, 2003

Hey guys. Well almost the end of another uneventful day in Iraq. Good news. My stomach is better. Thank God for that. Life is bad enough without those problems. It happened just in time to, because tonight we had a steak for dinner and it was actually pretty good. That's like the third day in a row we have had a good dinner. It's kind of nice.

I went to the PX the day before yesterday and bought a portable DVD player. It is really cool and surprisingly, Kristen didn't kill me when I sent her an e-mail and told her. She said she didn't mind. So if anyone would like an idea on something to send me, a DVD would be nice. I would ask that they just send the DVD in like a CD holder or something that doesn't take up too much space. I am concerned that with all of the stuff I am collecting I won't have room to get it all home. That would really suck. So as you send me stuff just try to keep it kind of small if you can.

Other than that not much to tell you. We lost 2 more soldiers the other day. They were working at a traffic control point when 2 vehicles pulled up. They stopped both of them and as they searched the first one people started shooting at them from the second one. Two soldiers were killed, but they killed two of the gunmen and captured 6 others. I guess things are still dangerous here. am told that there is an increased threat of female suicide bombers right now. Apparently that is the latest trend. In fact, someone shot a lady the other day who was carrying 2 grenades and going toward some soldiers. It's all pretty scary because who knows who is friendly and who is not.

Well I need to go. I hope I didn't scare you. I promise that when I leave the compound I always wear my helmet, my flak vest and I am very careful. I will try to write again soon. I love you all.

Love,

Jeremy

Walter "Bud" Stuhldreher

Sent: Monday, June 2, 2003

Hey guys. Not much news to report today. I went to a meeting this morning with the guy I am getting ready to replace. It was the start of my transition into the new job. It was a pretty boring meeting, a lot of which I didn't understand. I guess that is why I need to transition into the job with the guy who is in it now.

My life should get a lot more comfortable starting tomorrow. I will live in a hotel that we are using. It has bathrooms with running water, sinks, hot water heaters, showers, and even real toilets. That will be really nice. The windows all have screens on them so I shouldn't have to fight the nightly battle of the mosquitoes. I don't think they have air conditioning because we are not allowed to spend army money on air conditioners, but they do have fans since we can buy as many of those as we want. I may try and share the cost of an air conditioner with whoever I am staying with since I am probably going to be there for a while.

One of the cool things is that they just opened a "Cantina" where I am going. They contracted with a local restaurant owner to come in and set up sort of a restaurant right there. They sell smoothies, Iraqi pizza, sandwiches, soda, and ice cream. They have tables, chairs, a T.V., DVD player, fans, ping pong tables and pool tables. Would you believe it? It should be nice.

They are still working on the phones and email, but at the place where I went to my meeting this morning (and where they have it everyday) they have both that I can use, so I will try to do that as much as I can. Over all, this should be a really good transition that will hopefully help time pass by faster. Well I need to go. I will try to write again soon. I love you all.

Love,

Jeremy

Walter "Bud" Stuhldreher

Sent: Wednesday, June 04, 2003

    Hey everyone. Christy, I read your email and the info was mostly correct. I support 2nd Brigade not 1st Brigade. The base where I went to Airborne School was Fort Benning. I am going to attach to this email a Battalion History that was written in my Battalion. It is pretty much correct and has a few technical terms you may not understand, but it will give you a real good idea of what we did during the war. I will reread it again and make whatever corrections need to be made and resend it to you. I hope you enjoy it and that it gives you some more info.

    To answer mom and dad's question; yes, I have been to Washington D.C. I really enjoyed it. I went with Kristen for a TCC [Tallahassee Community College] trip one time. She can give you all the details if you call her. I don't have enough time to type all that.

    I don't know how often I will be able to write emails but I do come to this location everyday so hopefully it will be that often. If you get a chance, please thank Grandma and Granddaddy as well as Joe and Judy. I got packages from Grandma and Granddaddy and from Joe's Church yesterday. I never thought I would get a package from Joe's church but it was really cool.

    Anyway, not too much news from me. I like the restaurant where I live now. The chicken and the pizza is really good as well as the smoothies. I am staying pretty busy, but it makes time pass faster. I got a chance to call Kristen on Monday night. I really enjoyed that, and it was nice to hear her voice. Well, I need to go. I love you all and I will write again soon.

Love,

Jeremy

SOUR M.A.S.H. AT SEA - SECOND WAVE

Sent: Tuesday, June 10, 2003

Hey guys. I didn't think I would ever get to send this email. Every time I tried, either the Internet wasn't working or there was such a long line and I couldn't wait. I finally got a chance to write you a long letter on Microsoft Word so that I am not on a time constraint like I normally am.

I am on my Tactical Operations Center (TOC) Battle Captain shift right now. It is one of those less than pleasant things I get to do in my new job. Basically what it means is that I sit here from 4:00 p.m. till midnight listening to radios, making sure we send accurate reports up to Brigade, and just about whatever else needs to be done involving running the Battalion. It is not very fun. I usually get asked questions about things that happened before I came on shift and get yelled out when I don't have the answer. makes life less than enjoyable during that time of day.

My day usually consists of this: 6:30 a.m. wake up; 8:00 a.m. battle captains meeting (This is where the battalion commander basically tells us what he wants us to have answers for when he gets back at the end of the day (example: we have this project today, and I want to know what happens with it when I get back; etc.); 9:00 a.m. Brigade Targeting Meeting (This is where Brigade tells each Battalion what they want us to look at and update us on the latest intelligence that we have collected (example: this guy told us that this mosque is anti-U.S. so I want X unit to go talk to the Imam (preacher) and ask him if and why he is anti-U.S.). From the end of that meeting (about 10:00 a.m.) until I go on Battle Captain Shift (4:00 p.m.) is when I usually use the Internet, eat lunch, and anything else I want to do. That is my life everyday. It is not very exciting.

I was extremely sick on Thursday night and Friday. I had a real bad problem with diarrhea and I was throwing up. I also had a fever of 100.0. I haven't been that sick in a long time. It kept me up all night and purged all food and fluids out of my stomach. At times I think part of my stomach even went with it.

Considering that I drank a bottle of water with raspberry ice drink mix (which I got from mom in a package that day; thanks it was awesome going down) it made for a really grotesque sight coming up. I thought my body was bleeding out one stomach heave at a time. Sorry for the grossness, but you want details. Anyway, several diarrhea pills and a shot in the butt for nausea later I was feeling a little better. The shot (which I am still sore from) knocked me out for most of Friday and that really helped. Saturday I woke up feeling much better except that I was really weak from having no food or fluids in my system.

All that sickness went away Saturday thanks to a good nap that afternoon, lots of water, and a great meal that evening. We collected money from everyone at the TOC and some NCO's went and bought food to cook. Dinner consisted of lamb (grilled and kabobs), potatoes (with onions and seasonings), watermelon, and soda. It was very good. I live in what used to be a communications center for the power company. It is pretty nice. It has all tile floors, concrete walls that are painted white, and it is 3 stories tall. The best part is it has electricity and running water. At least it is the Iraqi version of running water. It doesn't work quite the same as the U.S. All plumbing in Iraq is driven by gravity. We have huge (at least they would be huge if 45 guys weren't all using it) 500 gallon tanks on top of the roof that supply water to the building. There are pipes attached to pumps that supply water to the water tanks on the roof. It's pretty annoying because occasionally you have to go outside and turn the pumps on to fill the tanks with water. If an unusually large number of people use the shower at one time then the tanks run dry and you no longer have running water.

That's how things are in Iraq. They are almost modern but not quite. It makes us all feel like Iraqis are pretty stupid because they have the technology to make themselves modern and they are only one step away from it, but they are just too lazy to make that last step. Here is a good example. Right now we have a program going called Task Force Neighborhood.

Basically we are picking points in the city that need to be cleaned up because Iraqis like to throw trash on the ground. We send an engineer unit to the location we pick on the day we are doing this so that they can transport the trash to a landfill. We send a small group from the unit that owns that part of town to provide security while the clean-up is going on. We even pay any Iraqi who shows up and helps clean 4,000 Iraqi Dinar (about $4.00) as a "tip" for helping to clean up their streets. We send a psychological operations vehicle out into that area the day before which has a loudspeaker on it that broadcasts a message telling civilians we are going to do this. In other words we are paying them to clean up their area and providing everything they need to do it like gloves, shovels, etc. and they still refuse to participate. We only get about 10-15 kids (8-12 year old boys) to participate. All of the adults say it is beneath them to do this. It's like dealing with rich snobs except they are all poor. It doesn't make any sense.

I saw an article from the Washington Post dated June 6 that someone got off the Internet today. It said there is a good chance we may end up being here for 9 months. I hope it isn't true because I don't think I can handle this place much longer. The funny thing is that when we ask the Iraqis why they are attacking our soldiers they tell us it is because they want to run their own country. I'm not sure they will ever be ready to run their own country without handouts from the rest of the world. They are too lazy for that. I wouldn't tell the wrong people that or else we will be here forever and I really want to go home. Oh well.

By the way, I got the power converter on Saturday and I got the Xbox on Monday. That was great timing. I don't have the screen or "Fisher what are you doing" yet but I hope to soon. I didn't realize Stephen was sending all the stuff he did. I got the Xbox with 4 controllers, 5 copies of Half Life for Playstation 2 signed by all the people at Gearbox, 2 games that came with the Xbox as part of the system, and they sent me a copy of Halo which I absolutely love almost as much as Splinter Cell. That was awesome. Can you all send me his email address so that I can thank him myself? He would probably really appreciate that. Anyway, I need to go. I hope these details help. If you have questions please ask. I will try to answer them. I love you all and I will write again soon.

Love, Jeremy

SOUR M.A.S.H. AT SEA - SECOND WAVE

Sent: Thursday, June 12, 2003

Hey guys. I read some of the questions you asked in your email and I decided to answer them with another long email in Word while I am on shift. I am also sending you some pictures that I found on the computer I use (with views) of the building I live in, as well as the surrounding area. I know that one of the pictures shows you an Iraqi toilet, but don't worry, we actually have real toilets here (no those are not Iraqi urinals; you do the math). I hope they help you understand my surroundings a little more.

I did not get a chance to find a digital camera because I was too busy, but I do know of some people who have them.

I will try to answer as many of your questions as I can. As far as food, I have been meaning to write about that. I am still being swamped with stuff from you guys which is awesome, but I am a little overwhelmed. That's another reason I want the digital camera so that I can take a picture of the amount of food I currently have stored. I am thinking of opening my own Publix right here in Mosul and my aisles are almost fully stocked:-).

I usually grab something on my way out the door for breakfast because of my 2 meetings first thing in the morning. That's where the Pop Tarts, cereal bars, and Nutri Grain Bars have come in real handy. There is a T-ration breakfast (eggs, sausage, waffles, etc. in various combinations and styles which come in packages which are boiled to cook them) made every morning but I usually don't have time to eat it. They also usually have small boxes of cereal, fruit (apples, oranges, bananas which are not green:-(etc.), and other side breakfast items. For lunch I usually have a few options because of the break in my schedule. Sometimes I cook the stuff you guys have sent me. Obviously macaroni and cheese with beanies and weenies is my favorite.

Sometimes I go to the cantina here and have a pizza (Iraqi pizza has no tomato sauce and is basically a normal crust with

Walter "Bud" Stuhldreher

meat (I don't know what kind and may not want to know) and cheese (could be regular cheese, could be goat cheese, who knows and who wants to) or a lamb sandwich (roll with lamb meat, onions, tomatoes, cucumbers, and some kind of sauce that tastes good (I don't know what it is and probably don't want to). Sometimes I have a whole chicken with bread (kind of like pita), and a vegetable plate (cucumbers, black olives, pickles, and some other stuff I don't eat because it looks too exotic).

I have noticed that the vegetables here taste really good. It's probably because they are so fresh which we all know is always better. The cantina also offers smoothies made from different fruit (I usually have banana and melon). They also sell things like soda, fruit drinks, ice cream, cookies, chips, and other snack foods a convenience store would sell in the states.

I usually don't eat dinner because I am not hungry. I don't know if that is because of the weight I have lost or because I am busy because I am on shift. When I do eat I either snack on some stuff you have sent me like the tuna and crackers or I eat the meal that the cooks make. They usually have a T-ration dinner (different meals like spaghetti, lasagna, beef with noodles, etc. with some kind of vegetable (usually mixed vegetables), fruit, sometimes rice, and Kool-Aid or some kind of drink from a mix; both the main meal and side items come in a bag (which are boiled in order to cook) but on occasion we do get A-rations which is actual food that the cooks make (steak, chicken and rice, on rare occasions shrimp, even rarer lobster tail, etc.). A-rations are the best and usually attract a crowd. T-rations are all right but are just one step above MREs. I have not eaten an MRE in several weeks (thank God).

Right now I live in a room with one of my NCO's (Staff Sergeant Madden) but that is just temporary until the guy I am replacing leaves on 15 June. SSG Madden is a great Christian man and he knows a lot about army intelligence (he should; it's actually his job and he is the only person in my small section who is trained on intelligence). The guy I will be rooming with permanently is LT Drury. He is our Battalion Physician Assistant. He is a great guy and we get along really well. I will be very pleased when this change is made because I want to settle in. Right now my stuff is just laying everywhere and I hope to eventually be able to make some shelves out of empty MRE and T-ration boxes and put my stuff in them. This may not sound like much, but our food comes in very sturdy cardboard boxes (some of the sturdiest I have seen) and when you mix that with some well placed tape you can make some pretty sturdy storage shelves. I will try to take a picture of these and send them to you.

I currently sleep on a litter (device used for carrying wounded patients which is fabric attached to two poles) that I acquired from the medics. It has a 3 inch thick pad made of sponge like stuff that we bought locally for everyone. The Iraqi's use it for padding on their beds and I guess now so do we. I put my inflatable mat that the army issued me on top of that for a little more padding. For a pillow I use a folded fleece the army issued me with a pillow that Kristen made for me on top of that. I don't use any kind of covers or anything because it stays extremely hot all night. I usually wake up completely sweaty because the fans just can't keep up with the heat. It is pretty comfortable, and other than the heat I really can't complain.

Well, I need to go. I hope these details help. I will try to write you again soon.

Love,

Jeremy

Walter "Bud" Stuhldreher

Sent: Friday, June 13, 2003 2:41 AM

Subject: Ancient History (Is this a better subject line?)

    Hey everyone. Not much news to report today. I learned something really interesting yesterday that I thought all of you would find really neat. First of all let me tell you that the source of my information is our Battalion Chaplain. He is a really interesting guy. He is Jewish which makes things really interesting for us because we can't let any of the Iraqis know that because they are Muslim. If they knew that they would stop having anything to do with him and may even try to persecute him.
    On a side note. We have found maps of the middle east in buildings here and did you know that Arabs are so anti-Israel that their maps don't label the country of Israel as Israel. All it says is Palestine. In the maps that do label the country of Israel that we have captured they actually take a marker and black out the label for the country.
    Anyway, the information I found out is that apparently the chaplain has found 5 Jewish synagogues from the 15th century inside the city of Mosul. He said they are people's homes and one of them is just full of trash. He said they have Hebrew writing on them that proves they are Jewish. Not only that, but apparently Jonah (as in Jonah in the belly of the whale) is buried right here in Mosul. This is also where Ninevah is. I don't know if I will get to see any of this stuff but I would love to try. We'll see. I will keep you updated as to whether or not I get a chance to visit those places.
    I don't know if I told you but the city of Al Hillah were we fought a battle is the ancient city of Babylon. Imagine that; another battle at the old city of Babylon. Anyway, there is your history lesson for today boys and girls. I need to go. There were a lot of riots that started in this area yesterday about this

time so I need to get out of here in case it happens again. I love you all and I will write again soon.

Love,

Jeremy

Walter "Bud" Stuhldreher

Sent: Saturday, June 14, 2003 2:39 AM

Subject: Another day in Iraq

    Hey guys. I got Splinter Cell yesterday but unfortunately I can't play it :(Oh well. At least my Playstation works and I have the new Matrix game and another army game that Kristen sent me. The Matrix game is really cool. I am enjoying it a lot.
    Things have been crazy here the last few days. The ex-Iraqi army soldiers are still trying to protest and cause trouble here in Mosul. We had 5 soldiers get injured yesterday, mostly from grenades. It is still a dangerous world. I really look forward to the day when I can ride down the road without having to wear a flak vest and helmet, and I don't have to worry about people shooting at me as I drive by. It makes me really nervous, but I still pay attention and should be fine.
    I do get to see my soldiers every once in a while. In fact I saw SSG Kallgren this morning. It's good to see them because I really miss them. I do get to interact with the Iraqi people everyday. Mostly the ones who work for us like the interpreters or the teenagers who clean our building that I live in. Most of them annoy me because of how they talk and act towards us. I can't really explain it in an email because it isn't as annoying as telling someone in person.
    Anyway, don't really have anymore news today. Obviously, I can't wait to go home, and I think about it everyday. Hopefully it will happen soon. I love you all and I hope to see you soon.

Love,

Jeremy

SOUR M.A.S.H. AT SEA - SECOND WAVE

Sent: Wednesday, June 18, 2003 2:51 AM

Subject: Rough Days

Hey guys. Sorry I didn't write you yesterday. After my meeting I had to pick up 2 Australian reporters and take them right back to where I live because they were going to a school with my former battery. They were going to teach a class on American culture to Iraqi school children and it makes for a pretty picture.

Yesterday was just a rough day in general. About 9:30 p.m. last night one of my soldiers shot himself in the foot on purpose. He is fine. He had to have surgery done today in order to repair the shattered bones in his foot. I don't really know why he did it. I talked to SSG Kallgren for quite a while last night because he had to come to the TOC to answer a bunch of questions about it. SSG Kallgren told me that he had mentioned he was pretty mad that they changed his End of Time in Service (ETS) date from Aug 20 to Dec 20 because of the stop loss we were all under. I don't really know if that is why he did it or not. It doesn't really surprise me though. He is kind of a weird guy who seems fine and then suddenly just doesn't like anyone and wants to do something extreme to sort of get everyone's attention.

Needless to say, he is going home and will be facing punishment under the Uniform Code of Military Justice. I am being told he could even go to jail. We'll see what comes of that. It definitely made us all mad that he did that. SSG Kallgren told me that even as he lay there being stabilized by the medic some of the soldiers commented on how stupid he was. They were immediately told to leave the room, of course, because they were busy working on him at the time. I don't know how he can be so selfish. Oh well.

Other than that I don't have too much else going on. Just one excitement after another. There is never a dull moment over

Walter "Bud" Stuhldreher

here. It's kind of like a soap opera. Just one drama after another. Anyway, I need to go. have a pretty busy day today. I love you all and I hope to write again soon.

Love,

Jeremy

    p.s. I have been getting a lot of mail with the wrong unit on it. I am in HSB/1-320 FA not SHB. I would also like it if I could be sent some sugar to go with all of the unsweetened Kool-Aid I have been getting. I can get sugar but it involves me opening about 4,000 sugar packets. If anyone wouldn't mind, I sure could use some help.

SOUR M.A.S.H. AT SEA - SECOND WAVE

Sent: Saturday, June 28, 2003 3:41 AM

Subject: I GOT AIR CONDITIONING!!!

    Hey guys. Did I mention I GOT AIR CONDITIONING? We finally got it yesterday. I got back from a change of command rehearsal and there were boxes with air conditioning units and glass windows all down the halls. They installed most of the air conditioners and some of the windows yesterday. I didn't get a glass window yet so I still have a screen window, but they did install my AC unit. We just covered the windows with cardboard and let the room cool off. My roommate brought one of his oral thermometers up and it registered 79 degrees this morning. I actually had to use my poncho liner as cover last night because I was a little cold. It is absolutely awesome. I am sooooo happy about that.
    Life just keeps getting better and better. Not that I wouldn't leave in a heartbeat because it is still not America, but it is still better. Last night was the first night in 2 months I didn't sweat all night long. Between that and all the DVD's and games I have now it is much easier to pass my time. Hopefully I will be able to come home soon. I need to run. I will try to write again soon.

Love,

Jeremy

Walter "Bud" Stuhldreher

Sent: Friday, July 04, 2003 3:02 AM

Subject: Sorry about not writing for a few days.

Hey guys. Sorry I haven't emailed in a while. I have been really busy and haven't been able to get onto the email computer. I did, however, get a chance to use a digital camera and take some pictures that you will probably enjoy. I put the pictures into a Powerpoint presentation so that I could describe what you are seeing. I hope you like them. They should help you understand more about where I live.

Not much news here today. I now have windows in my room which allows me to make it even cooler in there. I now get cold at night and have to use covers. It is awesome but I am afraid it has given me a cold. I really don't mind because it is nice just to not be hot for a while.

The mail sucks again. We haven't gotten any mail in a few days. I don't know what happened. It was working pretty good for a while but it just suddenly stopped. Hopefully it will start flowing again soon. All anyone is talking about now is when we are going home. The consensus here is that we don't care if we are here a year we just want a date to mark on the calendar. Without that date we feel kind of hopeless. We are just stuck here. The new joke is to ask someone what they are going to do on their mid-term leave. Mid-term leave is something you get when you go to Korea for a year. Since you can't bring your family with you, at the six month mark you get about 3 weeks of leave to go see your family. I hope it doesn't come to that. No one knows when we are coming home.

Of course 04 July is a holiday which doesn't help. I don't think we will be watching/shooting fireworks here. I just hope no one tries to attack us on that date because of its significance.

Eight July will mark 4 months since I left. It feels like I have been in Iraq my whole life. The helmet and flak vest I have to put on when I leave to go somewhere is no longer a burden to me. It just feels normal. It's like that is what you do when you leave your house or something. I can't wait to leave this place but I don't know how long it will be before this place is stable enough to stand on its own. Anyway, that is enough complaining. I need to go. am sorry about not writing sooner. I hope I didn't worry you. I love you all and I will write again soon.

Love,

Jeremy

Jeremy being promoted to Captain on October 1, 2003

A SCREENPLAY TREATMENT

Walter "Bud" Stuhldreher

INTRODUCTION

A *screenplay treatment*, like the one which follows, is no more than ten pages long. It is a synopsis of the principal events in the story line of a proposed film script. It is a resume of the outstanding visuals, a rundown of the characters, and a description of the crucial moments of the script. Also, the screenplay treatment will almost always be written in the present tense, to give it more reality and immediacy. An old Hollywood joke: Why is a screenplay treatment less than ten pages? So the producers' lips won't be tired out after reading it!

A *screenplay* is 120 pages long - never one page more, never one page less. Why? It's because the script length of 120 pages equals a two hour, full-length feature film — and that means the running time of each screenplay page is approximately equal to one minute of actual film time.

Hollywood is a strange place. If you ask a producer to read a screenplay *treatment* he will refuse, and ask to see the *screenplay*. Being offered the screenplay, he will then refuse it and read the screenplay treatment. Strange place, strange people. All are more slippery than WD-40.

This screenplay treatment is an adaptation of an article I had published in 1968 in a professional Navy journal, *The United States Naval Proceedings*. It was based on the original court proceedings of a 1916 court martial of a young Navy officer, Ensign Oliver O. Kessing, Jr., USN. I first became interested in the court proceedings because they described a court martial where the defendant was awarded the Navy Cross, second only to our nation's highest award, The Medal of Honor. It is the only time in the Navy's history when this happened. Then I became intrigued with the larger story; one which included a cowardly commanding officer and a brave young woman who didn't receive recognition for her heroic actions. President Woodrow Wilson felt it would be a political mistake to honor a woman at a time when the suffragette movement was making waves. And many of the voters, as well as almost all of the politicians, didn't want women to be able to vote.

Add in General John J. "Black Jack" Pershing, the hero of WW I, and Pancho Villa, a well-known Mexican guerrilla, and I felt it had the ingredients of a terrific story. Read the screenplay treatment and see if you don't agree with me.

(As this book went to press, the process of converting this screenplay treatment into a screenplay for a TV mini-series had begun.)

Walter F. Stuhldreher
Tallahassee, Florida

THE MAZATLAN INCIDENT

A screenplay treatment by Walter F. Stuhldreher

Registration # 8616262
The Writers Guild of America, West
Expiration Date: 04/01/2007

3709 Longford Drive
Tallahassee, FL 32309
850 / 893-3561
Bettiebud@aol. com

Walter "Bud" Stuhldreher

Date: January, 1973   Location: A home in Virginia Beach, Va.

In the living room of a modest home in Virginia Beach, Virginia, a woman, in her early 80's is looking at a glossy brochure advertising the joys of "Vacationing in Mazatlan, Mexico." Smiling to herself, she reaches for a scrapbook and turns to a page which contains a letter dated August 19, 1916. The letter is addressed to Mrs. A. Gordon Brown, commending her for her actions at Mazatlan, Mexico, on June 18, 1916. It was signed by the Secretary of the Navy, Josephus Daniels. She leans back in her chair as she recalls what happened that terrible day.

Date: March 10, 1916   Location: The White House, Washington, D.C.

Woodrow Wilson, elected President in November 1912, is three years into his first term and preparing for reelection later that year. His campaign slogan is to be "He Kept Us Out of War." (World War I had started two years earlier, and America is not yet involved.) Wilson was informed that on March 9, 1916, the Mexican revolutionary Pancho Villa, with 600 troops, attacked the tiny American border town of Columbus, New Mexico. Villa burned the town to the ground, killing 18 Americans. Wilson has a tough decision to make. This first attack by foreigners on the U.S. mainland since the War of 1812 is sure to generate a tremendous wave of controversy as the nation debates how to avenge this massacre.

In Congress, Senator Henry Ashurst shouts, "Hunt out these red-handed bandits, bring them back to Columbus, and shoot them on the spot."

360

Senator Albert Fall wants 500,000 troops sent to seize every one of Mexico's ports and rail lines. Other Senators are equally outspoken.

President Wilson fears a war along the border will distract from his reform agenda at home. Also, a war would sidetrack his reelection campaign, which is set up with peace as its main thrust. Complicating his choice of options is Wilson's realization he was partially to blame for the political unrest in Mexico.

In 1913 Wilson told Congress there could be no peace in Mexico while General Victoriano Huerta ruled Mexico as dictator. Huerta had gained control by assassinating the elected President, Francisco I. Madero. Then Wilson permitted Huerta's enemies, who had begun a revolution, to obtain arms in the United States. Wilson let the Mexican groups fight it out for a while. But in April 1914, when Huerta's forces arrested 14 American sailors who had gone ashore at Tampico, Mexico, Wilson took action. After Huerta had refused to apologize, Wilson ordered American forces to occupy the Mexican port of Veracruz. Eighteen Americans were killed in the occupation.

Huerta soon fled from Mexico, and Venustiano Carranza, backed by Wilson, became acting President. Francisco "Pancho" Villa, one of Carranza's chief generals, then quarreled with Carranza and led a revolution against him. Carranza's soldiers drove Villa into northern Mexico where he began raiding American settlements across the Rio Grande. Many Americans called for war, but Wilson would not yield to their pressure. "Watchful waiting" became his policy. Wilson did send a "punitive expedition" of 10,000 men under General John J. Pershing to patrol the border, settling for something short of the political middle ground. For the next two years Mexican forces harassed Americans living in the area.

Walter "Bud" Stuhldreher

Date: April and June 1916: Location: The White House, Washington

Wilson orders General Pershing to pursue Villa deep into Mexico. Pershing's totally inadequate force of 10,000 Americans chase Villa around Mexico without making contact. Carranza warns that he would resist any further invasion, and his troops attack the Army's 10th Cavalry in June, killing 14 Americans.

Fed up with Wilson's continued indecision about what America should do, and with Mexican forces killing American military personnel and civilians with no retaliation, the politicians are howling for all-out war. Forced into action, Wilson mobilizes the National Guard and sends 112,000 American troops to the border.

Date: April 28, 1916 Location: *USS Annapolis* (PG-10)

The *Annapolis*, a 168-foot, three-masted gunboat with steam as her main power, is anchored off Mazatlan, a district in the state of Sinaloa, Mexico. Sent by the American government, she has two main duties to perform: 1. Keep up with the situation ashore. (Relations between the United States and Mexico are strained, communications are difficult, and the news is often contradictory.) 2. Be ready to provide asylum aboard the *Annapolis* for all Americans in the Mazatlan district in the event of war. The recent attack on Columbus, New Mexico by Villa, unanswered by the American government, has added to the tension.

During the next two months, the relations between Commander A.G. Kavanaugh, the commanding officer of the *Annapolis*, and the Mexican military authorities at Mazatlan remain friendly. The *Annapolis* sends boats to Mazatlan regularly, and officers are repeatedly granted permission to go ashore. They also deliver press reports, received by radio, to Angel Flores, the Governor and Military Commander of Sinaloa, at his request.

Date: June 17, 1916   Location: Mazatlan, Mexico

About 4:00 p.m. Governor Flores, who lived in Mazatlan but is now in Culiacan, 120 miles north of Mazatlan, issues a proclamation. Dated from Culiacan, it states that a telegram has been received and that Mexico and the United States will undoubtedly go to war! It calls on the Mexican inhabitants of Sinaloa to rally to the defense of the area. This proclamation results in arms and ammunition being issued to the civilian population of Mazatlan that evening.

The medical officer of the *Annapolis*, Assistant Surgeon J.A. Omer, happens to be spending the night ashore with a patient in the hospital where they learn of the proclamation.

Date: June 18, 1916   Location: Aboard the *USS Annapolis*

Ensign Kessing, whose nickname as a midshipmen was "Scrappy," almost didn't make it back to his ship, the 168-foot composite gunboat *Annapolis*, after the 1916 Mexican incident

Dr. Omer returns to the *Annapolis* on its 9 a.m. boat, commanded by Ensign Oliver O. Kessing, a recent graduate of the Naval Academy. Omer and Kessing immediately realize the officers and crew of the *Annapolis* are unaware of the changed situation, and that arms and ammunition have been issued to the civilian population of Mazatlan the previous evening.

Omer and Kessing report to Commander Kavanaugh's stateroom as ordered. Omer reports that he spent an anxious night on the beach, because of hearing the discharge of firearms in Mazatlan throughout the night. Also, people had come to the private hospital where he was attending his patient, with rumors that war between the United States and Mexico had already begun and that there was severe fighting along the northern frontier. Further, Doctor Omer states that he experienced some difficulties in getting to the pier to meet the 9:00 a.m. boat commanded by Kessing. In fact, Omer reports, some armed civilians, drunk, grabbed and searched him, looking for money. Omer feels that had he been armed, things might have gone very badly for him. Omer next gives Kavanaugh a copy of the proclamation. Kessing adds that when his boat came alongside the pier, an official notified him that no one from the *Annapolis* will be allowed to go ashore in the future by order of General Flores.

Commander Kavanaugh has heard nothing from U.S. Vice Consul Alfred G. Brown, who lives in Mazatlan, concerning the proclamation issued the previous night. From the copy Omer gave him he comes to two conclusions:

1. The Mexicans are about to begin hostilities, and,
2. The Mexicans have probably done something to prevent the Vice Consul from communicating with the *Annapolis*.

Kavanaugh knows the *Annapolis* is the only hope the Americans ashore have of being rescued, since it is the only American military presence within hundreds of miles. Kavanaugh now decides it's time to take action, as required by his orders issued over two months earlier and still in effect. It will be necessary to send an officer ashore to make an effort to get in touch with Brown, the American Vice Consul, recommending that all Americans in the Mazatlan district take asylum on the *Annapolis* as soon as possible. Kavanaugh is very concerned by Omer's report of numerous Mexican civilians firing weapons the previous night. Obviously the Mexican military forces in Mazatlan have been enlarged by issuing arms to civilians. These civilians are bolstered by drink and not subject to military authority. Influenced by Villa's, Huerto's and Carranza's ability to kill Americans and not pay a price for it, they are a grave danger for Americans in Mazatlan. A massacre is not only possible, but probable. And the one Mexican who could possibly restrain the civilians is elsewhere, Governor Flores being in Culiacan.

Ensign Kessing previously volunteered to go ashore in case anyone was sent ashore from the *Annapolis*. Kavanaugh, having decided he is the best officer for this dangerous duty, gives Kessing instructions to go in close to the pier and ask the Mexicans to send for the U.S. Consul; to ask one of the Mexican officials how American refugees could be embarked; to be careful not to show any disrespect or to argue with the Mexicans, but to be very polite to them. At this point, Kessing volunteers to go to the consulate, but Kavanaugh is adamant about rejecting this proposal:

"Mr. Kessing, I will not send anyone into the town under any circumstances since the Mexicans have issued an order forbidding our landing. You should lay off the wharf so that the

Mexicans cannot seize the boat, and carry on a conversation from there with the parties ashore."

Kavanaugh directs Kessing to take Assistant Paymaster Andrew Mowat, USN, with him as interpreter. While not fluent in Spanish, Mowat has the best Spanish of anyone on the ship.

Ashore

Kessing, after hiding arms and ammunition in the boat, proceeds to the pier, laying off as instructed. Due to the noise of the boat's engine, Kessing cannot talk with the Mexican officials on the pier, so he has the boat go alongside the pier. The Mexicans refuse to send any messages to the Vice Consul, but state they have been ordered to give the American officers a safe escort to and from the consulate if they care to go. Kessing and Mowat go up the stairs, and are immediately grabbed by several Mexican soldiers. Kessing yells at the boat to return to the ship and report to the Captain. Kessing and Mowat are surrounded by twelve soldiers and hustled off the dock, hearing shooting start. Instead of taking the Americans to the consulate as promised, the soldiers take them to Fort Vienta dos de Deciembre, forcing them to run the whole way. On the way they see numerous soldiers and civilians behind rocks and bushes firing at the boat, whose colors are flying. The crowd repeatedly shouts, "Viva Mexico," "Viva Carranza," "Kill the Gringos," "Lynch them," "Shoot them," as Kessing and Mowat are pushed into a room in the fort and lined up against a wall. Soldiers form up against the opposite wall and load their rifles. Mowat asks what is going to happen and is told they are going to be shot.

Luckily, a Colonel Miranda passes the door at this time and Mowat shouts for him to stop the execution. Miranda does so, and agrees to take them to see General Mexta. After a difficult

SOUR M.A.S.H. AT SEA - SECOND WAVE

passage to Mexta's quarters, Kessing and Mowat are told by Colonel Miranda the Americans started the firing, and since the *Annapolis* was seen putting out to sea, he is very sorry for them. The firing squad is re-forming. At this time, 50-year old Vice Consul Brown and his wife, 26-year old Maria Brown, enter the room. Mrs. Brown, the former Senorita Maria de la Vega, of Mazatlan, Sinaloa, Mexico, had married Brown two years earlier.

Meanwhile, after Kessing and Mowat leave the ship's boat, it shoves off from the pier, intending to return to the *Annapolis*. The treachery of the Mexicans now becomes apparent. Earlier, a Mexican Captain had called General Flores when he saw the boat approaching the pier. He was ordered to shoot any Americans who tried to land. The Mexican Captain now pulls his revolver and shoots one of the Americans in the boat. The shot signals the crowd of Mexican soldiers and civilians to open fire on the boat. The American sailors grab their hidden rifles and return fire. Before getting back to the *Annapolis*, several sailors are killed and several others are wounded. The Mexicans have 17 fatalities and approximately 30 wounded. (The Mexican Captain, who fired the first shot, is mortally wounded and dies the next day.)

Aboard the *Annapolis*

The *Annapolis* is safely anchored 2,200 yards from shore, well outside firing range of the Mexicans, but when Captain Kavanaugh sees and hears the fighting, he orders the crew to general quarters. The ship's boat pulls alongside with its dead and wounded sailors, and Captain Kavanaugh is told Mowat and Kessing are prisoners of the Mexicans. Kavanaugh immediately gets the *Annapolis* underway and out of the harbor of Mazatlan. Several officers protest this action, not wanting to leave Mowat, Kessing and the American refugees behind. They tell the Captain the Mexicans would take great satisfaction in seeing the

Annapolis leaving, and the ship is in no danger. They strongly believe a massacre would result if they depart. Captain Kavanaugh refuses their pleas and continues putting more space between his ship and Mazatlan, not stopping until the ship rounds Black Rock, out of sight of Mazatlan.

Ashore

Back on shore Vice Consul Brown, Colonel Miranda and General Mexta discuss the situation in a hall outside of the room where Mowat and Kessing are still lined up against a wall. General Mexta decides Brown should go out to the *Annapolis* to demand an apology from the Captain, and that Mowat and Kessing will be released if he gets the apology. Brown and his wife leave, but Mrs. Brown hurriedly returns a few minutes later, nearly hysterical. She stands between Mowat and Kessing. She says she overheard the soldiers say they will shoot the Gringos as soon as Mrs. Brown left. Vice Consul Brown, not wanting to leave his young wife in front of a Mexican firing squad, argues with Mrs. Brown to leave with him, but she repeatedly refuses. Mrs. Brown tells him her duty is clear: stay with the two Americans. She remains standing between Mowat and Kessing for several hours. *The firing squad remains in firing position.*

Around noon, Brown finally returns, saying he has a letter of apology from Captain Kavanaugh to Mexta and that Kessing and Mowat are now free to return to the ship. However, Colonel Miranda tells Kessing and Mowat that Vice Consul Brown will first have to see General Mexta. While Brown is seeing Mexta, Colonel Miranda talks with several of his officers, and these officers leave immediately.

About 3:00 p.m., Brown and Miranda return. Brown tells Mowat and Kessing they are free to go, that Miranda will provide an escort to the pier and they will be sent out to the *Annapolis* in a Mexican boat. As Mowat and Kessing leave the building, the Mexican boat crew comes in saying they will not take them out. Brown asks why, and the boat crew replies that they are afraid because the Americans are going to be shot on the way to the pier. Brown asks them if anyone would shoot if Mrs. Brown was with them; they reply no. Then Vice Consul and Mrs. Brown decide to accompany Mowat and Kessing to the ship. After passing many angry Mexican soldiers and civilians, they arrive safely at the pier. One man on the pier tells Mowat that if Mrs. Brown had not been with them they would have been shot, either before getting to the pier, or on the pier. He adds that, war or not, the Mexicans would get them the next time they came ashore in Mazatlan. When the four Americans board the boat furnished by the Mexicans, Colonel Miranda refuses to let it proceed until Brown pays him ten dollars in gold.

Aboard the *Annapolis*

As Vice Consul and Mrs. Brown, Mowat, and Kessing, board the *Annapolis*, the crew, which had feared them dead, breaks out in a spontaneous cheer. Captain Kavanaugh is not so happy. After escorting Vice Consul Brown and Mrs. Brown to a cabin, he returns to the deck where Mowat and Kessing are still being congratulated by their shipmates.

"Ensign Oliver O. Kessing, you are hereby directed to remain in your cabin under close arrest. You are going to be court-martialed for flagrantly disobeying a direct order that resulted in the deaths of American sailors, your shipmates. Further, your failure to obey orders has resulted in a flagrant insult to the United States by Mexico. You are hereby relieved of your duties. Dismissed."

Ashore

With the hated American military gone, tensions abate. Many American refugees hire boats to take them out to the *Annapolis*, but most return to Mazatlan when they realize conditions have improved and are as normal as could be expected. Back in Washington, D.C., however, things are different, very different.

A week later in Washington, D.C.

President Woodrow Wilson is very unhappy with the Secretary of the Navy, Josephus Daniels. Wilson wants the American public to forget about Mexico. He particularly wants to bring back the large American military forces uselessly chasing Mexican guerrilla forces, doing no damage except to American pride.

(Wilson) "Daniels, I don't understand why you can't have that court martial called off. The Navy has the wrong man on trial. It should be that yellow-tailed Captain who scooted with his ship. All it's doing is keeping the mess in that Mexican town — I forget the name — on the front page of the papers. Just where I don't want it."

(Daniels) "Mr. President, the Mexican town is Mazatlan, and stopping a court martial is not that simple. Once a court martial gets put in motion, it takes on a life of its own. I'm sorry to tell you that it will start on July 10, and I can't do anything to stop it."

(Wilson) "I don't want to hear that. But if you say so, OK. Maybe we can get this court martial to work for us, not against us. What this country needs now is a hero. Was there one?"

(Daniels) "Yes sir, there certainly was; a Mexican native, the young wife of our Vice Consul there, a Mrs. Alfred Brown. She stood between a Mexican firing squad and some American officers for several hours, thus saving their lives."

(Wilson) "Are you crazy? We can't have a woman hero. The suffragettes are marching up and down the Eastern Coast, including here in the nation's capital, demanding the right to vote. I'm not about to help their cause with a female hero. That would be political suicide. Is there anyone else?"

(Daniels) "Yes sir, the officer being court martialled. He showed great courage facing death several times that day. He's young and looks good in his uniform."

(Wilson) "Now we're getting somewhere! Here's what I want you to do..."

Date: July 10, 1916   Location: Aboard the *USS San Diego*

The court martial of Ensign Oliver O. Kessing, USN, commences aboard the *San Diego*, flagship of the U.S. Pacific Fleet. Called for by Admiral C. McR. Winslow, Commander-in-Chief, Pacific Fleet, it was preceded by several telephone calls and telegrams between Daniels and Winslow. Seven officers, the members of the court, file in and take their places, The senior officer, Admiral Winslow, occupies the middle seat; the others are seated as their rank dictates. Also, as tradition demands, Admiral Winslow's sword lies on the table before the board, pointing sideways.

The court martial moves along at an astonishingly fast clip. Witnesses are only briefly interviewed. Even Ensign Kessing isn't asked much. However, it was a different story with the Captain of the *Annapolis*, Commander Kavanaugh. He is

Walter "Bud" Stuhldreher

subjected to a rigorous examination of his actions that fateful day. His answers are noticeably disliked by the members of the court. The business is concluded that day, with the members of the court meeting in seclusion to make their decision.

July 11, 1916, aboard the *San Diego*

Kessing is called in to hear the verdict. His eyes, and those of the other participants in the trial, immediately look to see in which direction the sword is pointed. If toward the members of the court, the defendant has been found innocent, but if it pointed at the defendant, then he has been judged guilty. To Kessing's obvious relief, the sword is pointing at the Admiral! The following is read: "Ensign Oliver O. Kessing, you have been found not guilty of all specifications contained in the order of court martial. Further, this court finds that you acted in the finest traditions of the U.S. Navy, bringing glory to the nation. Accordingly, you have been recommended to be awarded the Navy Cross which, as you know, is our nation's second-highest honor. This court is pleased to make this recommendation, feeling strongly it reflects our pride and the nation's pride in your heroic actions at Mazatlan, Mexico. You are congratulated and dismissed."

The board calls in one other officer, Commander Kavanaugh. "Commander Kavanaugh, you are hereby immediately relieved of your command of the *USS Annapolis*. You will be assigned a shore billet waiting further assignment. Dismissed."

The board has one other remaining duty. Secretary Daniels is immediately informed of the outcome of the court martial by Admiral Winslow. Daniels is not surprised.

Date: August 1916 Location: The White House, Washington, D.C.

(Wilson) "See, Daniels, it happened just as I said it would. The public got their hero, they have forgotten Mexico, and we can go ahead with the nation's business. Now that's what I call a good ending to a difficult situation."

(Daniels) "I agree with you, Mr. President, but I still feel badly about our ignoring Mrs. Brown, the only real hero in this whole business."

(Wilson) "Can't be helped, Josephus. You know my reasons. Any politician who helps the suffragette movement will never be reelected, but make sure Mrs. Wilson doesn't find out about how I treated Mrs. Brown. (Wilson had married Mrs. Edward Bolling Galt, a widow, on December 18, 1915, just a few months earlier. The second Mrs. Wilson was known to be an intelligent and strong-minded woman.) She would be angry with me and I don't want that. Now, Josephus, this is the last time I'm going to tell you to forget Mrs. Brown. This administration is done with her."

The next day   Location: The Secretary of the Navy's office

Josephus Daniels, the Secretary of the Navy, 1913 to 1921, is troubled. It just is not right to ignore Mrs. Brown. She performed heroically and the administration did not. He decides to disobey President Wilson and write her a letter, officially recognizing her efforts in saving the lives of two American officers. He does so, commending her in flattering, yet justified, terms. Daniels hopes President Wilson, and especially Mrs. Wilson, will never hear about the letter.

Walter "Bud" Stuhldreher

Date: January 1973   Location: A Home in Virginia Beach, Virginia

The old woman lays down the letter from Secretary Daniels, sent so many years ago. It was the only recognition she ever received for her actions that terrible day in Mazatlan, Mexico, almost 60 years ago. Until now. Today she received a magazine from a friend of the family. A professional publication of the Navy, it contained an article describing "*The Mazatlan Incident.*" Mrs. Brown had finally received public recognition. She was content.

SCRAPBOOK

An unexpected bonus from writing my previous book, SOUR M.A.S.H. AT SEA - And Other Stories, was receiving comments on it from relatives, friends and strangers. In some instances, from shipmates I hadn't heard from in fifty years. Some were received while I was writing the book; other comments were received with orders for the book, and finally, some came after the book was published. Here are a few of them. Some poignant, many humorous, one startling. At least it startled me — a blind person ordered the book.

Walter "Bud" Stuhldreher

****

Alexander Rearick, Fishers, IN:

Please autograph as follows: To my brother-in-law Alex Rearick whom I have never managed to offend.

Dear Bud:

At breakfast this AM I opened your crass commercial letter while drinking imported Kona coffee from my "**Colon & Rectal Care Center**" coffee mug.

I am pleased to know you are doing something beneficial with your retirement instead of leading an "Indolent Life of Leisure."

Now that Nancy [his deceased wife] is no longer looking over my shoulder trying to keep me from "frittering away money" I can buy your book.

Have to close now. Broke a tooth today & scheduled for dental repair tomorrow, Warm regards.

****

Gene Tanzy, Tallahassee, FL, a retired Florida State University Professor:

You haven't heard from me about your picturesque tales for various reasons, the main being that I've been in the hospital fighting a sudden fierce attack of pneumonia. Now home, and kept from the public by a tigress named Regina [his wife], I've been convalescing with the stories of that natural author, you. What a way to recoup, laughing with you.

No kidding, you are a natural storyteller. You missed your calling, I swear, and maybe you ought to take it up in these riper years. I admire the way you write. Direct, vivid, getting us in with you on the spot. That's hard to do. Actually I think you write like you drive — with verve — and taking in just about everything along the way, commenting, scaring the people you're with, who don't know just what's what (and that my friend is what makes a story great), but always with a destination you know you're heading for and are going to get to.

Slap dash. Flynn, take cover. Tom Jones, yes. A rogue, oh yes! You haven't changed your spirit, thank God. A real life picturesque hero if there ever was one. You must have come from great parents. I love the way your mother laughed.

****

Doris Gyorgyi, South Bend, Indiana:

Bud!!! You will never know how much you have entertained the Gyorgyis with your emails. In fact, I shared them with my family and friends. Our daughter's comment was, "I just wonder how he survived — no, I take that back, I wonder how the Navy survived during his tour of duty." I sent a copy of the first one to my friend at Notre Dame and she called me to find out if there were more to come. My brother in law said he was laughing all the way through that email — would being a Marine have anything to do with his laughing?

Then you sent one on the Ups and Downs of a Magician and the comments got better. They all want to meet you because compared to you the people they know are dull, including themselves.

Walter "Bud" Stuhldreher

****

Comments on the *Honeymoon From Hell* story

Niece Jennifer Greene, Chicago, Il:

Uncle Bud: I have a new aspiration in life — to develop as much patience as Bettie obviously has. It's a miracle she still speaks to you at all! And, as a side note, I cannot wait for the one about the Japanese mermaids — sounds too good to be true but then, so do the rest of the stories you've been sending.

I have to tell you these stories just about kill me — it's hard to believe they are even true. Uncle Bud, you may be the unluckiest person at times, but your "adventures" have brightened many a day lately. Just so you know, I often share these with friends who feel I may have the most entertaining family around! I couldn't agree more.

Niece Mindy Greene, Chicago, IL:

I wasn't sure anything could be funnier than the chimpanzees in the state fair story — but this one beats it by far. I just sat here at work and laughed out loud. Hilarious! Bettie is a good sport — and it must be true love!

Nephew Mike Stuhldreher, Columbus, Ohio:

Uncle Bud, this one really takes the cake. Like Jen has said, it's almost too good to be true.

****

SOUR M.A.S.H. AT SEA - SECOND WAVE

Comments received with book orders

Former Haven patient Altone Lathrop, Willimantic, CT:

I was a patient on the USS Haven having been wounded at Charwon April 26, 1952, and spent over a month on the Haven before being sent back to the front. I recall a Navy Corpsman Milo Pearsom from Aransas Pass, Texas and a Dr. Pearsom. I don't think they were related.

Looking forward to reading the book.

Nurse Mary Shafer Cermak said one of the toughest things for her was sending the boys back to the front after patching them up. WFS

****

Niece Mary Connerton's, Oak Harbor, Washington, autograph request. Mary was sending the book to her Dad for a Father's Day present.

May this book help you to remember the good times, life's misadventures, and all other special times during your lifetime. Enjoy this Father's Day from your daughter. Love, Mary.

****

Jack Bradshaw, Indianapolis, Indiana:

I am happy to enclose an order form for one copy. You will note I have even popped for the hardback version. Despite the unexpected dent that this outlay will put into the net spendable portion of my next month's Social Security check, I am indulging in this bit of extravagance for a special reason. Since I

Walter "Bud" Stuhldreher

preceded you by one year at Cathedral High School and Notre Dame, I doubtless had a profound and exemplary impact on your psyche during your tender and formative years. As a result I can look forward with confidence to seeing my name approvingly mentioned in your book. If, however, I am destined for disappointment in this respect, you can make suitable atonement for this oversight by appropriate comments in the author's autograph page. Then again, I could be persuaded to settle for a bit part in your book's forthcoming movie, or perhaps the television series that is sure to follow. Move over Seinfeld, here comes Stuhldreher.

Sorry to disappoint you, Jack, but since I have absolutely no memories of you ever having a favorable impact on my psyche, indeed, just the opposite as I recall, you missed the Acknowledgments section. But you did write a damn funny letter! WFS

****

Isabelle Rodwell, Rochester, NY:

Robert was pleased to meet you on the MS Noordam and equally pleased to hear from you. I tend to be the secretary in this marriage, he has never been one to write letters, so I will suffice, and hope you can read my writing.

Thank you for sending us the short story, *A Monkey Named Lazarus*. If all the stories in your book are as good as that one, you will have no trouble selling your book. We really enjoyed it and got many laughs.

Thanks again, we know we will enjoy your book when we receive it.

Hope I see you at the reunion. Best wishes.

****

Captain Frank B. Shemanski, USN (Ret.), San Diego, CA:

Dear Walt: (Lord High Everything Else in USS Haven) Got your mailing and I am ordering a copy of your book.

I was on the Haven during 1954/55 as an Ensign and JG and managed to accumulate 21 collateral duties. Have service record entries to prove it. If you were as much of a "Badass" as you imply, you and I would have met officially since I was legal officer and prosecuted all courts-martial. Not too many, because after a few folks went to the brig four hours after their court, sailors stopped screwing up on the Haven.

P.S. Your last name coincides with one of the 4 horsemen of the Notre Dame football team christened by Grantland Rice, a pretty good sportswriter. Are you related in any way? Always intended to write the great American naval novel but never got around to it. Glad you could do that which I could not. (gr)

Best of luck and keep scribbling!

****

Donna Beckman, Floodwood, MN:

I'm ordering this for my husband, Marvin. He served on the Kleinsmith right after he graduated from high school in 1949. Maybe you could autograph as you see fit.

****

Walter "Bud" Stuhldreher

John Cicogna, Senior Chief Petty Officer, U.S. Navy, Retired, Saunderstown, RI:

Walt, happy to order your book. I served aboard Kleinsmith after you, 1958-59, as an RD2, and made the Great Lakes cruise. Simply endorse the book "Shipmate" or something appropriate.

****

Captain Richard M. Baker, USN, Ret., Tallahassee, FL:

Dear Bud, please autograph your book as follows.

Time, as we know, is the destroyer of youth, strength and beauty. This axiom applies to most, but not all, men. In the case of Richard M. Baker, Ph.D., Captain, USN Retired, FSU Athletic Hall of Fame (1977), M. Litt., BS., Professor Emeritus, and a host of other honors and benefices too numerous to mention in this allotted space, time has been his friend. Whereas time tends to savage the vast majority of men, it has been so very kind to Dr. Baker. One only has to remark him a single time to disbelieve that he has witnessed Mother Earth in her annual voyage about the sun a full eighty-two cycles. To view him one is moved to exclaim, "Here is a young, strong, handsome man." How can this be, given his alleged span on this soul-wrenching, mind-numbing, body-destroying coil? The answer, alas, resides in the heart and mind of God Almighty alone. Nevertheless, this scribe shall attempt to unravel an explanation sufficient to bring understanding to this mysterious phenomenon.

The world has been embarked on a never-ending search for the secrets of perpetual youth and even, perhaps, eternal life on this side of the curtain that separates us from the realm where one must go to take his own chamber in the silent halls of death.

Conjecture leads me to believe that the aforementioned Dr. Baker has, indeed, unlocked some, if not all, of the secrets that Nature has so carefully husbanded and held close to her breast. This writer yearns to probe, to delve into the life and times of the subject, but quails at the thought that he may be treading on sacred and hallowed ground. Even so, one has to ask, "Could it be Viagra, Zocor, Preparation H, Grecian Formula for Men, or perhaps it is not chemical at all?" It now comes down to this: To learn one often has to beard the lion, to risk all by confronting the source and to ask the crucial question. I have decided to go directly to Dr. Baker with my question, and if the sonofabitch fails to reveal to me what I must know, I will not autograph his stinking book.

Your name

Needless to say, I didn't autograph Dick's book as requested. Too much crap for me to put my name to! W.F.S.

****

Mel Hendrickson, Las Vegas, NV:

Walt: Please autograph (a little tongue in cheek!) as follows:

To Mel Hendrickson, who single-handedly planned and directed the atomic tests at Bikini in 1946.

P.S.: Did you have a relative that coached at University of Wisconsin?

****

Walter "Bud" Stuhldreher

Frank Cermak, Tallahassee, FL:

Mary was a nurse on the Haven. Mary is blind - so I'll be reading it to her.

****

Frances Klein, San Diego, CA:

Dear Mr. S:

So happy you're writing your memories of the service. I'm anxious to read of your experiences in Sour Mash At Sea & other Stories.

I served as a navy nurse during and before the Korean War. Later it grieved me to realize these little boys went to fight a war in Vietnam that I helped bring into the world.

****

Joseph McConville, Quincy, MA:

Please autograph as follows: To SK2 McConville from your former Supply Officer.

Hello, Mr. Stuhldreher. I can't believe it is almost 50 years now that I left the Kleinsmith. Did see Frank Rizzuto, my striker, for the first time at the last reunion. Have seen Richie Ciullo, and his son came into Boston Gear one day to verify our Workers Comp liability. I had 8 years service when I returned, and retired as Personnel Manager with 48 plus years. Took LTJG Davis's advice and got my BBA nights at Northeastern on the G.I. Bill. Meanwhile, I got married and we have 4 sons and a daughter. Two sons graduated from Providence, one from

Mass. Maritime (MBA from B.C.) who is the Project Engineer/Manager for the U.S. Navy's flagships, and my future general per his own unbelievable resume (enclosed). My daughter is an oncology nurse with her masters. Needless to say how proud I am for what they have done.

So as I finish my remarks, I am looking out the window where I can watch every ship enter Boston Harbor or planes land at Logan Airport. Life has been good and I am very grateful for the many blessings I have received over the years. Best wishes.

****

Captain J. H. Armstrong, USN, (Ret.), Tallahassee, FL:

Please autograph as follows: From one sand bagger to another!

Dear Bud:

Congratulations on sitting still long enough to write a book. Am looking forward to reading it.

****

John P. Casey, St. Petersburg, FL:

Dear Walt:

If you're the Walt Stuhldreher we affectionately knew as "Waldo," then indeed I'm the same Casey who served with you on the Kleinsmith lo those many years ago. It was good to hear from you.

Walter "Bud" Stuhldreher

So you've turned into an author; congratulations and of course I want a copy of your latest book — look forward to reading it.

After the Navy I went back to work for GE and stayed there until I retired in '92. Was most fortunate in that my division supplied propulsion equipment (steam turbines and reduction gears) to large ships of all types — both Navy and commercial. Most of my years were spent in Engineering but I concluded my career in program management.

I married in 1960, had 5 children, 4 girls and a boy in that order. All but one are married and have graced me with six grandchildren from Georgia to Virginia to Massachusetts. Divorced in 1991 after straightening their teeth, music/dance lessons and putting all five through college. My ex-wife and I are on good terms.

Your memory is better than mine - I could never remember Norm Feldpush's name.

Let me know when your next book is published as I'll definitely want a copy. Thanks again for writing and giving me a chance to revive old memories.

****

Shem Blackley, Jr., Charlotte, NC:

Dear Walt:

Indeed, I do remember you, even though our tours on the Kleinsmith overlapped only a few months. I look forward to reading Sour Mash. I regret that I did not keep a journal during those days — there were some pretty notable and exciting times.

I served from August '54 until August '57, then was assigned to the Naval Academy as an instructor until August of '59. Kleinsmith had one deployment to the Med during my time — officers during that time were Dave Miller, Norm Feldpush, Tom Megan (your relief), Captain Kelshner (a lush), Jerry Hamilton, et al.

Several years ago I visited the Navy Memorial in DC and through some computer manipulation found that the Kleinsmith was still operating in the Taiwanese Navy! I think I caught a glimpse of her on the news sometime later — at least [it was] an APD in Formosa.

I spent 30 years with Duke Power Company in engineering. Martha and I have been married 49 years in June. We have 4 kids and 12 grandkids — all near by. Life has been good to us.

Great to hear from you. Drop us a note when you can. Have you done other writing?

I enjoyed your interesting letter of April 7, and look forward to getting your book. I feel sure that Dave and Pat Miller would appreciate hearing from you. Let's keep in touch. I'm certain that reading your book will sharpen my recall of events.

P.S. I recall my father (long deceased) had some acquaintance with your uncle (or father?) through Notre Dame football. Four Horsemen, etc. Can you fill in the blanks?

Contrary to what many shipmates like Shem thought, I did not keep a journal. I simply have a quirky memory and can remember long-ago events with amazing detail. W.F.S.

****

Walter "Bud" Stuhldreher

Rex Raymond, Tacoma, WA:

Walt: Will use this copy for our reunion table - shipmates to look and order. USS Haven Reunion Seattle 2004 Reunion. Rex Raymond, USS Haven 1952-1955, Reunion Coordinator

****

Jackie Frazier, Cincinnati, OH:

Sounds like you must be related to Charles. He was a devil when he served in the Navy aboard the USS Montpelier during WW II, June 1942 to December, 1945. However by the time he was assigned to the Haven he was settling down. He served from Sept. 1950 until March, 1952. It was as the mailman. Also served on the USS Pine Island from 1947 - 1950.

He is fine, doesn't like to write.

****

June Marvin, Huntsville, AL:

Thanks for the opportunity to get your autographed copy of your book. I think it's wonderful! Can't wait to get to reading it. It should be a kick!

****

Dick Lorenz, Deerfield, IL:

Please autograph as follows:

(a) To my best friend

(b) To the smartest guy I ever met
(c) Something appropriate

****

Paul Harrawood, Fairfield, VA:

Bud: I served on the Kleinsmith 1951 - 54, just ahead of you. It will be interesting to compare experiences.

****

Mary Heaney, Battle Creek, MI:

Please autograph as follows:

To Mary Heaney, original Plank Holder - aboard USS Haven (AH-12) May, 1945 - January, 1946.

****

Floyd Norris, Pensacola, FL:

Dear "Bud":

Seems that about the time I was ending my approximately three year stint aboard the Haven, you were coming aboard. If you have access to old cruise books, it was I who wrote the text for the '52 and '53 editions. I hope those years are correct.

I too wrote a novel about my time aboard the "Galloping Ghost of the Korean Coast" but it was neither light-hearted nor humorous and I have never made a sincere effort at getting it published.

Walter "Bud" Stuhldreher

Am looking forward to receiving your book and wish you great commercial success.

****

Nephew Mike Stuhldreher, Columbus, OH:

Please autograph as follows:

"To Mike my nephew, I hope you enjoy reading this as much as I enjoyed living it. Love, Uncle Bud" Or whatever else you want to write. You're a better letter writer than I am.

****

Paul Pudenz, Sunset Beach, CA:

Please autograph as follows:

I served on the Haven from January, 1963 to June, 1966. To all Hospital Corpsmen, God Bless.

****

Dusty Rhodes, Tallahassee, FL:

My year in Hell on the Haven was March, 1956 - April, 1957. Was the H Division officer LCDR Warren David Decious, MSC, USN, during your tour? I was transferred to Haven as punishment for voluntarily dropping from O.R. tech course at Balboa.

****

SOUR M.A.S.H. AT SEA - SECOND WAVE

Betty Burkhalter, Orinda, CA:

Please autograph as follows:

To Dick and Betty who witnessed some of the "Honeymoon From Hell."

Also: Dear Bettie and Bud: Great to hear from you. Know your book will be lots of fun. Thanks for thinking of us.

****

Glenn Lambert, Monticello, Iowa:

Please autograph as follows:

To Glenn Lambert - Original Plank Owner - May 5, 1945 - USS Haven (AH-12) - NAGASAKI Evacuation - Magic Carpet Duty - Pacific Theater

****

Nephew David Tobin, Anchorage, Alaska:

Please autograph as follows:

To David, Val and Briana Tobin. Briana - these are tales from your grandmother's (Marge Tobin) brother.

****

Tom McCullion, Tallahassee, FL:

Please autograph as follows: To another Irish Fan!

Walter "Bud" Stuhldreher

Also: Walt, Best of luck with your first edition. Tom

****

Dave Miller, Warrenton, VA:

Pat and I enjoyed your letter and the news of your book. Yes, we would like to order a copy.

Since Kleinsmith days we have kept up with the Blackleys and Kirby Horton MacBrayer. Also, we saw Jean and Jerry Hamilton up until their divorce many years ago. Kirby and Phin Horton were divorced, and both remarried. The Blackleys spent a night with us several weeks ago, and we enjoyed catching up and reminiscing about old times.

We have enjoyed your wedding gift over the years. You gave us a Japanese woodblock print, showing cormorants fishing at night. The framed print now resides in our Texas daughter's house. We actually saw cormorants fishing at night on a trip to China a few years ago.

****

Adelmo Costantini, Yonkers, NY:

Please autograph as follows:

To Leanna, born when I was in Inchon, Korea!
Love, Dad

****

SOUR M.A.S.H. AT SEA - SECOND WAVE

Frank Cermak, USMC, San Diego:

Thank you for the Autographed copy of your book. I've just started reading it and find it hard to put down. Also, thanks for getting my Mom involved with it as well. She is a really super lady. What you guys did in Korea is truly heroic. I also want to thank you for keeping the spirit alive.

****

Wes Rhoads, Durand, MI:

Bud, I dropped a check in the mail today for a paperback copy of your book. I am having knee replacement surgery on July 10 and looking forward to reading as I am recuperating. When I was a patient on the Haven I was recuperating from surgery for hernia that was done at a Field Hospital near Munson-ni, not far from the railhead. Had spent the first 3-4 months with the 5th Marines. The great care, food, USO shows, regular showers, clean sheets — was really appreciated.

I'll tell my Vet friends about your book, hope you sell a million. Good Luck.

****

Glenn Shirley, Hubcap Heaven of Knoxville, Knoxville, TN:

I was aboard the Haven from January until July, 1954. Organized the baseball team, we played teams from Korea and Japan. Wish I had kept up with some of the guys. Do you have a roster? The book sounds great. Can't wait to get my copy!

****

Walter "Bud" Stuhldreher

Wilford Ruppenkamp. Dallas, TX:

Please autograph as follows: To Ensign Ruppenkamp - original crew member.

****

Owen Reuterwall, Jr, cruise mate on ms Noordam, Tampa, FL:

Please autograph as follows:
Yesterday is long gone
Today is a new day-
let's enjoy.

Good luck on your book. I look forward to reading same. Maybe will sail together again.

****

Ed Groth, via Internet:

I can remember flying on a chopper with a patient from Easy Med Co to the Haven. I was a corpsman in Korea from March, 1953 to August, 1954. I can remember some corpsmen from the Haven coming to a 4th of July party in Korea. Now for the long shot: did you know a non-corpsman on the Haven named L.W. "Bud" Trumbull? He was a red head who, according to the story, tore up a bar in Japan which put it off limits to the Haven crew.

Author's note: I was sorry I had to tell Ed I didn't know Bud Trumbull; he sounded like my kind of a guy! WFS

****

Anna Willitts, Portsmouth, RI:

Please autograph as follows: To an erstwhile shipmate.

Your book title is great! I joined the Haven in 1950.

Author's note: My brother Don, and nephew Kurt Stuhldreher, who named the book, will be pleased by Anna's remark. I think it's a great title also. Too bad I didn't come up with it! WFS

****

W.E. *Watkins, MD, Nampa, Idaho:*

Please autograph as follows: To HM3 Watkins, W.E. USS Haven (AH-12) from January 1954 - September, 1954.

Author's note: I received several letters like this one and they really touched my heart. An enlisted man on the ship, a corpsman, then going on to medical school after service and becoming a doctor. Wonderful! WFS

****

Virginia Brown, Fort Collins, CO:

Walter (Bud): I look forward to reading your book. We (my son and I) went on one of the military trips to Korea last May and had a great time.

Have you sent info on the book to the Haven reunion list?

I look forward to reading your book. Fond regards, Gin. Haven 52-53

Also, do you have my stories on Kay Keating?

****

Dr. James Alford, Tallahassee, FL:

Dear Bud: Congratulations! I can now add to my obituary, "He knew Bud Stuhldreher when." Trouble is, he could never remember when.

It must be a very rewarding experience to complete such an accomplishment.

I'm looking forward to receiving and reading the book. The second book ordered might end up as a gift to my neighbor, Jim Morin, a retired admiral.

I gave up playing golf about a year ago because I kept getting increasingly worse; although, I tell the inquisitive ones it was because of my knees and back.

Good luck and wishes for huge sales of your book.

****

Comments received from people who read book

Dr. Ron Downing, Tallahassee, FL:

I learned one thing from your book: never to go on liberty with you! Were you ever court martialled?

Several readers asked me this same question. My unequivocal answer: Yes and no. Shortly before my three years of obligated service were up, my last Commanding Officer decided to court martial me and initiated the required paperwork. While the paperwork was working its way through the system, my discharge date came and went. His bosses determined the court martial had no merit and dismissed it. My CO hated me for having refused to spring him out of jail one night after he had violated his wife's restraining order, forcing him to ask the Commodore of our Squadron to do so; not a career enhancing move. (I was the OOD and the only officer aboard at the time he called.)

But justice was served soon after. Within several months, my ship came out of dry-dock and the CO, drunk, piled her up on the shore in the river between the yard and the ocean. *He* was court martialled and thrown out of the Navy. WFS

****

Tom McCullion, Tallahassee, FL:

You were a disgrace to the Navy and Notre Dame! I laughed all the time I was reading your book and still am. Is there another book on the way? I hope so!

****

Dick Lorenz, Deerfield, IL:

I finished SMAS yesterday and thoroughly enjoyed it. Regarding your venture to the New Territories. I had heard of your trip but I thought you had your [golf] clubs with you and needed two rickshaws to get you and the golf clubs to the course. Such is how changes occur in hearing a story second hand.

Walter "Bud" Stuhldreher

Congratulations on a good book.

****

Marvin Goldstein, professional pianist, Tallahassee, FL:

I have been reading your book! Very interesting and quite compelling!

****

Dick Schreitmueller, Kensington, MD:

Hey, Bud, congratulations! I just finished your book and loved it. You've had some neat experiences and, more important, you really know how to tell a story (true or not)!

Your last chapter about putting on shows at nursing homes rang a bell with me. I do that a bit too, singing once or twice a month in a barbershop group at nursing homes, assisted living centers and senior centers. They sure love any outside entertainment, including our emcee's corny jokes.

Best of luck on your script project. Let me know if I can help edit it.

Author's note: Dick did help edit this book. WFS

****

Hank Schwarz, author, Hollywood, CA:

Bud — I got your book yesterday and was able to read the first story and wow — I loved it. If the first story is any indication, it's all wonderful material. Very vivid and immediate and I can see it all unfolding in front of me. I wanted to tell you, you are a real yarn spinner.

****

Betty and Hugh Shearer, Wichita, KS:

Thanks for the book. Received our copy and it is great! What an adventure it has been! Everyone could write a book but so few do. We're so proud of Bud for this! Best wishes on your movie deal.

****

Glenn Shirley, Knoxville, TN:

Hi Bud: Thanks for the reply. I will look forward to the next book. Please be sure and let me know when it will be available. Remember, keep the head down, left arm straight, etc., bullshit, just play and have fun.

****

Richard Blair, Kingsport, Tenn.:

Bud — my copy arrived while we were at the beach last week and even though there were a multitude of projects to do on our return, I have found time to enjoy your stories. I don't know if you had that many more exciting events in your life or just better at capturing the events and relating them. In any event, I'm glad you put them in your book. Now I can't wait to see the movie! How about a TV series? Best regards and I hope you sell a million copies!

Walter "Bud" Stuhldreher

Author's note: Started working on either a movie screenplay or a TV mini-series script on July 8, 2003 with a young man, Chris Bryant, a graduate student in Florida State University's School of Film and Theater. We shall see if lightning can strike! WFS

****

Robert Tanzy, Waxhaw, N.C., whose Uncle Gene Tanzy had sent him the book:

Hey, Uncle Gene: I am loving the book and the timing was perfect. It came last week and I needed an escape and Bud's stories have been great for getting me away from my "week from hell." To give you an idea of how bad my week was, and to show why I needed something good to happen like get a great book that can take you to another world and make you laugh, I will list some of the events of last week.

Monday our server went out at work; today is the first day I could get my mail in over a week, and my computer got that worm that was going around. Tuesday my dog Skippy of 12 years died. Wednesday Katie had all four of her wisdom teeth cut out and was not coping well. She is OK now! That afternoon Caroline had a car wreck on the way home from school. She is OK but the car is a mess; so is the car she ran into and the one that [it] was knocked into. I don't remember Thursday but Friday Ann and I went out to dinner and a bar. Ann drove me home.

What a terrible week and what a great letter! I'm glad, Robert, my book helped you get through the "week from hell." Hope you're having a better week when you read this one! WFS

SOUR M.A.S.H. AT SEA - SECOND WAVE

****

Nephew Mike Stuhldreher, Columbus, Ohio:

Uncle Bud: Just wanted to say that I think the book is a smash. It really is cool having it on my shelf, not to mention reading it. You really did it. It's a fine book. It's funnier than hell right now, but also an entertaining and great description of the time and place of the US Navy in the Korean War for posterity. Thank you for that.

Thought I'd pass on the first review I've received, from my friend Mike Davis in Cincinnati: Mike: I read your uncle's book this past week. That's some funny stuff. Passed it on to my Ma and Pa as well. It was enjoyed by all. Sounds like that dude was trouble with a capital T as far as the Navy went. Very suave though.

Looked suave up in the dictionary. He must have been referring to my nephew Mike. WFS

****

Frank Nipper, Lisle, Illinois, to whom Gene Tanzy had sent the book:

Gene T.: I have finished reading your friend's book and must report that I enjoyed it very much. As with you, I also laughed out loud at certain humorous parts of the book. Being an old Navy guy myself, I could appreciate some of the B.S. he went through with his superior officers. I was particularly entranced by his powerful description of being caught in an unexpected storm in a fairly small boat. This also happened to me in Guam. Anyway, tell Bud that I enjoyed his book a lot. I can't wait for the movie!

Walter "Bud" Stuhldreher

****

Alexander (Tex) Rearick, Fishers, IN:

Bud, your military career makes mine look bland and colorless by comparison. I almost broke a rib in mirthful laughter over your various escapades. Persons in authority seemed to be your special targets. Your book is a masterpiece of wild misadventures.

Just think, I recommended you to Grandma Crow as a good prospective husband for her daughter Barbara. Of course, I didn't know about your Navy career at the time!

Tex's military career was anything but bland. He served in the Pacific as a waist gunner in the Air Force and completed more than 25 missions enduring enemy fire many times. WFS

****

ABOUT THE AUTHOR

Before beginning the *Sour M.A.S. H at Sea* series, the author had written over two dozen articles which were published in professional journals, and had published one short story. The author is collaborating on a TV/movie script based on this story, The Mazatlan Incident.

The author has also commenced work on a novel set in the 50's and 60's involving a former naval aviator, his marriage to a rich young woman and subsequently, working for her father in his Coca-Cola distributorship. His hobby, flying a refurbished Navy two-seat trainer, the SNJ-6, commonly called a "Jenny," causes a rift in the marriage and places his job in jeopardy. How he resolves his marital and work problems furnishes a challenge to the author not yet solved!

The author has taught at Baldwin-Wallace College, Berea, Ohio, the University of Alabama in Huntsville, Alabama, and Florida A&M University in Tallahassee, Florida, where he currently resides. A professional speaker, he has conducted over

500 seminars/presentations in many states. He has performed as a magician in the United States and other countries. He is an avid golfer and reader.

Printed in the United States
19266LVS00003B/37-132